An OPUS book

The impact of English towns
1700–1800

P. J. Corfield

The impact of English towns 1700–1800

Oxford New York Toronto Melbourne

OXFORD UNIVERSITY PRESS

1982

Oxford University Press, Walton Street, Oxford OX2 6DP

London Glasgow New York Toronto
Delhi Bombay Calcutta Madras Karachi
Kuala Lumpur Singapore Hong Kong Tokyo
Nairobi Dar es Salaam Cape Town
Melbourne Auckland
and associates in
Beirut Berlin Ibadan Mexico City Nicosia

First published 1982 as an Oxford University Press paperback
and simultaneously in a hardback edition

British Library Cataloguing in Publication Data
Corfield, P.J.
The impact of English towns 1700–1800.
1. Cities and towns–England–History
I. Title
942'.009'732   HT133
ISBN 0-19-215830-9
ISBN 0-19-289093-X Pbk

Library of Congress Cataloging in Publication Data
Corfield, P.J.
The impact of English towns, 1700–1800. (OPUS)
Bibliography: p. Includes index.
1. Cities and towns—England—History—18th century. I. Title.   II. Series.
HT133.C67   307.7'6'0941   81–16979
ISBN 0-19-215830-9   AACR2
ISBN 0-19-289093-X (pbk.)

Printed in Great Britain by
Richard Clay (The Chaucer Press) Ltd.
Bungay, Suffolk

HT
133
.C67
1982

Preface

This volume dicusses the history of English towns during a century of many complex and interlocking changes. It argues that the towns themselves underwent a variety of transformations – in terms of their numbers, size, physical form, economic role, and political, social, and cultural significance. These changes helped to consolidate a powerful, if often ambivalent, urban tradition in England. It was a tradition that celebrated the capacity of the towns to allure many outsiders, such as the country gentleman who compained that 'living in the country was sleeping with one's eyes open'. But it was also one that incorporated the townsman's own characteristic and growing preoccupation with urban 'problems' and the manifest need for improvements, as well as a certain idealization of the countryside.

The book further suggests that English towns contributed to wider structural changes in the economy and society as a whole. The accelerating pace of urbanization accompanied that of the world's first Industrial Revolution. And that, in turn, was closely linked with other important, complex, and sometimes subterranean, social and political changes, under the veneer of an unchanging 'age of oligarchy'. It is not intended, however, to unmask here yet another long-lost 'first cause' of industrialization. That search evidently has many attractions, as shown by the number and variety of candidates for the honour. But single-cause explanations for multiple transformations have rightly come under critical scrutiny – not least from development economists. If, on the other hand, complex structural changes are thought of as the outcome of simultaneous equations of change, then the dynamic growth of English towns was a major component variable in England's industrialization and its wider ramifications. (A select bibliography indicates further reading on these themes.)

Most of the discussion relates to the English experience, although the aggregate population figures are the most commonly used totals for England and Wales together – not through any disregard for Wales but because its substantial urbanization was chiefly a nineteenth-century phenomenon. Scotland and Ireland also fall outside the direct scope of this study.

Grateful acknowledgement is extended to the staff of all libraries and record offices who have provided assistance over the years; to R. C. Halfhide and his team in the Geography Department Drawing Office, Bedford College, for the production of maps and diagrams; and, especially, to Sheelagh Taylor, for invaluable secretarial support. Warmest thanks also are due to many friends and colleagues for advice, information, and criticism; particularly to Peter Clark for constructive help, as also to Dr. F. Capie, Dr. J. A. Chartres, Prof. F. R. H. DuBoulay, Prof. F. J. Fisher, Dr. R. B. Outhwaite, Prof. F. M. L. Thompson, Prof. E. A. Wrigley; and, irrefutably, to Tony Belton.

London   P. J. Corfield
May 1981

Contents

Maps and plans

Graphs

Tables

1 Introduction

The history of towns goes back to ancient Babylon, if not before. The emergence of fully urbanized societies, on the other hand – societies in which a majority of the population live and work in towns – is a very recent development in human history. Many large and expanding towns in agrarian societies had housed only a tiny proportion of their country's population. In the history of urbanization, therefore, the English experience has an important place, for England and Wales was the first large country (as distinct from region or city-state) to become urbanized. It is still today one of the most highly urbanized countries in the world. The census of 1851 was the first to show a majority of the population of England and Wales as town-dwellers; but that novel state of affairs had not come about overnight. The epic transformation – from Babylon to Babylonia – had been the result of at least a hundred years of urban growth and change.

This study is concerned with the early stages of those changes: the gradual but distinctive process of urbanization in eighteenth-century England. It is argued that the towns were themselves part-agents, as well as part-products, of the economic and social changes that constituted the twin phenomena of urban and industrial revolution in England. Large towns are often thought of as the creations of modern industrial society, as dependent variables of independently determined economic factors. But urban growth also helped to promote and stimulate the process of social and economic change in eighteenth-century England. The early stages of urbanization therefore provide an interesting case-study of the close interrelationship of cause and effect in history; and, indeed, of multi-dimensional rather than simple processes of change.

Throughout the eighteenth century the urban inhabitants of England and Wales constituted a minority of the total population. They lived in a countryside patterned typically with very small village settlements, many of which contained only a few hundred inhabitants. The majority of the towns themselves were small, apart from the huge capital city and the leading provincial centres. Yet this description, although true in the most general terms of England in 1800 as in 1700, conceals some important changes which took place during the century as a whole. Towns were expanding both in number and in size, so that the town-dwellers were a growing minority – increasing not only in absolute numbers (as might be expected when the total population of England and Wales multiplied from some five to nine million between 1700 and 1800) but also in proportionate terms. By the end of the eighteenth century over two and a half million people, or about 30 per cent of the country's population, lived in towns of 2,500 inhabitants or more. A century earlier the towns had accounted for fewer than one million people, less than 20 per cent of the total. And those are conservative estimates, excluding the network of small 'Casterbridges of England' that constituted in turn 'the pole, focus, or nerve-knot of the surrounding country life'. The process of urbanization was clearly under way, and it quickened appreciably in the later decades of the century.

Furthermore, the urban minority of eighteenth-century England was becoming increasingly influential and important, notwithstanding the continuing and well-entrenched hegemony of English landowning society. The new importance of the towns stemmed initially from their growing economic and social significance rather than from any formally enshrined political or constitutional power. The claims of traditional rural England in these years were at first uneasily complemented and later superseded those of the new urbanized world it had nurtured. It was a long-drawn-out but unmistakable transformation.

Many contemporary observers in eighteenth-century England were vividly aware of the distinctive qualities of town life, although its implications were very variously appreciated. Poets and dramatists made much of the contrast between town and countryside, and noted the insidious diffusion of city culture into rural England. 'In my Time', rasped the old squire in Goldsmith's *She Stoops to Conquer* (1773), 'the Follies of the Town crept slowly among us, but now they travel faster than a Stage-coach.' Moralists and divines condemned the greater opportunities for religious laxity and consumer choice in manners and morals in the towns. Bishop Porteous of Chester warned his flock in *A Letter to the Inhabitants of Manchester and Macclesfield* in 1777, after the shock of an earthquake (a not uncommon stimulus to literary and philosophical meditations in the eighteenth century), to beware the perilous nature of their urban follies, of which he gave a formidable list: 'Intemperance and Licentiousness of Manners; a wanton and foolish Extravagance in Dress, in Equipage, in Houses, in Furniture, in Entertainment; a Passion for luxurious Indulgences and frivolous Amusements; a gay, thoughtless Indifference about a future Life...; a Neglect of divine Worship, a Profanation of the Day peculiarly set apart for it; and perhaps, to crown all, a Disbelief and Contempt of the Gospel.' It was a weighty charge, also endorsed by Wesley and the evangelicals. Wesley, for example, had earlier in a letter of 1731 described London in particular as 'the worst Place, under Heaven, for preserving a Christian Temper', but he later decided that Bath ran it close.

Nor did urban patriots necessarily deny the worldliness and animation of the urban environment, although they tended to describe it in rather different terms. The sober Dissenter William Hutton recounted, in a famous passage in his *History of Birmingham,* his exhilaration on first encountering the bustle of that town (in 1741) as a youth of eighteen: 'I was surprised at the Place but more at the People. They were a Species I had never seen. They possessed a Vivacity I had never beheld. I had been among Dreamers, but now I saw Men awake.' There was something of the enthusiasm, and even the terminology, of a convert in these words – perhaps a recruit to a new secular doctrine of 'getting ahead'. Birmingham at that time, it might be added, was still a relatively small town, with perhaps twenty thousand inhabitants; but already it seemed very different from village society.

Others, in more sober vein, had also begun to analyse the economic implications of urban development. It was a subject that had been debated by a number of the 'political arithmeticians' in the later seventeenth century, chiefly with reference to the growth of London. Later, many of the celebrated economic journalists and commentators of the eighteenth century, such as Defoe, Arthur Young, and William Marshall, had perceptive comments to make on the economic role and social impact of the towns they visited on their travels round England. Sir James Steuart in 1767 speculated on the differential factors that caused some towns to grow more rapidly than others. The political scientist, Dr Price, attempted to distinguish between what he considered to be the unfavourable economic implications of London's expansion and the more satisfactory consequences of the growth of the 'middling' towns (1771); while, most famous of all, Adam Smith devoted a chapter of the seminal *Enquiry into the Nature and Causes of the Wealth of Nations* (1776) to an extensive analysis of 'How the Commerce of the Towns contributed to the Improvement of the Country'. Notably, it was the role of the towns in promoting agricultural innovation and improvement upon which he laid most stress; but at the same time he recognized the towns' capacity to act as a generator for wider economic changes.

Politicians also took cautious note. The eighteenth century was not a period when general schemes for franchisal or municipal reform were adopted, but nonetheless some administrative and political steps were taken to accommodate the growing urban society. Many private Acts of

Parliament were introduced to permit individual town improvement schemes, often including the creation of a new administrative authority or commission for that specific purpose. Much parliamentary time was taken up with urban issues, lobbyists, and pressure groups. Rather less to the delight of town residents, the younger Pitt's schemes for fiscal reform, including the eventual introduction of income tax (1799), were prompted by the need to tap new forms of urban and industrial wealth, neglected by traditional sources of revenue, such as the land tax.

Finally, and considerably to the alarm of urban magistrates, it seemed at times (particularly in the 1790s) that discontent among the urban masses might be organized and radicalized into a new political force. Their fears proved groundless, at least in the short term. Thwarted radicals, however, looked to social and economic change for the hope of eventual emancipation. John Thelwall, for example, was critical of most of the urban environments he knew, but mused, in *The Rights of Nature* (1796): 'Man is, by his very nature, social and communicative – proud to display the little knowledge he possesses, and eager, as opportunity presents, to increase his store. Whatever presses men together, therefore [he instanced particularly workshops and manufacturing towns], though it may generate some vices, is favourable to the diffusion of knowledge, and ultimately promotive of human liberty.' Something of the same combination of hope through a dialectic with disenchantment was expressed in William Blake's soaring vision of the fight to build 'Jerusalem in England's green and pleasant Land' (*Milton*, 1804–8). The dream was of a spiritual awakening, but the metaphor was also urban.

The abundance of published references to the urban experience in the eighteenth century to some extent reflects simply the great volume of surviving documentation from an era when the press was both relatively free and prolific – in contrast to earlier times. Many other themes – both sacred and profane – were also canvassed extensively in print in these years. That vigorous public exchange of views, news, and information was, however, in itself a quintessential sign of a city-based culture. 'A great City', Samuel Johnson observed in characteristically rotund style in 1778, 'is, to be sure, the School for studying Life.' The growing communications industry in eighteenth-century England (in Johnson's terms, the 'superfoetation' of the press) was therefore a product, as well as the chronicle, of urbanization.

There was no simple definition of what constituted a town. People in the eighteenth century, as now, were confident that they could identify a town when they saw one; and for many purposes a purely subjective but commonsense definition is quite satisfactory: a town is a human settlement known to contemporaries as a town. It is sometimes helpful, however, to establish a more precise gauge, to measure change over time – particularly when contemporary terminologies themselves alter in meaning. Originally, a 'town' (from the old English 'tun', an enclosed place or piece of land) was any nucleated or clustered settlement, however small. This usage prevailed into the sixteenth century. At the same time, the term had acquired a more precise and specialized meaning, with reference to settlements with certain independent rights and privileges in their local government. Later, in the seventeenth and eighteenth centuries, the modern emphasis was emerging: a 'town' increasingly referred to a settlement of a certain size and political autonomy, while 'village' (in the language since the late fourteenth century) gained currency for the smaller places. But the dividing line was very uncertain. Many small or decayed settlements still held the ancient title and legal privileges of a town, while some rapidly growing places lacked the formal title, although it was often given to them in general parlance. Dr Johnson's *Dictionary* (1755) was confident that a 'village' was 'less than a town', but recorded six different contemporary usages of 'town' – including one based on size alone, as 'any collection of houses larger than a village'.

Furthermore, within the ranks of the 'town', there were many additional distinctions. As Blackstone pointed out in his *Commentaries* (1765–9): 'The Word *Town*, or *Vill*, is, indeed, by the Alteration of Times and Language, now became a generical Term, comprehending under it the several Species of Cities, Boroughs, and Common Towns.' 'City' was used loosely of any large town, but technically referred to an urban centre that was, or had been, a cathedral town (Dr Johnson recorded both the general and specific usages). A borough was an incorporated town, with its own independent institutions of local government. A parliamentary borough, by contrast, was a place with representation in Parliament, but not invariably one that was incorporated. A plain market town was also not necessarily incorporated but held, at least in theory, a regular market. But here there were further problems, as some of these very small traditional markets were inactive by the eighteenth century. It was noted in 1750, for example, that 'Several of the Market-Towns . . . being very small, can be reckoned little more than country villages.'

Diversity of terminology mattered little at the time. Historians, however, have to pick their way through the profusion of names. Indeed, there has been a long-running debate among historians, sociologists, and demographers over the criteria for 'urbanity', in order to facilitate comparative surveys. Among the specifications often mentioned are population size, density of habitation, proportion of residents engaged in non-agrarian employment, social diversity, and distinctive 'way of life'.[1] Few of these variables can be studied systematically for England's eighteenth-century towns because the information is simply not available (and can be reconstituted only with great difficulty and without precision). The very urban art of social analysis and statistical survey work was barely inaugurated in the eighteenth century. On employment patterns, in particular, information is exceptionally scarce.

For the purposes of this study, a definition couched solely in terms of legal and constitutional title will not suffice, as many sizeable and clearly urban settlements (notably Birmingham, Manchester, and Sheffield) were not incorporated and furthermore had no direct representation in Parliament. Defoe ironically termed Manchester the 'greatest mere Village in England', although in practice few people talked of it as that. Here, therefore, the towns of eighteenth-century England are defined by the social and economic realities – while the sluggish adaptation of legal and political forms in the light of those realities is a matter for subsequent discussion (see ch. 9). In other words, town are taken to include all settlements of a certain size, that were based on a non-agrarian economic function, and had a distinctive social and cultural identity; tiny places that solely retained an ancient title have been excluded.

One of the few variables that can be examined at all systematically for eighteenth-century towns is that of population size, which may be taken to stand proxy in a very general sense for other aspects of urban identity. Urbanization was, however, not a matter merely of numbers; there is little merit in worrying too much about a rigid cut-off point between town and country. Selection of a uniform 'threshold' figure is useful merely to provide some comparative information about the scale and pattern of urban growth that is under scrutiny. If, therefore, a figure of 2,500 inhabitants is selected as the minimum size of a town, the resultant picture is shown in Table I, and summarized in percentage form in Table II. A higher threshold figure would produce a smaller urban population, and vice versa; but in both cases the broad trends in eighteenth-century urban growth remain the same.[2] A settlement of 2,500 residents is, of course, small by modern standards; but in the sparsely populated countryside of pre-industrial England, it was a distinctive unit.

It is true that there are many difficulties in establishing accurate population figures. All evidence from pre-census times is scrappy in form, capricious in incidence, and only partially reliable in content. A polite scepticism is often needed in response to eighteenth-century estimates, for it was not uncommon for those to be unwittingly exaggerated by local patriotism. Residents in more than one town expressed disbelief in 1801, when the first census showed their populations to be much smaller than they had expected: the response in Newcastle upon Tyne, for example, was 'universal surprise'. On the other hand, there was a growing interest in the compilation of accurate demographic data, and an impressive number of local enumerations were carried out by town governments and private individuals in the course of the century. Returns from over 125 such listings have been recorded, although usually without the detailed survey material from which they were compiled. It is possible, therefore, with the aid of enumerations, and circumstantial evidence from demographic, topographical, economic, and literary source material, to make informed estimates of the population size of individual centres in 1700 and 1750. These can then be compared with the 1801 census, to establish the broad contours of aggregate urban growth.

The figures in Tables I and II show clearly that the urban population grew more rapidly than the population as a whole. That in itself was a considerable development, as even the initial level of urbanization in 1700 was a relatively high one for a non-industrialized economy to sustain. A cumulative and long-term process was at work. It had certainly begun before 1700. In the seventeenth century it had been fuelled chiefly by the massive growth of London, which accounted for fully 11 per cent of the country's population by 1700. But a broadly based urban growth was apparent at least by the 1680s – and it continued throughout the eighteenth century. It could be observed in the early decades, before the Industrial Revolution was strongly under way, as well as in the later decades, when industrial expansion, population growth, and urban development alike accelerated. The urban population, in towns of 2,500 inhabitants or more, therefore grew from 18.7 per cent of the total in 1700, to 22.6 per cent in 1750, and to over 30 per cent in 1801.[3] The number of towns similarly expanded from 68 in 1700 to 188 in 1801.

These estimates are broadly corroborated by the testimony of informed contemporaries in eighteenth-century England, who certainly thought of theirs as a relatively urbanized society when compared with other countries. Gregory King, the great pioneer of social statistics, calculated in the 1690s that about 25 per cent of the country's population lived in towns, including the smallest market towns as well as the great towns and cities. Disregarding the very decayed townships, his figures suggest that perhaps 22–23 per cent of the country's population lived in settlements of approximately 1,000 inhabitants or more – a figure that provides a lower benchmark for comparison with those put forward in Table I. King, however, had no direct heir in the early eighteenth century; and while there are many literary references to the vigorous, if selective, urban

Table I Population of England and Wales living in towns of 2,500 inhabitants or more in the eighteenth century*

Size of towns	1700		1750		1801	
	No. of towns	Urban population	No. of towns	Urban population	No. of towns	Urban population
Over 100,000	1	575,000	1	675,000	1	948,040
20,000–100,000	2	52,000	5	161,000	15	702,473
10,000–20,000	4	55,000	14	175,500	33	428,040
5,000–10,000	24	168,000	31	201,900	45	313,759
2,500–5,000	37	120,000	53	167,500	94	332,859
Total	68	970,000	104	1,380,900	188	2,725,171
Total population		5,200,000		6,100,000		8,892,536

* Figures for 1700 and 1750 based on county-by-county survey of local sources; for 1801 from the first census returns. For the purposes of these calculations, each town or conurbation is counted as one, whatever the number of administrative authorities within its bounds.

A pattern of 'clear, if modest and interrupted, population growth between 1701 and 1751' is confirmed by calculations in E. A. Wrigley and R. S. Schofield, *The Population History of England, 1541–1871: A Reconstruction* (London, 1981), esp. pp. 207–10, 577, and 587. Their figures for England only (excluding Monmouth and Wales) show a total of 5.1 million in 1701, 5.8 in 1751, and 8.7 in 1801.

Table II Percentage of the population of England and Wales living in towns of 2,500 inhabitants or more in the eighteenth century*

Size of towns	Percentage of total population in:		
	1700	*1750*	*1801*
Over 100,000	11.1	11.1	10.7
20,000–100,000	1.0	2.6	7.9
10,000–20,000	1.1	2.9	4.8
5,000–10,000	3.2	3.3	3.5
2,500–5,000	2.3	2.7	3.7
All towns	18.7	22.6	30.6

* *Source*: As Table I

growth of the following years, there were few attempts at measuring the magnitude of the change.

A century after King, however, Arthur Young confidently reported the general opinion among educated society that the 'towns' (undefined) accounted for as much as 50 per cent of England's population – a fact that Young admired as a sign of economic advance. 'It is commonly observed, and doubtless founded on certain facts,' he wrote in his *Travels* (1792), 'that in flourishing countries the half of a nation is found in towns. Many writers, I believe, have looked upon this as the proportion in England.' Young was then contrasting the relative urbanization and wealth of England (and also of Holland and Lombardy) with the less developed and less urbanized economy of France. His estimate was too high, but, given the vagueness of the definition of a 'town' and the prevailing exaggeration of the actual size of urban populations before the first census, it was not implausible. It certainly indicated that the phenomenon of urban growth had been noted. Indeed, Young added a glowing tribute to its impact: 'Now, it deserves notice that the great resort, which is everywhere observable on the highways of England, flows from the number, size, and wealth of our towns, much more than from any other circumstance. It is not the country, but towns that give the rapid circulation from one part of a kingdom to the other.' The growth of traffic and towns were counterparts of the same social and economic changes, although their causation was more complex than Young's cheerful generalization implied. By the end of the century, therefore, England had developed into one of the most densely populated countries in the world. In Europe, only the early-commercialized (and much smaller) Dutch Republic and some north Italian city states could stand comparison; but there urbanization was not still intensifying.

The figures in Tables I and II also demonstrate some of the changing components of England's urban growth. There was a marked change in the relative status of London. Certainly, the capital city retained an unchallenged pre-eminence as the single largest urban centre in England and Wales. Throughout the century it was the largest city in western Europe; and by 1801, with almost a million inhabitants, it was one of the largest cities in the world – surpassed by Edo (Tokyo) and Peking, but probably few others. But, at the same time, its relative importance within the domestic economy had been cut back by the growth of England's provincial towns in the course of the eighteenth century. Its share of the country's total population remained broadly unaltered between 1700 and 1800, at about 11 per cent of the whole, whereas by 1750 the combined populations of all the provincial towns more than matched that of London, and by 1801 their populations came to almost double that of the capital city. The general impact and relative importance of London cannot, however, simply be measured by population statistics. It was, after all, one giant conurbation with key political, social, and cultural significance as well as economic importance, while the provincial towns were many in number, and individually much smaller in size.

But England's urban world was becoming notably multi-centred rather than focused upon a single city. The new confidence and claims of the 'provinces', much articulated in the later eighteenth and early nineteenth centuries, coincided closely with the growth in numbers and size of the provincial towns. Their assertiveness now expressed not so much the age-old jealousy of the countryside for the town, but a strengthened competitiveness between the provincial towns and the metropolis.

Some of the most novel and dramatic developments, therefore, in eighteenth-century English urban history were to be found in the growth of the provincial towns. Their increasing share of the country's population came about partly through the simple multiplication of the number of towns, but, more importantly, as the figures in Tables I and II also show, through the growing size of a number of larger provincial centres. Between 1700 and 1800 the proportion of the population living in provincial towns of between 10,000 and 20,000 inhabitants, and especially in those of 20,000 inhabitants or more, increased significantly more than did the proportion living in the smallest urban settlements. Particularly when viewed as a proportion of all town-dwellers, their share increased markedly, while those of both London and of the smaller towns with fewer than 10,000 inhabitants fell away (see Table III). By the end of the eighteenth century, then, there were many more urban residents, living in a greater number of towns; and instead of the stark contrast between one giant metropolis and many small towns, there were a growing number of sizeable provincial centres.

Table III Distribution of the urban population of England and Wales between towns (by size), 1700–1801*

Size of towns	Percentage of urban population in:		
	1700	*1750*	*1801*
Over 100,000	59.3	48.9	34.8
20,000–100,000	5.4	11.7	25.8
10,000–20,000	5.7	12.7	15.7
5,000–10,000	17.3	14.6	11.5
2,500–5,000	12.4	12.1	12.2
	100.1	100.0	100.0

* *Source*: As Table I

There was also an important geographical dimension to change, as illustrated in Figs 1–3. The shift from the urban predominance of the south of England in 1700 to the new significance of the industrial north and Midlands was manifest by 1801. It marked the emergence of a 'new frontier' in England's economic life. London meanwhile was left in comparative isolation from other very large towns; but the process of urban growth had greatly increased the total number of towns even within its powerful orbit. One of the major factors behind the changing distribution of England's leading towns was the increasing economic development of the coalfields of the north and Midlands. In the same way, the nineteenth-century urbanization of South Wales was built upon the later exploitation of its coalfields. River transport, for so long one of the influential factors in the growth of the larger inland towns, ceased to be a major determinant in their siting. Sheffield, Birmingham, Leicester, for example, were not on navigable rivers. Instead, river improvement schemes and, later, the canals took water-borne traffic to the emergent towns. A strategic siting at the original head of the Aire and Calder Navigation (1699–1701) reflected as well as further consolidated the growing pre-eminence of Leeds among the West Riding textile towns. Similarly, the canalization of the Avon between Bristol and Bath in 1727 acknowledged as well as compounded the expansion of the resort city.

A mantle of growth did not, therefore, fall evenly on all towns alike. Particularly before 1750, the process was very selective; and, throughout the century, the picture remained highly fluid and dynamic. Relative rankings among the leading provincial towns changed considerably. Some long-established centres were eclipsed for the first time: York, Exeter, Chester, Norwich lost their pre-eminence. Indeed, the eighteenth century was one of the most mutable periods in English urban history, in terms of the fluctuations in relative standing of individual towns. In 1700

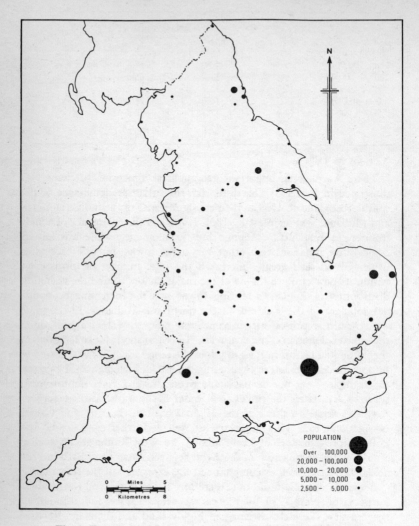

Fig. 1: Towns with 2,500+ inhabitants in England and Wales, 1700

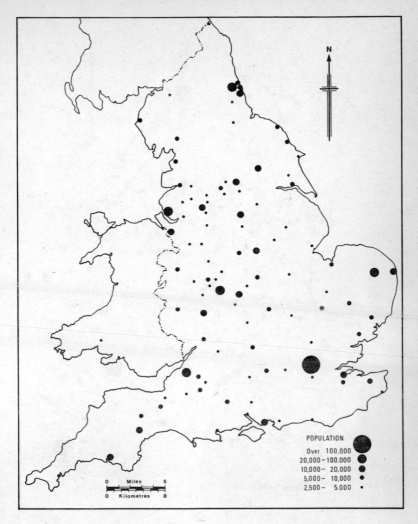

Fig. 2: Towns with 2,500+ inhabitants in England and Wales, 1750

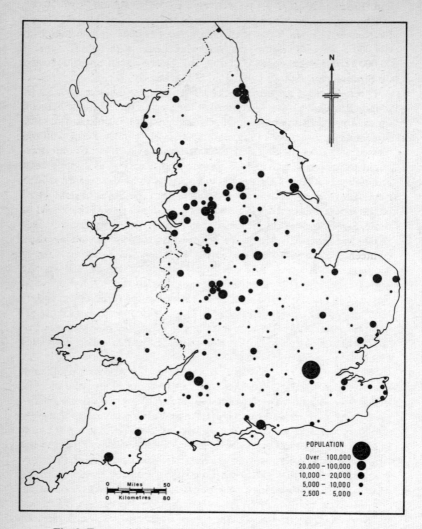

Fig. 3: Towns with 2,500+ inhabitants in England and Wales, 1801

the largest centres outside London were Norwich (30,000 inhabitants) and Bristol (20–22,000) respectively. By 1750 Bristol with 50,000 inhabitants had surpassed Norwich; and they were both followed closely by Newcastle upon Tyne with Gateshead (29,000) and Birmingham (24,000). By 1801, however, it was Manchester with Salford (almost 90,000) and Liverpool (83,000) that led the provincial towns, followed by Birmingham, Bristol, Leeds, and Sheffield.

The most rapid growth rates of all tended, naturally enough, to be found among towns that were small at the start of the century. Sheffield, for example, with a population of perhaps 3,000 in 1700, had grown some fifteenfold in the course of the century. Bath, of a similar size in 1700 and blessed with a location on that 'Spot of Ground which our Countrymen ought to esteem as a particular Favour from Heaven', as a guide-book rhapsodized in 1769, some twelvefold. None of these were record growth rates. They did not compare, for example, with the hectic 'instant cities' of the nineteenth-century American gold rush. The most celebrated of those, San Francisco, mushroomed from under 1,000 inhabitants to over 50,000 within a single decade. Yet the pace of urban growth among many eighteenth-century towns was brisk and persistent; and it sharply accelerated in the later decades. In 1774 Arthur Young had already noted, for example, the frontier-like expansion of the Pottery towns (it was his comparison). And in 1783 an enthusiast for Birmingham and its building industry suggested that 'The Traveller who visits her [Birmingham] once in Six Months supposes himself well acquainted with her; but he may chance to find a Street of Houses in the Autumn, where he saw his Horse eat Grass in the Spring.'

Such fluidity of experience began to change the way people talked of and classified towns. Definitions in terms of status alone were increasingly bypassed by changing circumstances. Many traditional county towns were now overshadowed by larger neighbouring centres that were regional capitals in all but name. It was not possible to identify a neat hierarchy of towns in eighteenth-century England, ranging from the one metropolis, to the few provincial capitals, to the many 'simple' country towns. Indeed, it is doubtful whether such a translucent model can be identified in England in earlier periods; and it certainly cannot be considered as universally typical of pre-industrial urbanism. There are many difficulties in forcing the great variety of non-industrialized societies into one analytical mould. Certainly, in the case of England, the earlier hierarchy of towns was already coming under considerable pressure by the sixteenth and seventeenth centuries. Peter Clark and Paul Slack have demonstrated how the growing numbers of 'new towns' were rapidly distorting the older pattern.[4] In the eighteenth century that process was extended. Some of the earlier 'new towns' were now well-established regional centres in their own right; and urban networks themselves became increasingly complex. There was now a plurality of patterns. In some of the less-urbanized regions – such as parts of southern England – the traditional hierarchy could still be detected. Elsewhere, in many of the urbanizing regions – in Yorkshire's West Riding, as in Lancashire, the Potteries, the west Midlands – there sprang up veritable constellations of towns, each with its intricate local network.

A new and more specialized terminology began to be adopted. Towns were now talked of in terms of their leading economic functions. As well as traditional concepts of market towns and ports, other places became identified as dockyard towns, manufacturing towns, spas, holiday resorts, university towns, as well as 'thoroughfare towns' on the main roads – anticipating the nineteenth century's canal and railway towns. These were the mutable terms of a dynamic urban world, rather than the timeless language of a stable hierarchy. The growing specialization of urban economies paralleled the growing trend towards regional specialization in English agriculture, both reflecting the gradual integration of the regions into one national market. It should be stressed, however, that the naming of towns in this way did not imply that their economic functions were completely uniform: a manufacturing town no more consisted entirely of manufacturers than a holiday town consisted entirely of landladies. As in modern classifications of towns, these descriptions refer only to leading specialisms, defined in terms of the predominant form of employment in the local economy. Many commercial and service centres in eighteenth-century England also had a sizeable manufacturing sector – although none quite achieved the dramatic dualism of modern Oxford, advertised in the 1960s for its University and as the 'Home of Pressed Steel'.

The chapters that follow, therefore, analyse the dynamics of urban growth from a number of perspectives. Chapters 2–5 look at the diverse experience of different towns, from the small market centres to the great metropolis. They examine the extent of differentiation between towns, their diversity of experience and economic fortunes. Chapters 6–10 change the focus, and consider a number of distinctive themes in their collective history. This section considers the wider social, economic, political, and cultural impact of urbanization; and identifies the important urban dimension to change in eighteenth-century England.

2 Market and manufacturing towns

Fundamental to the very existence of urban life was the role of the town as a centre of exchange. The market place for trade and town walls for security are two of the oldest images associated with the history of towns. In eighteenth-century England many ancient town defences were being pulled down or allowed to decay; but with the expansion of England's economy at home, and its acquisition of an empire overseas, trade flourished. It was the prime business of many urban residents. Gregory King calculated in the 1690s that there were 50,000 families in the country headed by merchants and shopkeepers: with their dependents and servants, their households accounted for some 244,000 individuals – fully a quarter of the population estimated to be living in towns (of 2,500+) in 1700. The calculation is not exact, since it cannot be assumed that all shopkeepers and merchants lived in towns, although probably most of them did; and to these must be added the many urban craftsmen, who combined retailing with craft production, as well as the many professional men, and the porters, carriers, waggoners, bargees, innkeepers, ostlers, and countless others, who all helped to service trade.

The very ubiquitousness of urban commercial life paradoxically makes its impact in some respects difficult to examine. Inland trade, in particular, has been relatively under-studied, although its importance has often been acknowledged. The small inland market towns were, however, the predominant components of the urban network. They were to be found scattered across the countryside – in greater densities in much of lowland England, more sparsely in highland and marshland terrain. Some were settlements of great antiquity, and their survival and continued evolution form one of the major strands of overt continuity in English urban history. Even here, however, there were changes in the course of the eighteenth century.

The economic life of the market towns centred on the exchange and distribution of goods – particularly the agricultural produce of their hinterlands – on regular market days. In the smallest centres markets were held weekly; in the larger towns more frequently. Market days were the busiest days of the week and important social occasions for both town and countryside. Observers were fond of contrasting the crowds and bustle in town on these occasions with their usual relative peace and quiet; and pickpockets had a field day. The growing volume of trade often made markets difficult to organize. A visitor to Chester in 1812 was amused at the vain attempts of the constable to control the stallholders: 'frequent scuffles ensued between him and some of the old ladies, who snatched up their stools and ran away.'

Physically, as well as economically, these towns centred on a large market place or broad-spanned commercial arena in the main street. Markets were held in the open, where wooden stalls (sometimes with colourful awnings) were easily erected and dismantled. They furnished a cheap and flexible venue for trade, where urban tradesmen and craftsmen as well as country producers could rent stalls or simply display their wares in baskets or panniers. In the larger markets separate sections were often reserved for different commodities – fish, dairy produce, corn, livestock. Most places dealt in a wide range of staple agricultural produce, for both the retail and wholesale trade, while further market specialisms were dictated by the nature of their agricultural hinterlands and the requirements of inter-regional trade. Cirencester, for example, was a celebrated market of national importance for wool: 'it is sold here in Quantities, so great, that it almost exceeds Belief', reported Defoe enthusiastically; and Farnham in Surrey was, 'without Exception, the greatest Cornmarket in England, London excepted'. Many places were embellished with a fine market cross or market house, where the official weights and measures were kept and tolls and dues collected. The cross was a symbolical and actual monument to the meeting of the ways in the busy town centre.

Such scenes had existed for centuries but were now accompanied by some important new developments. There was a growing tendency for many whosesale dealings to move from the open market to private rooms and chambers close at hand. The great urban inns were favoured centres for such transactions, providing neutral ground for the private meetings of producers and dealers: *'Half-way Houses* for this Purpose, where they meet and cabal', as a critic described them in 1718. The trend had already begun in the sixteenth and seventeenth centuries and continued apace in the eighteenth – notably for long-distance and non-local trade, and especially for commodities (such as wool or grains) that could be bought and sold by sample. These markets served increasingly as venues for settling the prices and terms for wholesale dealings, rather than primarily for the display and inspection of the goods in bulk. Countrymen with grain to sell, the same critic noted in 1718, 'bring only Parcels of Corn in a Bag or Handkerchief, which are called *Samples*; and these are expos'd, perhaps, in private Houses, to a few *Jobbers* or *Engrossers*.' Farmers or their servants began to travel greater distances to attend the larger markets; and wholesale dealings became more streamlined and highly organized. In the later eighteenth century some of the most important wholesale markets for grains instituted official Corn Exchange buildings. And, throughout the century, the number of specialist middlemen and dealers expanded considerably.

Not only were wholesale markets streamlined, but retailing became more firmly established with the emergence and diffusion of permanent shops – a term now used in the modern sense to refer to places that sold goods not made on the premises. Specialist shops had long been found in London and a few of the most thriving provincial towns, whose size had early guaranteed a regular and appreciable demand for shopping facilities. In the later seventeenth and eighteenth centuries the number of specialist retail shops multiplied, in towns both large and small. Luxury provisions were, of course, better provided in the resort and society towns; and the rapid growth of manufacturing towns in the later eighteenth century sometimes outpaced the expansion of shopping facilities; but no centres were without some shops.[1]

So marked was their growth that it was claimed, wrongly but excitedly, that they had by 1760 superseded the open markets entirely. In fact, the shops complemented the retail markets, and clustered close to the market place in the town centres. Stylish new barrel-shaped glass shop windows enhanced the display of wares. It was noted in the 1720s that some ambitious shopkeepers spent substantial sums on decor and fittings alone: 'Never was such Painting and Gilding, such Sashings and Looking-Glasses, among the Shopkeepers as there is now.' Fashions spread from London to the provincial towns. And with the growing volume of routine shopping, the practice was gradually introduced (initially by the Quakers) of quoting fixed prices for all comers – instead of the slower and traditional bargaining and higgling over every sale. Credit was, however, virtually universal, as anguished shopkeepers complained when large numbers of their customers defaulted in periods of slump or depression. In some of the larger towns, Courts of Conscience were established during this period to assist traders in the recovery of small debts. It marked the adaptation of commercial and legal procedure to mass custom.

With the growing refinement and complexity of marketing arrangements came a streamlining of the market network. The success of many inland trading towns in the eighteenth century entailed a focusing of the commercial economy. There had been in the course of previous centuries a great number of market grants – some merely speculative, some highly successful. In the sixteenth and seventeenth centuries there were over 800 known markets in England and Wales, although they were by no means equally active in trading terms. The process of market creation (usually in response to local initiative) continued into the eighteenth century – very often, in the later decades, to provide markets for newly expanding manufacturing centres. Lists of markets in this period continued to record some 700 places in England and Wales with regular market days (there were many slightly differing editions and versions of these listings, which were compiled for travellers and tradesmen). But the number of operationally significant markets – that is, catering for more than very local traffic – began inexorably to decline.[2] Trade concentrated in the established urban markets in the most accessible towns, especially as improvements in transport and communications reduced travel time and correspondingly increased mean distances travelled.

Similarly, as trade became organized into a regular routine, the great seasonal country fairs (some located in or near great towns, others in small villages) began gradually to lose their commercial significance. Instead, those that were held close to large centres of population concentrated on the entertainment aspects of their role. The critical *Essayist* of 1718 observed: 'The Fact is undeniable, that in many of these Places, once populous and flourishing, the *Fairs* and *Markets* are become strangely thin; and where one can see little else besides Toy-shops and Stalls for Baubles and Knicknacks.' The speed of change to both markets and fairs was, in fact, much more gradual than these phrases would allow; but many observers made similar comments. A letter in the *Gentleman's Magazine* in 1758, puzzling at the changes, alleged that: 'The great Declension of Trade in the Market Towns, occasioned by the Decrease in the Consumption of our Manufactures, is become a Subject of Universal Complaint.' In reality inland trade, far from being in decline, was in process of transformation.

Patterns in the 'shake-out' of the very smallest markets varied from region to region, as transport and marketing conditions changed only patchily. The commercialized eastern counties probably led the field. For example, the *Suffolk Traveller* (based on a survey in 1733–4) accorded words of praise to only nine markets in the whole county, while recording that fully 13 were facing economic difficulties (well over a third of the 33 markets active there in the years 1500–1640). Later, in 1771, Arthur Young found the village markets in Norfolk 'very inferior' to the great urban markets at Norwich, Yarmouth, and King's Lynn. Similar changes have been identified in eighteenth-century Dorset, Essex, Lincolnshire, Oxfordshire, and Warwickshire. In Derbyshire, too, three new markets were established in growing manufacturing centres, while six traditional markets lapsed completely. The changes were slowest in the highland north, though in Westmorland in 1794 it was noted again that 'There are weekly markets at eight different towns . . .; but the only one of any note, is held at Kendal.' The rationalization of the market network in the eighteenth century did not defer to antiquity or novelty of foundation, or to the nature of the market grant (whether to private patron or to a chartered body). It was certainly no longer possible, by the eighteenth century, to equate possession of a market grant with urban status – if indeed it ever had been. All towns had markets, but not all markets created towns. Indeed, as the established urban networks strengthened, so the minor markets declined.

The eighteenth century, then, was a period of consolidation and prosperous expansion for an array of strategically sited inland trading towns. Success depended on good transport services: Lincoln's commercial revival in the later eighteenth century, for example, followed improvements to its river communications. For many of these towns it was a period of considerable building activity. Shops, inns, coffee-houses, and new housing were constructed around the market place and in the main streets; and old properties (very often including the market house and the town hall) were rebuilt, refronted, or otherwise refurbished. Many market crosses were embellished, some were rashly destroyed. The configuration of the eighteenth-century inland commercial centre can be glimpsed to this day in the high streets and market places of many smaller towns – and seen in its full architectural splendour in the case of Blandford Forum, Farnham, and Stamford – all successful commercial centres whose subsequent development has not been of sufficient magnitude to erase the eighteenth-century legacy.

Despite the flurry of rebuilding and the steady expansion of business in these trading towns, however, they did not experience exceptionally rapid population growth during the eighteenth century. In many cases their population history matched that of the country as a whole, with only modest recruitment of new residents between 1700 and *c.* 1760, followed by a more rapid expansion thereafter. Many had thus less than doubled in population during the century; and few towns that were dependent chiefly upon inland trade were of very great size. The slow-growing York, with a population of *c.* 16,000 in 1801, was probably the largest of these. On the other hand, the number of essentially commercial centres expanded in the course of the century, as the total population and volume of trade grew. It may seem surprising at first sight that these places did not expand as dramatically as did some of the great ports and manufacturing centres; but inland trade was not as labour-intensive as overseas trade or industrial production. It was, nonetheless, the efficiency of the increasingly streamlined trading system that underpinned the whole process of urbanization.

It was often by extension of their commercial activities that a number of eighteenth-century towns developed also as industrial centres. They were markets and commercial centres for the trade in manufactured goods as well as in primary products. Some specialized craft industries had therefore long congregated in the towns, for ready access to their clientele. In the eighteenth century expanding consumer demand encouraged a considerable multiplication of these specialisms. Furthermore, as headquarters and market centres for a number of rural industries, the towns also drew strength from change in the countryside. Much production, indeed, continued to be carried on outside the towns. In some of the country's woodland and pastoral regions, for example, part-time industrial work was regularly undertaken to supplement low earnings from agricultural labour.

Yet with the intensification of production in the course of the eighteenth century, some of these regions came to specialize increasingly in industry. As they did so, they stimulated the growth of towns in their midst. It is, indeed, by this time misleading to talk of industries moving in aggregate 'into' or 'out of' the towns. Expanding rural settlements that were acquiring an industrial specialism attracted labour so rapidly that they themselves grew into towns. 'Manufactures make Towns large and rich which they found small and poor', a pamphleteer commented in 1752. 'From the Establishment of Manufactures, we see Hamlets swell into Villages, and Villages into Towns', concurred Sir James Steuart in 1767.

The proliferation of specialist industrial towns in the course of the eighteenth century constituted, therefore, one of the most distinctive and novel elements in the urban transformation. Indeed, many products were known generically by the name of the major town of their industrial region. Not all Manchester fustians (or, later, cottons), Norwich stuffs, Sheffield knives, or Birmingham 'toys', were actually made in the towns; but their reputation was already stamped upon their local industries.

By 1757, in a notable poetic outburst, John Dyer in *The Fleece* had identified four of the eighteenth-century's most celebrated manufacturing towns. He admired the growth of 'busy Leeds', where:

> ...Some, with even line,
> New streets are marking in the neighbouring fields,

and he added:

... So appear
Th' increasing walls of busy Manchester,
Sheffield, and Birmingham, whose reddening fields
Rise and enlarge their suburbs.

Despite the poetic licence (not all were built in red brick), his words felicitously depicted their atmosphere of bustling growth. Others too had noted the phenomenon. The observant Defoe had exclaimed in 1728: 'let the Curious examine the great Towns of *Manchester, Warrington, Macclesfield, Hallifax, Leeds, Wakefield, Sheffield, Birmingham, Froom, Taunton, Tiverton,* and many Others. Some of these are meer Villages; the highest Magistrate in them is a Constable, and few or no Families of Gentry among them; yet they are full of Wealth, and full of People, and daily encreasing in both; all of which is occasion'd by the meer Strength of Trade, and the growing Manufactures establish'd in them.' In fact, not all of Defoe's individual growth points were well chosen, but his general observation was important. Their growth was not owed to ancient title or to gentry patronage, but to expanding industrial and commercial life. Defoe was one of the first, indeed, to use the term 'manufacturing town', which was in growing currency from the 1750s onwards. In 1774 Dean Tucker further observed that 'the Towns of *Birmingham, Leeds, Halifax, Manchester, etc.,* being inhabited in a Manner altogether by Tradesmen and Manufacturers, are some of the richest and most flourishing in the Kingdom.'

Nucleated manufacturing centres grew in number – and also in size. Their importance became increasingly marked among provincial towns with populations of 20,000 or more, as shown in Table IV. Not only had the number and average size of the large inland manufacturing towns expanded considerably, but so had their share of the total population living in the larger provincial towns: from under 40 per cent (37.3) in 1750 to virtually 50 per cent (49.6) in 1801. The accession of urban-industrial might to the earlier pre-eminence of the ports is very striking. It indicated that, in a growth economy, like that of eighteenth-century England, a number of industries could derive advantage from a location in or near to large towns. Relatively cheaper labour costs in the countryside were not necessarily then more advantageous than the external economies to be derived from an urban location. Prompt access to markets, merchants, transport, news of fashions, professional services, all conferred advantages – let alone the abundant labour resources of the growing towns, and their developing reservoirs of craft skills. Hence it was that the growth of manufacturing towns preceded the factory and the mechanization of industrial production. It is true that England's first modern (water-powered) factory was erected at Derby in 1719; and there was a growing crop of spinning-mills in Lancashire and the Midlands from the 1770s onwards. But these were not all initially sited in urban locations; it was only with the development of the steam-engine that factories congregated increasingly into the manufacturing towns. So powerful then was their impact upon the Coketown of Dickens's *Hard Times*, a place 'of machinery and tall chimneys, out of which interminable serpents of smoke trailed themselves for ever and ever', that it has obscured the fact that the growth of manufacturing towns preceded the factory.

Many industrial regions fostered a cluster of medium-sized towns – demonstrating the fine balance between forces for the concentration and dispersal of population. Often there was one larger commercial and industrial centre to the region. Manchester, with its ring of satellite towns, was at the heart of the Lancashire textile industry. Leeds, on the other hand, was a gateway town, on the border of the West Riding textile-producing region to its south and west, and the pastoral economy of the Vale of York: 'Not a single Manufacturer is to be found more than one Mile east and two north of Leeds', it was remarked in 1795. Yet these capitals did not predominate – either socially or economically – as easily within their manufacturing regions as did some of the old-established regional capitals in the purely rural counties. Some small producers in the industrial villages in the shadow of Sheffield, for example, traded directly to their market outlets in London and elsewhere. The big towns led but did not monopolize. There was often a fierce rivalry between close neighbours within these urban constellations. The smaller places were zealous to assert their independent identities – identities that survive to this day, even where subsequently several towns have coalesced into one large conurbation.

One industrial generator of urban growth in the eighteenth century was England's textile industry, in all its varying and diversifying branches. In 1700 one of the two major provincial towns was the city of Norwich, a textile centre as well as a commercial and regional capital. And in 1801 four of the fifteen largest provincial towns – Manchester, Leeds, Norwich, and Oldham – owed their importance primarily to the production and marketing of textiles. By the end of the century Manchester and Salford, together straddling the River Irwell, 'that here flows turpid, black, and deep', had already acquired the ingredients for their reputation as the 'shock city' of early industrialization. Contrasts of wealth and poverty on a large scale attracted dramatic emphasis. 'Our Streets swarm with distressed Objects of every Kind; Hunger and Nakedness, abject Misery, and loathsome Poverty may be found in every Neighbourhood; and, notwithstanding the pious Liberality of the Rich,

Table IV Population of leading provincial towns classified by economic specialism, 1750 and 1801*

Provincial towns with populations of 20,000 + (by leading economic specialism)	1750			1801		
	Number of towns	Population	Percentage	Number of towns	Population	Percentage
Manufacturing towns	2	60,000	37.3	7	348,462	49.6
Dockyard towns	–	–	–	2	76,360	10.9
Ports	3	101,000	62.7	5	242,661	34.5
Spas and resorts	–	–	–	1	34,990	5.0
TOTAL	5	161,000	100.0	15	702,473	100.0

* Based on figures in Table I

the Complaints of the Poor are as loud, their Distress as grievous as ever', wrote a Manchester magistrate in *Friendly Advice to the Poor* (1755), suggesting a tonic of regular work and less dissipation – especially less drinking and gaming.

The construction of the great Cloth Halls in the textile towns of the West Riding of Yorkshire in the later eighteenth century provided vivid testimony to the central importance of the staple business. Leeds began early to specialize in the merchandizing of woollens. Already by 1707 it was claimed to hold the largest cloth market in England – eclipsing the older regional and commercial capital of the area, traditionally known as 'Merry Wakefield'. Early markets were held in the open; but in 1755 Leeds institutionalized the trade with the building of the White Cloth Hall (rebuilt extensively in 1775) and the Coloured Cloth Hall in 1758. Isolated Huddersfield, of whose inhabitants Wesley in 1757 declared that 'a Wilder People I never saw in England', emulated Leeds with an unusual oval-shaped Cloth Hall, funded by the local lord of the manor, Sir John Ramsden, in 1766. The adjacent rivals for predominance in the Yorkshire worsted industry followed suit, Bradford with two Halls in 1773 (extended 1780) and Halifax with the magnificent, and sole surviving, Piece Hall in 1774. Wakefield, still an important grain market, also began to develop a manufacturing specialism of high-quality 'tammies' (worsteds), for which it constructed the Cloth or Tammy Hall in 1778. These huge industrial marts demonstrated the importance of the towns as commercial headquarters for rural industries. They were venues where the many industrial producers could meet the smaller numbers of dealers and traders, although, as in other wholesale transactions, far from all exchanges actually took place on the floor of the markets. As the industries expanded, therefore, much of the industrial production even prior to mechanization began to move down from the scattered homesteads on the hills into the valleys and close to the towns.

Not all textile towns, though, expanded equally successfully. An industrial specialism was by no means an invariable passport to growth, if the economic rationale of a regional industry was vulnerable to erosion by competition elsewhere. That happened to a number of old-established textile towns in eighteenth-century England, in response to industrial change. Exeter, the economic capital of the Devonshire serge industry, provided a case in point. Undercut first by the Norwich industry and then by Yorkshire, Exeter experienced economic difficulties and probably some population loss in the mid-eighteenth century, before stabilizing at a lower pace of growth as a commercial and banking centre. Tiverton, its smaller industrial satellite, had fewer alternatives. Its economic and demographic difficulties in the mid-eighteenth century

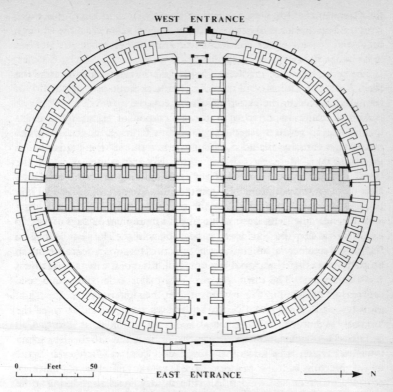

Fig. 4: Ground Plan of Huddersfield Cloth Hall, 1766. Adapted from plan in W.B. Crump, *History of the Huddersfield Woollen Industry* (Huddersfield, 1935).

The unusual oval-shaped Huddersfield Cloth Hall was promoted in 1766 by the manorial lord, Sir John Ramsden, to provide a centralized venue for dealings in the staple industry, and thereby to attract business to the town. Without windows in the outer wall, the Hall looked rather like a bull-ring. It was brick-built, with a distinctive clock tower and cupola over the eastern entrance, and was initially only one storey high. A second was added in 1780; and in 1864 the new north–south axis (shaded on plan) was added, raising the number of cloth stands from 82 to 114. The Hall was dismantled in 1930 and partially reconstructed in nearby Ravensknowle Park.

underpinned the noted radicalism of its weaving workforce. Much the largest place, however, to experience the onset of relative eclipse through industrial change in the eighteenth century was Norwich. Its worsted weaving industry faced complex difficulties in the later decades, compounded by loss of markets overseas and the new challenge from the rival Yorkshire industry. Again, its political militancy in the 1790s similarly testified to the extent of discontent.

Also of major importance in the generation of eighteenth-century manufacturing towns were the metal-manufacturing industries, whose products eventually included, among other things, the hardware for mechanization. Metalware districts flourished in those parts of the country where workable deposits of coal and iron ore were available, although iron was additionally imported from Sweden. Many production processes were still carried out in the countryside. In 1747 a clerk from Wortley, near Sheffield, was unable to send more than 52 bags of nails to London, because 'the Naylers have been busy in the Harvest'. But again there were commercial and industrial pressures towards a degree of urban growth within these industrial regions. Mightiest of the metalware towns was Birmingham. The town was at once a major social and commercial centre for its region, the organizational headquarters for the rural industry, and an industrial centre in its own right. Jovially termed the 'toyshop of Europe', making metal goods and trinkets, it also had an extensive armaments industry. It was the gateway town to the urbanizing industrial region later known as the Black Country, where even in the mid-eighteenth century visitors gaped at the number of smithies, crowded with men and women 'All with smutty Faces, thundering at the Anvil'.

Elsewhere, the fast-growing 'old smoky Sheffield' was also famed for the production of metalwares, especially cutlery and tools. From the 1740s onwards it also made crucible-cast steel; and in the later eighteenth century large-scale iron works were established at nearby Barnsley and Rotherham. The social impact of such large-scale foundries was, however, undoubtedly greatest in the early urban growth of South Wales, an area without any antecedent industrial traditions. Merthyr Tydfil, by 1801 the second-largest town in Wales, had sprung up from a poor and sparsely inhabited parish of under 1,000 in the mid-eighteenth century to a town of almost 9,000 by 1801. Visibly a one-industry town, it was termed, perhaps ironically, a 'metropolis of iron-masters' in 1807. Its youthful population of recent migrants from the Welsh countryside was described by a nervous magistrate as 'naturally turbulent'; and an assize judge on circuit in 1790 recommended the soothing influence of matrimony.

Above all, it was the depth and range of emergent manufacturing specialisms that was notable. In the east Midlands three hosiery towns showed continued expansion. Largest of these was Nottingham, a county capital that also specialized in the framework knitting of silk and cotton stockings and fancy hosiery, and later in the century diversified into lace-making, using an adaptation of the stocking frame. Leicester was similarly a textile town and county capital, specializing in the production of coarser and cheaper worsted stockings; while Derby, the smallest of the three, was the site of Lombe's pioneering silk mill and a centre for the hand-knitting of silk stockings. Its industry faced initial difficulties, struggling with technical problems and patent restrictions imposed by the early factory masters; but by the 1790s there were some twelve mills in existence employing over 1,000 workers. William Hutton's memoirs recounted his dislike of the monotony and strict discipline he faced there as a youthful mill-hand.

Further west, the Potteries provided graphic illustration of the generative power of industrial growth, for there the towns emerged almost by default, as a result of a growing density of industrial settlements in the coal and clay district of Staffordshire. The townships gradually merged into a long, sinuous conurbation, with plural centres rather than a single focus. Indeed, a visitor to Hanley complained in the 1790s that 'to a Person in the midst of it, it has scarcely the Appearance of anything beyond a moderate Village; yet if the Houses had been properly joined together, it ... would make a capital Town.' Elsewhere, too, industrial diversification in the later eighteenth century saw the origins of other celebrated specialisms: brewing at Burton upon Trent, soap- and glass-making at St. Helens in Lancashire.

Industrial development, in all its manifold guises, therefore played a cardinal role in eighteenth-century urban growth. Many of the urban specialisms of later industrial England were already established or developing in the early eighteenth century. Others emerged in the course of these years, as in, for example, the establishment of beer-brewing at Burton. Some towns were visibly in transition from one industrial specialism to another. For example, Northampton, traditionally a commercial centre and one of the smaller Midlands textile towns, began from the later seventeenth century to move gradually into boot- and shoe-making, taking advantage of local supplies of hides and oak bark (for tanning). Industrial transition and commercial difficulties in the early eighteenth century meant that it grew very little between 1700 and 1750, but Northampton expanded more vigorously thereafter, success-fully undercutting the London industry in the production of cheap footwear and standard army boots. Furthermore, the economic foundations for several others towns' later industrial development were already becoming apparent, as a result of regional economic specialization. Leicester's eventual diversification into boot- and shoe-making in the early nineteenth century, for example, was encouraged by the success of Northampton and its hinterland. Rochdale's transition from traditional woollens to cottons was also clearly responding to the pull of the Lancashire industry. Coventry's growing reliance upon watch-making and light engineering, especially after a crisis in its ribbon-weaving industry in the mid-nineteenth century, was similarly aided by its proximity to the expansive metal-manufacturing region of the west Midlands.

The many emergent manufacturing towns in eighteenth-century England differed in some obvious externals. The clack of the loom in the textile towns contrasted with the pall of smoke associated with the metalware towns. But they shared a number of common characteristics. Their economies were strongly dominated by the fortunes of their industrial staple. A depression in the dominant industry could lead to extensive economic problems throughout the whole urban community, as demand for other goods and services was dampened. The organizers of local poor-relief schemes, for example, often found that ratepayers were least able to contribute at the very time when demand for assistance was greatest – and for the same reason. The extent of these fluctuations varied according to the degree of dependence upon one industry, and with the nature of that industry and its markets. Those reliant chiefly on unstable overseas markets tended to experience more dramatic fluctuations than those cushioned by home demand, although that too was a variable factor. Equally, the impact of industrial depression could be absorbed more readily in the case of towns with additional economic functions as commercial and/or consumption centres. The headquarters towns in the urban-industrial regions often had a more diverse economic role than their purely industrial satellite towns, and were better protected against rapid downswings in economic activity.

Without reliable figures for levels of employment and industrial output, the extent of individual towns' economic specialization cannot easily be measured. Partially-surviving occupational data suggest, however, that the proportion engaged in the staple industry in all its branches could rise in some cases to as high as 40 per cent or more of the adult male workforce. Probably, too, a broadly similar proportion of the female workforce shared in that labour, given the prevailing system of production in domestic units. Individual jobs were still, however, relatively unspecialized, particularly at the start of the century, and plurality of occupation was not uncommon. Nonetheless, a large proportion engaged in the staple industry has been noted in a number of manufacturing towns. In mid- and late-eighteenth-century Nottingham, for example, it has been estimated that as many as 50 per cent of the whole working population were engaged in hosiery production and its associated occupations of finishing and marketing. In Leicester in 1740–9, 41. 3 per cent of the men admitted to the freedom of the city were active in the hosiery business, as were an even higher proportion of new apprentices (54 per cent) in the years 1730–49. The freemen and apprentices in Leicester were, admittedly, both relatively select groups; but, if figures for the number of stocking frames at work in the city are at all accurate, the proportion of stockingers among the workforce as a whole must have been similarly large.

In Norwich, with a wider municipal franchise, the proportion of freemen engaged in the production and finishing of worsted stuffs at the time of their admission to the freedom generally accounted for between 40 and 60 per cent of the total throughout the eighteenth century – with the exception only of the 1720s, when the proportion rose briefly to 64 per cent (after local legislation to encourage all potential candidates to apply for the freedom), and the 1790s, when it fell dramatically to 19 per cent (in a decade of economic problems for the Norwich industry). Even in the smaller and less specialized town of Northampton, a survey of the occupations of 1,139 male voters in the 1768 parliamentary election (the extensive scot-and-lot franchise meant that the electorate amounted to about 75 per cent of the adult male population) showed that 31.4 per cent were engaged in the town's leading industries (13.3 per cent in the declining textile industry, 18.1 per cent in the emergent boot- and shoe-manufactures), compared with 15.5 per cent in the provision of food and drink, and 7.0 per cent in the building trades.

These figures reinforce the point made by many contemporary observers, that the concentration of urban occupations upon one leading industrial specialism could be very marked. Indeed, these figures are comparable with those found in twentieth-century manufacturing towns, where a proportion of between 39 and 50 per cent of the employed population may be found in the manufacturing sector of an urban economy.[3] Comparisons cannot be pressed too far, as early job designations were by no means standardized. The creation of the factory was therefore itself partly an organizational response to the employers' need to regulate and discipline these growing aggregations of industrial producers, as well as the outcome of the eventual mechanization of production.

In some cases, the advent of the factory altered employment patterns by a relocation of the manufacturing labour force. In central Leeds, for example, the proportion of the working population engaged in the textile industry was probably higher in the 1740s than it was in the 1790s, as the town centre itself took on commercial and warehousing functions, and the new factories were built in outlying hamlets and industrial suburbs. In the industrial satellite towns, on the other hand, and in some new industrial centres, the core of manufacturing concentration was retained and even strengthened by the advent of the factory. Cotton-spinning, -dyeing, and -printing works, owned by the Peel family, were said to provide 'constant employ for most of the inhabitants of Bury and its neighbourhood, of both sexes and all ages', according to an observant (if somewhat euphoric) visitor in 1795. And the Crawshays' huge Cyfarthfa iron works at Merthyr Tydfil, probably the largest in the Europe of their day, employed a workforce of about 1,500 men, amounting to approximately 65 per cent of the estimated adult male population of the town.

These manufacturing towns, with their large artisan and labouring populations, were therefore distinctive places in the context of eighteenth-century England. Their populations developed a wide range of knowhow and expertise. 'The Mechanics [= craftsmen] are not . . . as in other Countries, mere Machines, who give motion to other Machines. Some of them even write themselves, in a bad Style no doubt, but good Things, upon the Trade which they respectively exercise', declared a French observer in 1754, admiring England's acquisition of technical skills.

The industrial towns also appeared to be evolving a relatively more disciplined and orderly workforce than did the great ports or the capital city, with their extensive reliance upon casual labour. The sharp-eyed Defoe commented on the absence of people out of doors in the manufacturing towns and villages, in contrast to the crowds to be seen on Sundays and holidays. The emergence of standardized and regular work patterns was, however, a lengthy process. Different industries and regions evolved their own marked patterns, and masters often bewailed the idleness of the domestic worker. Samuel Roberts, a Sheffield merchant-manufacturer, later recalled difficulties in finding skilled labour for the new silver-plating industry in the 1760s. The first recruits were the 'most unsteady, depraved, and idle of all other workmen . . . a pest to the town'; but gradually, he decided, regular work and good earnings had proved the 'means of purifying our plated working-class at Sheffield'. In some areas a communal work discipline was enforced. A poem on the Yorkshire clothiers, written about 1730, refers to the horn that was sounded early in the morning to waken the apprentices and journeymen – anticipating by many years the later factory whistle. Regularization of work practices was prompted by growing economic specialization and the increasing subdivision of labour. Some early 'manufactories' indeed were simply large workshops, where work could be supervised and/or industrial secrets protected.

This is not to say that the manufacturing workforce was particularly cowed or repressed; on the contrary, it was noted for independence and lack of servility. These towns fostered some of the most active traditions in union organization and political radicalism. The urban artisans, especially those in sedentary occupations, had a long tradition of literacy and religious nonconformity. Reactions to this emergent social force were often hostile or contemptuous, but also wary. The Reverend Thomas Whitaker, an early historian of Leeds and its region, described the population of Halifax parish (in 1816) as 'wretched beings', with what he described as savage grins, squalid countenances, bare feet, and dejected appearance. On the other hand, he also decided that the liveliness of the manufacturing population was preferable to the 'heavy ox-like stupidity of the mere husbandman'. 'Little partial as I am to manufactures', he therefore resolved that he could not wish for the decay of Halifax's industry, though anticipating its ultimate likelihood, given 'the general mutability of human things'. Ambivalence, such as that expressed so frankly by Whitaker, was often displayed by eighteenth-century observers of the growth of the manufacturing towns. Particularly by the later decades of the century, when the pace of change accelerated, cries of triumph at economic progress were mingled with apprehension at the social implications. The exchange and production of goods could also be accompanied by similar traffic in ideas and opinions.

3 Ports and dockyard towns

The creative force of trading and commercial life was certainly visible in the case of the provincial ports (London's experience is discussed subsequently). Here, too, there were major changes in the eighteenth century. Expanding and diversifying trade generated bigger concentrations of population at the ports, and an increasing specialization between the larger international ports and naval dockyards, and the smaller local havens. The carriage, transhipment, and merchandizing of goods in bulk, as well as the associated finishing and servicing industries, were all highly labour intensive. Undeniably, a considerable amount of the eighteenth-century port expansion was promoted by the growth of inland trade. Many heavy goods were moved around the country by water-borne transport, using rivers, and later canals, to the coastal route. Newcastle upon Tyne and Sunderland, for example, owed much of their early development to the coastal trade in coal. Indeed, a high proportion of the tonnage of all English shipping at that time was accounted for by the specially built fleet of colliers, plying between English ports with cargoes of 'black gold'. The coastal trade in goods other than coal was also sizeable, and growing in volume – indeed, in the early decades of the century it may have been growing as fast as, or faster than, overseas trade.

At the same time, the cumulative growth and changing orientation of foreign trade in the later seventeenth and eighteenth centuries also constituted a highly dynamic force for port development. That was so in the case of a number of Europe's major Atlantic ports – from Hamburg to Cork to Cadiz – but was pre-eminently the case in England, and indeed in Scotland. The widening range of goods – especially of English manufactured goods – for export, and the geographically expanding network of overseas markets, serviced by English shipping, fostered important changes among the country's provincial ports. Collectively, the outports, as they were termed, had begun to erode the massively established commercial predominance of London. Regionally, the ports of the north-east and west of England sprang into new importance; and, individually, many centres exhibited brisk rates of growth. Bristol, Exeter, Newcastle, Great Yarmouth, were now joined – and in some cases overtaken – by ports such as Liverpool, Whitehaven, Sunderland, and Hull.

There are difficulties in comparing the varying commercial fortunes of the provincial ports during these years, for different indices yield different answers. In terms of total population size, Bristol was without doubt the largest outport in 1700 and for most of the eighteenth century, but it was overhauled by the faster-growing Liverpool in the 1780s. In some other respects, on the other hand, the relative eclipse of Bristol had begun rather earlier. Whereas in 1709 Bristol had been the outport that owned the greatest tonnage of merchant shipping engaged in overseas trade, it was already surpassed for total tonnage (i.e. including coastal and fishing vessels) by Scarborough, not commercially of much importance albeit a favoured port of registration among owners of colliers. By 1751 Bristol was overhauled among the outports not only by three north-eastern collier ports (Scarborough again heading the list) but also by its west-coast rival, Liverpool. By 1792 the rankings had changed again. The coal port of Newcastle had moved into first place, now followed by Liverpool, while Bristol ranked only seventh, although it was still the second largest provincial port in terms of population.

Ship-ownership, of course, was not invariably indicative of a port's commercial importance: very little of the Scarborough-registered collier fleet, for example, actually traded from the home port. The figures in Table V, drawn from contemporary compilations of shipping tonnage made in selected years for the customs office, nonetheless show something of the evolving regional balance between England's ports in the course of the eighteenth century.[1] The growing strength of the outports collectively *vis-à-vis* London, for example, is readily apparent, although it is possible that the tonnage of shipping attributed to London in 1751 may be slightly too low and its share by the mid-century therefore understated.

Among the outports themselves, the early importance and growing strength of the north-eastern coal ports stands out. So does the emergence of the ports of the north-west. In contrast, there was a slight decline in the proportion of English shipping tonnage variously owned by the ports of East Anglia, and by the many small ports and harbours of south-western England. Among the individual ports to increase their shipping tonnage significantly in the course of the century were Newcastle, Sunderland, Hull, Liverpool, and Whitehaven; while the decline of Chester as a port (although not as a regional commercial centre) was emphatically signalled by the fact that it was the only sizeable trading port to own less shipping tonnage in 1792 than in 1709.

Table V Tonnage of merchant shipping owned in English ports, 1709–92*

| | 1709 | | 1751 | | 1792 | |
| | Tons burden ('000) | | Tons burden ('000) | | Measured tons† ('000) | |
Outports**		% of total		% of total		% of total
North-east						
Newcastle upon Tyne	11.5		21.6		121.2	
Sunderland	8.1		24.2		57.6	
Whitby	10.6		14.3		50.8	
Scarborough	27.1		33.3		25.8	
Kingston-upon-Hull	7.5		15.9		58.0	
5 others	3.8		10.1		17.6	
	68.6	21.45	119.4	28.42	331.0	27.90
East Anglia						
King's Lynn	6.5		9.1		16.8	
Great Yarmouth	11.4		14.7		35.8	
Ipswich	1.5		2.8		4.4	
Harwich	2.0		2.9		6.5	
Colchester	1.9		2.4		4.0	
8 others	5.8		7.7		16.6	
	29.1	9.10	39.6	9.42	84.1	7.09
South-east						
Faversham	1.0		1.2		6.4	
Dover	2.1		1.3		6.5	
Sandwich	2.2		1.9		5.0	
Southampton	1.6		2.7		9.2	
12 others	9.3		15.6		27.4	
	16.2	5.07	22.7	5.40	54.5	4.59
South-west						
Poole	4.1		7.6		19.2	
Exeter	6.9		7.1		13.4	
Barnstaple	3.1		4.4		6.8	
Bristol	15.5		19.0		43.9	
Swansea	2.3		1.2		6.3	
25 others	18.8		27.1		65.7	
	50.7	15.85	66.4	15.80	155.3	13.09
North-west						
Chester	2.7		1.3		2.4	
Liverpool	6.4		21.3		92.1	
Lancaster	1.0		2.3		10.7	

continued opposite

Table V continued

Outports**	1709 Tons burden ('000)	% of total	1751 Tons burden ('000)	% of total	1792 Measured tons† ('000)	% of total
Whitehaven	4.6		18.4		56.0	
7 others	0.5		9.4		26.2	
	15.2	4.75	52.7	12.54	187.4	15.79
All outports	179.8	56.22	300.8	71.58	812.3	68.46
London	c.140.0‡	43.78	119.4	28.42	374.2	31.54
Total	c.319.8‡	100.00	420.2	100.00	1186.5	100.00

* From contemporary listings of shipping tonnage (i.e. weight-carrying capacity) per individual port: British Library, Add. MSS. 11,255 and Add. MSS. 38,432.

** Regions as adopted by R. Davis, *The Rise of the English Shipping Industry in the Seventeenth and Eighteenth Centuries* (London, 1962), p. 33:

North-east = Lincolnshire northwards
East Anglia = Norfolk, Suffolk, Essex
South-east = S. bank of Thames estuary to W. border of Hampshire
South-west = Dorset to Pembrokeshire
North-west = Cardigan northwards

† After 1786 a more accurate system of measuring tonnage was introduced, which means that the later figures are not strictly comparable with the earlier ones.

‡ Estimated only: see Davis, op. cit., p. 35.

Little systematic comparative research has as yet been done into the extensive, but intractable, material in the surviving provincial port books, which recorded collection of customs dues.[2] Most ports overall, however, probably shared in the long-term expansion of English trade during these years. The staple traffic, particularly for the smaller ports, was the growing coastal trade – in grains, fuels, raw materials, groceries, and the bulkier manufactured goods. That was supplemented, in many cases, by some inshore fishing. A number of the smaller ports – especially those on the south and south-western coasts – were also involved in the extensive, if unquantified, smuggling trades. The illicit importation, or 'free-trading' as it was pointedly termed, of popular consumer goods (tea, tobacco, spirits, silks) and the illegal export of wool were undoubtedly the part-time occupations of many people in the eighteenth century. Yet, in general, the scale, flow, and organization of the smuggling trades was so mutable, and their operations so carefully dispersed, that their direct impact on port development was relatively small. At times they prompted dramatic incidents that illustrated the value of these transactions. At Poole in 1747 a band of smugglers launched a full-scale attack on the Customs House to retrieve their contraband tea. Usually, however, smuggled goods were quickly moved inland, and much evaded detection.

Orthodox foreign trade, on the other hand, tended to become more distinctly concentrated in a small number of the larger provincial ports, with the facilities to handle ocean-going shipping. This trend grew in the eighteenth century as the mean size of shipping increased. The same specialization applied to deep-sea fishing, and to the nascent whaling industry, centred on Liverpool, Newcastle, and Hull. Six large provincial ports increasingly dominated the overseas trade of the outports in these years. In the north-east, Newcastle and Sunderland were strenuous rivals for the export of coal, while Hull was engaged prominently in the Baltic and north European trades. On the west coast, Bristol and Liverpool competed keenly for the Irish, Atlantic, and slave trades; and Whitehaven, much the smallest of the six but the most rapidly growing newcomer among the ports, was an entrepôt or distribution headquarters for the North American tobacco trade, as well as a coal port.

England's foreign trade, expanding gradually in the early eighteenth century and hectically in the later decades, was, however, by its nature liable to considerable fluctuation and disruption in the short term. 'I trading constantly every year to Virginia, and God be thanked have had a very good success, not being in any ship that miscarried either by Sea or Enemy', rejoiced a Whitehaven merchant in 1707, identifying briskly two of the major hazards to his business. Yet another endemic difficulty was that of assessing commercial fluctuations at long distance. Threats of disaster, on the other hand, could have their uses, pushing up prices by creating scarcity. Two Bristol merchants, for example, complained in their private correspondence in 1788: 'The sugar market does not get up, we sadly want the report of a war, a hurricane, or something, to give it a lift.'

Variations in patterns of trade are shown in surviving figures of the tonnage of laden shipping, engaged in foreign trade, that entered and left these six major provincial ports, in selected years between 1709 and 1790. The information shown in Table VI, as collected by the eighteenth-century customs office, certainly has flaws. The records cover only twelve individual years and, most importantly, they are a guide only to the volume of goods carried and not to their value.[3] Nonetheless, they suggest a picture of long-term growth; and, fragmentary as the figures are, they also indicate clearly the short-term damage inflicted by war upon overseas trade, through the dislocation of commerce and the diversion of merchant shipping and men into naval service. Furthermore, one of the perennial difficulties facing merchants engaged in long-distance trade is demonstrated – namely, the problems in achieving a reasonable balance in the volume of trade inwards and outwards, to utilize shipping capacity to the maximum. Merchants in ports that dealt mainly in bulky one-way commodities found that a particular difficulty. Hull, with its extensive imports of Baltic timber, tended to have an excess of bulky imports over exports. The coal ports had the reverse problem, but even more severely. Whitehaven in a single year, 1790, exported almost seven times as many goods (by volume) as it imported. A troublesome by-product, when a return trade could not be achieved, was the disposal of the ballast (usually gravel or stones) from ships returning without freight. At the river port of Newcastle, in particular, there were continued grumbles from shippers that rubble washed back from the ballast quays was silting up the estuary, although the Corporation always indignantly denied the charge.

The fluidity of eighteenth-century urban history is again suggested by the fluctuating fortunes of these major provincial ports. A massive growth in Whitehaven's export trade (mainly in goods to Ireland) heightened its imbalance between imports and exports, and contributed to its eventual eclipse as a major port in the later eighteenth and early nineteenth centuries. Without an extensive consumer hinterland, its possibilities for sustained expansion were limited. Liverpool's overhauling of Bristol, at least in terms of the volume of overseas trade, was also apparent by the 1740s and was maintained consistently thereafter. That comparison almost certainly antedates the eclipse of Bristol in terms of the value of trade, for Bristol dealt in imported goods of relatively small bulk but of great value (tobacco, spices, snuffs), while it also grew rich on the proceeds of the triangular slave trade, which was not of course registered in the English port books. In terms of the value of customs revenue collected from imports, Bristol still ranked second among the outports at the end of the eighteenth century, only just behind Liverpool and well ahead of Hull. Furthermore, the 'metropolis of the west' continued to serve a huge local traffic to the ports of the Severn and Bristol Channel. The complexities of dating Bristol's changing status, however, do not detract from the paradox that the city's 'golden age' was also the era that saw the start of its relative eclipse. Certainly, from the 1760s onwards, worries were being expressed there about the port's trading position, while eighteenth-century Liverpool merchants had scarcely overtaken Chester, their ancient rival and the former head-port of the region until 1699, before they were casting competitive eyes upon Bristol.

The context of the growth of these provincial ports was undoubtedly

Table VI Volume of overseas trade of six major provincial ports, 1709–90*

(a) *Merchant shipping inwards (British and foreign-owned)* ** *by tons burden ('000)*

Year†	Bristol	Hull	Liverpool	Newcastle	Sunderland	Whitehaven
1709	19.8	8.1	14.6	7.8	0.0	9.9
1716	24.0	10.6	17.3	7.7	2.2	10.3
1723	26.4	11.0	18.8	10.7	3.9	9.1
1730	29.0	12.4	18.1	14.4	2.5	15.1
1737	26.4	19.0	17.5	14.0	8.8	7.6
1744	19.5	11.3	22.1	11.5	3.8	8.3
1751	30.4	23.6	31.7	21.7	6.4	10.8
1758	30.3	20.7	43.6	14.4	11.3	13.3
1765	38.3	34.0	61.2	21.1	12.0	32.4
1772	38.7	44.4	76.6	21.5	12.7	33.0
1779	32.3	40.6	74.7	14.5	7.8	32.9
1790‡	70.7	96.0	241.1	35.4	105.3	34.8

(b) *Merchant shipping outwards (British and foreign-owned) by tons burden ('000)*

1709	21.2	5.8	12.6	40.1	18.4	24.6
1716	23.7	8.6	18.9	40.1	35.0	31.6
1723	20.6	7.1	18.4	40.1	42.4	36.9
1730	24.6	8.2	19.1	46.3	49.8	45.2
1737	25.4	9.2	22.4	42.5	54.4	64.3
1744	15.3	9.2	22.7	26.8	37.4	94.3
1751	27.3	15.8	33.7	57.9	75.8	113.2
1758	35.9	12.3	44.8	36.4	41.0	107.9
1765	33.3	15.9	63.6	69.9	70.2	139.2
1772	35.7	18.4	93.0	73.4	85.2	193.4
1779	27.6	23.6	84.2	32.2	58.0	167.6
1790†	63.7	51.1	237.9	96.6	102.4	230.6

* British Library Add. MSS. 11,256, Tonnage of Shipping, 1709–1781; and Public Record Office, Customs 17/12.

** Excludes shipping entering port in ballast only.

† In italics for years when England was at war, as shown in the original manuscript.

‡ 1790 figures are measured tonnage, and collected from a different source.

the opening up of world-wide trade in the later seventeenth and eighteenth centuries, just as, earlier, London's massive commercial dominance had been based on the trading axis between England and the Netherlands. All long-distance trade was, however, underpinned by the local short-haul traffic, and the new trading patterns did not affect all the outports equally. Two major factors seem to have assisted the emergence of a few leading provincial ports: in some cases, growth was commodity-led; in others, it was regionally based.

Among the ports dealing in one or more commodity or raw material were the coal ports of the north of England and, later, of South Wales; and the grain ports of East Anglia, notably King's Lynn and Great Yarmouth, the latter also being a centre of herring fishing and curing. Others were major ports of entry and egress for extensive regional hinterlands: Hull, with its developing contacts with the West Riding of Yorkshire, parts of Lancashire, and the north-east Midlands; Liverpool, servicing southern Lancashire, the Cheshire Plain, and the northern Midlands; Bristol, catering for an extensive hinterland throughout the south Midlands, South Wales, and the West Country. Yet the distinction between 'regions' and 'commodities' should not be made too rigidly. Some commodity ports also generated their own immediate industrial hinterlands. For example, shipbuilding and iron- and glass-manufacturing grew up around Newcastle upon Tyne and Sunderland; Liverpool and its environs developed an array of refineries and foundries; and in the later eighteenth century copper-smelting and iron-manufacturing industries were established in the hinterland of Swansea, attracted by the relatively cheaper production costs on the coalfield. The grain ports, by contrast, did not generate many subsidiary or related industries, grain being a relatively 'mobile' resource. Conversely, one of the concealed strengths of Liverpool's position was that it did have a major raw material to export, as well as manufactured wares from its industrial hinterland. That was rock salt from Cheshire, discovered in 1670 and developed commercially from the later seventeenth century onwards. One observer, indeed, claimed in the 1790s that: 'The Salt Trade is generally acknowledged to have been the Nursing Mother, and to have contributed more to the first rise, gradual increase, and present flourishing state of the Town of Liverpool, than any other Article of Commerce.' He was exaggerating, but only slightly. The broad base of Liverpool's trading role undoubtedly helped to explain its rapid rise to importance and its eventual triumph over Bristol.

The implicit competition between the two great west-coast ports for predominance in the Atlantic and slave trades continued throughout the century. It illustrates clearly the point already made that 'growth' did not shed its mantle evenly on all towns alike. Numerous factors have been canvassed to explain the outcome of the competition between Bristol and Liverpool. Some, such as the initial complacency and lack of competitive drive on the part of the Bristol merchants, are highly questionable. They seem much more like symptoms of early success than root causes of eventual failure. Other differential factors – such as higher local port dues at Bristol – were probably only marginal in their effect. They certainly had not prevented the port's seventeenth-century success. More important factors therefore were the diverse base of Liverpool's trading economy, plus its early initiative in implementing dock and harbour improvements in the course of the century. Its natural handicaps were thereby transmuted into effective assets. Most crucially, Liverpool not only serviced an immediate hinterland that was industrializing rapidly, but it also developed good communications with the populous and industrially expanding Midland counties. In 1720, for example, two Midland towns (Derby and Lichfield) joined in the campaign to improve the River Weaver navigation, urging that they imported a considerable range of colonial goods by river and road from Liverpool. Already much of the overseas trade to and from Birmingham and the Black Country was directed via Liverpool (and also via Hull), as well as through the port of Bristol. Midlands manufactured goods provided much of the staple cargoes for the first stage of the slave trade.

Subsequent transport improvements serviced and consolidated these new commercial realities. The advent of the canal era in the later eighteenth century strengthened Birmingham's trading contacts with the northern ports. A canal link from Birmingham to the Trent and Mersey canal was opened in 1772. The first Birmingham canal did also give access to the Severn at Stourport, but was used chiefly for the carriage of Staffordshire coals. Furthermore, construction difficulties in crossing the steep escarpments of the Severn valley delayed the completion of the more direct route from Birmingham to the Severn at Worcester for some twenty-four years after its authorization in 1791. Goods were also, of course, taken overland from Birmingham to Bristol, but the delay in canal construction was symptomatic. The growth and differing fortunes of the 'regional' ports were therefore closely connected to both the nature and the extent of their effective hinterlands.

Most unusual and most dramatic was the case of Whitehaven. That port was planned and promoted initially in the 1670s and 1680s by the patronage of a local coal-owning gentry family, the Lowthers. Their investment and enterprise continued apace in the eighteenth century, not always to the fullest enthusiasm of the local residents. Captain Walter Lutwidge, a Whitehaven merchant, kinsman and for a time business associate of the Lowthers, attacked them as monopolists. He denounced the head of the family in 1748 as 'an Inhuman Tierant' (*sic*). However, despite some friction and its remote location, Whitehaven was launched successfully, and rapidly increased its trading turnover. It was both a coal port, sending Cumbrian coals to Ireland, and, in the early eighteenth century, an entrepôt for the colonial tobacco trades, re-exporting goods to Ireland, Holland, Italy, and a number of other European countries. Its importance in that trade was particularly marked before Glasgow effectively took over as the great tobacco emporium of Britain in mid-century. Eventually, therefore, Whitehaven's development was limited by the lack of growth in its hinterland, leaving it with little return cargo to counterbalance the export of coals. Inspired, if sometimes heavy-handed, patronage could therefore succeed only within certain limits.

Within the context of England's generally buoyant commercial economy, there were many variations in the fortunes of individual ports. A very few experienced outright decline and decay as ports in these years. Sandwich, to Celia Fiennes in the 1690s a 'sad old Town', was one that faced irretrievable economic difficulties from the silting up of its harbour. And the once-mighty port of Chester also suffered a considerable decline, especially in overseas trade, as large ships were debarred by heavy silting in the estuary of the Dee. The close proximity of Liverpool additionally deflected pressures for improvement schemes. A New Cut through the sands was authorized in 1732 and opened in 1735–6, to assist the outfall of the Dee, but it did not prove very successful, discouraging further initiatives. Chester's continuing trade in the later eighteenth century was chiefly confined to the coastal traffic in local agricultural produce, notably in the famous Cheshire cheeses.

Some other small and medium-sized ports did not grow very rapidly, especially in the early decades of the century. Contemporary observers tended to describe their fortunes in terms of blight and decay, but on examination in most cases the decline was relative rather than absolute. Celia Fiennes, for example, considered Truro to be, in comparison with earlier times, a 'ruinated disregarded Place'. In reality, however, Truro's port books show it to have enjoyed a steady, if not wildly expansive, coastal trade, shipping copper and tin to South Wales and returning with coal from Swansea and miscellaneous goods from London, Bristol, and the south-coast ports. In the same vein, Celia Fiennes also drew a melancholy picture of Southampton: 'Now the Trade has failed and the Town [is] almost forsooke and neglected.' Yet, whatever the state of affairs at the turn of the century, the port books indicate a continuing volume of coastal trade in the eighteenth century, as Southampton merchants carried coals, salt, agricultural produce, timber, and some manufactured goods, to and from other south-coast ports, London, and the Channel Islands. Southampton also had a lively career at this time as a resort and holiday town.

The ports that were marking time most visibly in the early eighteenth century were to be found in East Anglia and the south, reflecting the shifting regional balance in England's commerce. Defoe in the 1720s also commented on the 'decay' or problems of the ports of Dover, Winchelsea, Rye, and Ipswich. Indeed, Ipswich was, with Chester, the largest port to face economic difficulties, although both places (like Southampton) were successful centres for local trade and the social life of the gentry. There was nothing as marked as a 'shake-out' of the smaller and medium-sized ports, although there was a growing differentiation between those dealing in international or long-distance trade and the local ports. Many found that they were catering for an increasing volume of trade (especially coastal trade) in the later eighteenth century, with the general growth of population and commercial activity. Some found additional roles as seaside resorts. At least one anciently blighted port was restored to active commercial life by engineering ingenuity: in 1764 the Grand Sluice was built to drain the Holland Fen and to scour the silted-up haven of Boston, whose trading activity thereafter recovered promptly. The picture was complex in detail, but in general the ports shared, some markedly, some less dramatically, in the urban growth of these years. As they did so, their roles, too, were streamlined, their functions more specialized and more highly organized.

Three other specialist ports fell into a category quite their own. These were the major dockyard towns: Chatham, Portsmouth, and Plymouth. They all attracted considerable increase in population in the course of the century. Already sizeable by 1700, both Plymouth and Portsmouth were among the largest provincial towns in England and Wales by 1801 – ranking eighth and twelfth respectively. Chatham was not far behind. All were much larger than many traditional county capitals or long-established market centres. Their growth rates were closely influenced by the fortunes of their staple business: in that case, the changing requirements of government foreign policy rather than the fluctuations of trade. War, or the expectation of war, signalled rapid growth. In the later seventeenth century, particularly during the wars against the Dutch, the dockyards of Chatham had been given priority. Investment continued in the following century, when the population of Rochester–Chatham approximately doubled. With hostilities against Spain and later France, the Admiralty's attention in the eighteenth century also turned strongly to the south-coast dockyards. Portsea, the plebeian suburb of Portsmouth, expanded rapidly; between them they housed over 30,000 inhabitants in 1801. Meanwhile Plymouth, initially a fairly small service station for the fleet, grew most rapidly of all, after the foundation of the new yards in 1689. Much of its growth occurred in an industrial suburb, known prosaically as Dock (renamed Devonport in 1824). The combined populations of the conurbation by 1801 came to 43,000, of whom over half lived in Dock.

The dockyard towns had from the start highly specialized economies. They were certainly also minor ports, but their essential functions were the building and servicing of ships for the fleet. The scale of the dockyards made them some of the largest business operations in the whole country. The assembly-line manufactures of shipping, sail, rope, chain, and other tackle, constituted some of the earliest quasi-factory organizations. The predominance of employment in the yards made these places the eighteenth-century's equivalent of the 'company town'. Indeed, so draconian was the work discipline (in theory, at least) that an opponent of the death penalty suggested in 1753 that confinement and hard labour in the dockyards would provide a satisfactory substitute punishment. Situated as they were at a distance from other very large towns, the dockyards produced societies that seemed inward-looking and secretive to outsiders. They did not, for example, generate a tithe of the contemporary literature, guidebooks, surveys, histories, or even ballads and songs, that recounted the growth of many other towns.

Employment in the docks was central to their local economy. A survey of fragmentary surviving information relating to occupations in eighteenth-century Portsmouth and Portsea (using inventories and legal records) has suggested that as many as 73 per cent – virtually three-quarters – of all recorded adult male occupations were in shipbuilding and related industries. That compared with only 18 per cent engaged in the clothing trades, and a mere 9 per cent in the provision of food and drink. Those figures were not necessarily fully representative of the whole labour force, but accounts of the dockyard employees furnished by the Naval Commission visitations in 1700, 1759, 1764, and 1783 indicated a similarly high proportion of the adult male population engaged in the yards. A figure of at least 50 per cent is suggested by a comparison of the Commission's records with the estimated populations of the dockyard towns. Here, however, unlike in many eighteenth-century towns, jobs for women were comparatively restricted. While in many cases women migrants to town outnumbered the men, in the dockyard towns it tended to be the other way around. Indeed, a survey of Hampshire's agrarian economy (1804) complained dramatically that 'Portsmouth and the shipyards of the coast afford a constant market for all the prime and picked labourers of the county, leaving little behind but feebleness and debility to carry forward the common labours.'

In the context of the large-scale organization of the yards, the dockyard workforce were notably well-disciplined and organized in defence of their own interests and work conditions. They were particularly tenacious of the traditional perquisite, in supplement of their pay, of being allowed to take wood chippings from the yards. In the course of numerous industrial confrontations in the eighteenth century, the shipwrights formed national associations linking yard with yard. 'Petitions and Remonstrances were sent up to the Navy Board,' reported a shocked MP to the House in 1781, 'Committees were appointed; and Delegates and Deputies were sent up to London, to treat with the Navy Board, in the Nature of a Congress.' Yet, in general, as a result of the isolation of the dockyard towns, the specialist nature of their employment, and the particular chronology of their trade cycles, their militancy proved difficult to co-ordinate with radicalism elsewhere in the country.

The dockyard towns, then, were by no means quiet and placid places, despite their veil of secrecy. Indeed, their rapid growth seems to have sharpened a considerable range of conflicts. There were tensions between the Navy Board and the workforce in the yards; there were disputes between the Board and the local municipal corporations, jealous for their independence; and there were often social hostilities between the older towns and their newly growing industrial suburbs. In the case of the emergent Rochester–Chatham conurbation, Rochester represented the traditional interest and looked down on Chatham. The two communities were old rivals, arguing over their respective market rights in 1674, 1687, and 1711. Later, they proved unable to agree on a joint scheme for street-lighting and paving in the 1760s. In Portsmouth and Plymouth it was the new industrial suburbs that were, illogically, resented. As often happened in the most rapidly growing urban areas, the supply of water became a contested issue. In the case of Plymouth, there was fierce opposition to a scheme to pipe fresh water thence to Dock. 'No, no! I am against the *dockers;* I am a Plymouth man. Rogues! let them die of thirst!' thundered Dr Johnson, in exaggerated espousal of the conservative cause. In the event, the residents of Dock were constrained to form their own Water Company in 1792, in rivalry to Plymouth's long-established municipal supply.

There were therefore manifold signs of change – of growth and adaptation – in the eighteenth-century ports. They too were crowded, bustling places. The great provincial ports in particular had some of the highest population densities to be found anywhere in the country. Housing was packed into town centres and around the docks. Even the relatively spacious layout of early eighteenth-century Whitehaven rapidly became submerged as back yards and gardens were built over. In Newcastle and Sunderland in 1801 the number of inhabitants per house (8.6 and 8.4 respectively) was unsurpassed elsewhere. Lodging houses, alehouses, inns, abounded in the ports, which were also notorious for their brothels. A Liverpool *Guide* (1800) lamented the number of prostitutes who walked the streets, 'elegantly dressed', and frequented 'infamous brothels...which are grown to such a height of refined wantonness, unknown to any period'.

There were constant reminders of the life of the sea. At Bristol, ships sailed up river into the heart of town, and Pope observed admiringly on a visit in 1739: 'in the middle of the street, as far as you can see, hundreds of Ships, their Masts as thick as they can stand by one another, which is the oddest and most surprising sight imaginable.' The quayside was a favourite spot for citizens to stroll in the evenings and on holidays. At Yarmouth the arrival of the Dutch herring fleet in late September was a great social event. An onlooker reported in 1785 that 'The whole Length of the Quay was crowded by People of all Ranks in their best Apparel'; and added candidly that 'The annual Visit is a welcome Thing here, not only on Account of the Money they [the Dutch] spend themselves, but from the Conflux of Strangers brought hither by the Novelty of the Spectacle.'

Considerable investment went into the apparatus of trade. Grand merchants' houses were built, as well as warehousing, stately Exchange buildings, and the ubiquitous customs houses. Above all, extensive funds were channelled into dock-building and harbour improvements. Little research has been carried out into early dock-building schemes, despite recent interest in other improvements to the transport network; but a considerable number of English ports in the eighteenth century, both large and small, devoted attention to the maintenance and improvement of their harbours. New docks were constructed at Hull, Sunderland, Whitehaven, Whitby, and Liverpool. New piers were erected at Great Yarmouth, Scarborough, Newhaven, Rye, Dover, Wells, Bridlington, and Ramsgate. And many smaller works of dredging and maintenance were carried out. Improvements were needed partly to cater for the increasing volume of shipping and the growing size of ships, and partly to combat silting and navigational hazards. In the case of Hull, dock-building in 1774 followed a much-contested campaign for a public quay, to supplement the many privately owned staithes. It is impossible to quantify the total investment in port improvements, but in the course of the century it must have reached several million pounds. Most magnificent of all was the dock-building programme at Liverpool, whose natural port facilities in the tidally-complex Mersey estuary were very poor. The first dock there was authorized in 1710 and opened in 1715. A century later the Dock Estate Company was responsible for some sixty acres of docks, all interlinked for tidal cleansing. By the early nineteenth century the Company had spent more than £2.5 million there, raised by borrowing on the security of the dock and tonnage duties. A local patriot exulted: 'The ancients may boast of their pyramids and their palaces,

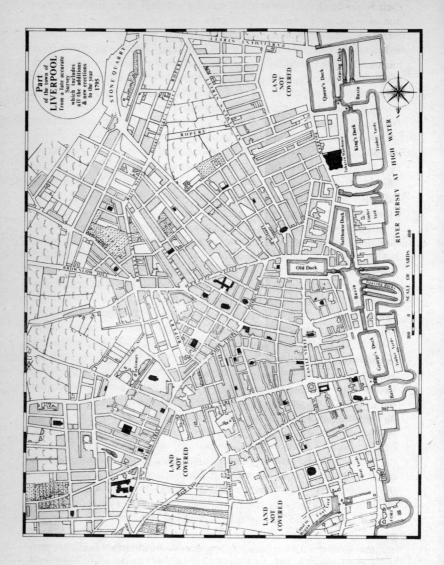

their towers and their temples . . .; but these works of modern construction will long be remembered as the most indubitable memorials of mercantile enterprise and transcendent utility.'

Trade was a predominant concern of the ports' inhabitants, the state of business a major topic of conversation. In eighteenth-century Bristol people professed '(to use their own Phrase) to care for no Body, but whom they could gain by'. A *Satire* of 1794 waxed sardonic:

> Discordant sounds compose the Babel hum
> 'Tis 'How goes Sugar? What's the Price of Rum?
> What ships arrived? And how are Stocks today?
> Who's dead? Who's broken? And who's run away?'

In fact, relatively few merchants traded on their own account. Many worked in partnerships to spread the risks, especially in the hazardous long-distance trades. They dealt in a wide range of commodities, although, notably in the larger ports, specialization in particular markets or in particular goods became more marked. Others were emerging as specialist shipowners. Overseas trade was especially risky and speculative, and insurance agents were also powerful and necessary figures behind mercantile enterprise.

The private letters of merchants were often case studies in nagging anxieties. Cries of woe abounded. News of the return of the fleet was eagerly awaited. The Hull merchant, Sir Henry Etherington, reputedly sat in his attic looking out to sea with a telescope, watching for the return of his ships. In late eighteenth-century Liverpool some ninety or so beacons stood on Bidston Hill, on the south bank of the Mersey, to hoist signals for the major shipping houses when a vessel was sighted. Even the coastal trade could prove troublesome. In the context of relatively glutted coal markets early in the century, fierce and complex rivalry for control of the trade was waged between the ports of the Tyne and the Wear, and also between the coal-owners, the shippers, and the London dealers.

◄ Fig. 5: Liverpool in 1795, from a contemporary survey. Eighteenth-century Liverpool's physical expansion still left the town a compact and densely settled centre, close to the river frontage. Many of the sites between the main streets were crammed with tenements, off narrow courts, yards, and passageways. Some of the earliest back-to-back housing was constructed to the south of the Old Dock, between St. James's Street and Wapping, in the 1780s. As yet, however, no part of town was far from fields and gardens. The port's facilities were greatly amplified by the programme of dock-building, beginning the transformation of the small harbour into a modern port. The original Pool was converted into the Old Dock in 1710 (completed 1715), followed by the first of many later docks in the channel of the Mersey, including Salthouse 1738 (completed 1753), George's 1762 (completed 1771), Duke of Bridgewater's 1762 (completed later 1760s), King's Dock 1785 (completed 1788), and Queen's Dock 1785 (completed 1796).

After one troubled year (1713), a mine-owner, Sir Henry Liddell, reported a general panic: 'The Masters run about . . . like so many craz'd People; they bellow, swear, and foreswear every Voyage that . . . they will be damn'd before they will load again.' In that context, the famed industrial militancy of the Newcastle keelmen, who were employed on a casual basis in a fluctuating trade, was readily comprehensible.

Certainly, despite vicissitudes, some huge fortunes were made in trade: for example, the West India merchants of eighteenth-century Bristol enjoyed some of the largest non-landed incomes in the country. The urban societies of the ports were dominated by the big merchant families: the Claytons, Ridleys, Blacketts in Newcastle; the Maisters, Peases, Standidges, and Wilberforces in Hull. Some moved into the countryside and established themselves as country gentlemen, some remained in trade but copied the manners and way of life of the country gentry. William Richards, a critic of the King's Lynn corporation, ridiculed in 1812 the local merchants' social pretensions: 'All the leading Families of this Town are in fact *tradesmen*; yet even these are very capriciously and superciliously distinguished into *Gentlemen* and *Tradesmen.*' Defoe had earlier asked rhetorically: 'How do our Merchants in *London, Bristol, Liverpool, Yarmouth, Hull,* and other trading Sea-Ports, appear in their Families, with the Splendour of the best Gentlemen?' Below these dizzy heights swarmed a host of hopeful small merchants, traders, factors, dealers, warehousemen, shippers, while the economy of the ports was underpinned by a multitudinous workforce of dock labourers and seamen. Demand for their labour was irregular, peaking in the summer months, slack in winter. It was not uncommon for large groups of out-of-work seamen to throng the streets of the ports, where they were, as a Hull chronicler noted disdainfully, 'left at leisure to exercise their dissolute Manners on the inoffensive Passenger in the public Street'. Their way of life was tough and testing, and could pose unforeseen moral problems. Samuel Kelly, a chief mate plying the Atlantic trades, recorded in his manuscript autobiography in 1786 that he had heard from a fellow sailor 'such an account of the iniquity practised in the slave trade that I determined never to go into that employ'. In wartime seamen also risked the hazards of enrolment into the navy by the press-gangs, whose activities added a further note of drama and danger to the bustle of the eighteenth-century ports.

4 Spas and resorts

Eighteenth-century towns had a key role to play as centres for the growing entertainments industry. Though London, by its size and diversity, retained its cultural pre-eminence, provincial towns began increasingly to constitute centres of social life and entertainment for their own inhabitants and those of the surrounding countryside. That included not only the larger regional capitals but also many middle-ranking towns, county capitals, attracting custom on the coat-tails of commerce and politics. Durham, Lincoln, Maidstone, Salisbury, Shrewsbury, Warwick, Winchester, York, were notable examples. 'Here we have Smoke, Noise, Scandal, Affectation, and Pretension!' exclaimed the heroine of *The Recruiting Officer* in 1706, affirming her devotion to Shrewsbury's urban charms. Indeed, even a relatively small centre (Shrewsbury's resident population was about 7,000 at the start of the century) could establish a lively social round, if its hinterland was wide enough. Other places of congregation for 'good Conversation and good Company' were popular through long-established tradition as regional magnets: Stamford, King's Lynn, Bury St. Edmunds in Suffolk, whose residents 'are supposed to live there for the sake of it', and 'Proud Preston', before its late eighteenth-century submersion by manufacturing. To these gentry centres, too, were added in the course of the century a growing number of specialist resorts, whose existence and development as towns was owed substantially to tourism and leisure industries.

Changing patterns of social life and entertainment sprang from the growth and diffusion of wealth in eighteenth-century England. A new and more broadly based consumer society created urban markets for specialist entertainments previously confined to courts, the capital, and great country houses. In the eighteenth century custom for the resorts came not only from the aristocracy and landed gentry – although they certainly joined in – but also from the growing urban middle class.

A number of towns therefore became the venue and showcase for social gatherings, where people could enjoy themselves in company with others. The 'conspicuous consumption' of leisure required not only the supporting services of the towns but also the mutual audience there assembled. As the ascetic Veblen pointed out in his mordant *Theory of the Leisure Class* (1899), goods and services were doubly valued in an acquisitive society, not only for their intrinsic worth but also for their publicly observed use and display. An appropriate urban environment (not all towns qualified) constituted an open and ostensibly neutral territory, where people could congregate in large numbers to see and be seen. Social display marked a claim for status; and simultaneously assisted social recognition in the impersonal urban environment. Beau Nash at Bath enforced rules of dress in order to achieve that effect. He removed an apron from the dress of the Duchess of Queensberry at an elegant soirée is the Assembly Rooms, announcing firmly that: 'None but *Abigails* [i.e. serving-maids] appeared in white Aprons.'

In the long term, the range of service specialisms demanded by wealthy societies has tended to broaden, but one of the earliest and most persistent demands to emerge has been that for the provision of accommodation, services, and entertainment, for people on holiday. The gradual specialization of work produced the obverse concept of specialized leisure. The 'holiday' came to be thought of as more than a single day – rather as a span of time. 'The more a Man is attentive to his Concerns, the more he has a Right to wish a Relaxation', decided the hard-working Hutton, introducing his *Description of Blackpool* (1789). The 'commercialization of leisure' to cater for that wish was, as its historian observes, increasingly an urban phenomenon.[1] It affected virtually all towns in the eighteenth century; and also fostered the specialized growth of the spas. In the course of the previous century the medicinal properties of mineral waters had been increasingly publicized. Serious scientific interest in their use was maintained in the eighteenth century; and a visit to the spas was strongly touted by the medical profession, especially for troublesome diseases that they could not cure. Satirists enjoyed laughing at the procession of gouty squires and vaporous ladies that made their way to Bath. But the spas did not grow as health resorts alone. It was their additional role as leisure centres that signalled the start of a sustained urban success.

The association of the early entertainment towns with medical services did not, however, stem from some particularly English association of entertainment and recreation with illness and disease. Many visitors to the spas were in fact *malades imaginaires,* as an observer noted wryly. The essential reason for the development of a vigorous entertainment industry was that these were places where crowds of people congregated for non-business purposes, thus offering a captive audience with time and money on their hands. As the author of a compendious guide to the English spas noticed in 1841, for the visitor, 'The mode of living is no longer the same at a Spa as at home. There is ... an end to all ordinary or fatiguing or worrying occupations.' Advocate of the spas as he was, he admitted that boredom would soon take hold, if the fourteen or sixteen waking hours were left unfilled. Not surprisingly, there developed an elaborate daily round of amusements. Entertainment became big business: 'Fools, Cullies, Squires, Beaus, and Criticks, resort as thick, as *Stock-Jobbers* about ... the *Royal Exchange*', reported a visitor to Bath's coffee houses in 1700. The initial association of the leisure industry with the health resorts was therefore readily explicable. Indeed, much the same progression occurred later in the development of both seaside and mountain resorts.

At 'the Bath' itself, as it was known in the eighteenth century, the number of invalid visitors was rapidly surpassed by the healthy. As early as 1698 a French visitor had noted that 'Thousands go thither to pass away a few Weeks, without heeding either the Baths or the Waters, but only to divert themselves with good Company.' By the mid-eighteenth century some critics of the services even argued that it was healthier not to join in the bathing, on grounds of hygiene. Nonetheless, the thermal baths remained an important focus for the social life of the resort. Crowds congregated at the three main baths every morning, either to drink the mineral waters, or to join in the bathing, or to view the fun. The King's Bath was for the genuinely sick; the Queen's Bath was for ladies only; while the Cross Gate Bath was the favoured venue for social bathing. Styles of immersion had changed considerably since the early seventeenth century, when the sight of the naked forms of the sick, the halt, and the lame of both sexes, had prompted thoughts of the Resurrection to a visitor in 1634. By the later seventeenth century, bathers were shrouded in canvas garments and helped into the water by attendants. If *A Step to the Bath* (1700) stressed the lascivious possibilities of clinging drapery and groping limbs, Celia Fiennes observed on a visit in 1687 the growing social ritual and decorum: 'There is a Serjeant belonging to the Baths that all the bathing Tyme walkes in the Galleryes and takes notice Order is observed, and punishes the Rude, and most People of Fashion sends to him when they begin to bathe.' In the eighteenth century some critical voices began to demur at the continuance of the practice of mixed bathing in two of the three baths; while others defended it as an essential part of the entertainment. Eventually, in the early nineteenth century, the practice was halted and separate days set aside for the different sexes, making bathing much less popular.

Other than a visit to the waters themselves, the social life of Bath centred around balls, assemblies, concerts, promenades, excursions, gaming, and intrigue. All resorts were famed as places with abundant opportunities for meeting the opposite sex; and Bath, as the premier spa, was particularly celebrated as a marriage market. The heroine of a romantic novel of 1761 trembled when an eligible *parti* took his time in coming to London: 'I am afraid he is gone to Bath only to show himself, and that he will be snapped up before he comes to Town', she lamented in businesslike tones. Young people from well-to-do families were therefore among the most enthusiastic devotees of a visit to Bath; social adventurers correspondingly often went there in search of a wealthy marriage.

Much of the early consumer demand came from affluent families in London and the south. London itself, of course, maintained its own winter season; but entertainments also demanded variety. Initially, many of the springs and wells close to the capital – Islington, Hampstead, Epsom, Streatham, Dulwich – flourished as resorts, but they were too close to London's sprawl to succeed as specialized holiday centres, although they were popular with Londoners for a day's outing. Entertainment demanded more than the commonplace to succeed; a fashionable resort needed accessibility – but also amenities, patronage, and constant promotion. Bath either had, or acquired, all four.

Improvements to the Avon in the early eighteenth century assisted the carriage of goods. And Bath rapidly established coach services, that were excellent by the standards of the time, for its many visitors. It is true that travellers in the early eighteenth century grumbled at the steep hills and bumpy roads just outside the city, but the road attracted some of the earliest investment in turnpike trusts. Though initially Bath drew custom mainly from London and the southern counties, as communications improved in the course of the eighteenth century and as travel times were reduced, its consumer hinterland became nationwide. The 1773 *Strangers' Assistant and Guide to Bath* listed an extensive network of regular services to and from the city. Passengers could travel to London on the three one-day 'flying machines' that left daily in the summer months, or on the six two-day coaches that left every two or three days throughout the year. Goods equally could be dispatched there either by the 'flying waggons' or the 'slow waggons'. Passengers for Bristol had a choice of five daily coaches, one of which went on to the Hotwells there, while goods for Bristol could be sent by the daily waggon or barge services. Coaches also left twice weekly directly for Exeter, Salisbury, and Oxford, although passengers for the north or Midlands had to catch the advertised connections at Bristol. If each coach took a full load of (on average) eight passengers, it meant that approximately 608 people entered and left Bath each week (or over 31,000 journeys in a year) on these scheduled services. Many grand visitors, furthermore, travelled by private equipage, and others by hired coach and four, while poorer travellers made their way on foot or got a lift with the carriers' waggons. The provision of all these transport services expanded rapidly in the later eighteenth century, particularly as middle-class demand increased.

Accessibility alone, however, was clearly insufficient to promote a spa. Indeed, many places were closer to London and other major centres of population than was Bath. A second necessary ingredient was the provision of suitable amenities, and it was to the quality of its new development that Bath owed much of its appeal. The building of eighteenth-century Bath created nothing less than a magnificent urban stage for its comedy of manners. A first requirement was good-quality accommodation. In the course of the century Bath's housing stock was greatly augmented, and the new building incorporated some striking and important developments in urban design. Rebuilding in the old lower town, around the Abbey, was complemented by the growth of an upper town to the north and west. The architect-developer John Wood's ambitious projects for the creation of a new Rome at Bath found no backers. But the developments he was able to carry out made the city a showcase for new standards of urban design and interior decoration. Wood's earliest project was the building of the stately Queen Square (built between 1728 and 1735), where he himself lived. He was aware of the social uses of public space. Explaining his formal design of the square, he wrote: 'I preferred an inclosed Square to an Open One, to make this as Useful as possible: for the Intention of a Square in a City is for People to Assemble together....' The aim was to enable polite society to promenade in 'Decency and good Order'. The same principles lay behind his building of the Grand (North) and South Parades, to the south-east of the old city (1740–3). John Wood the Younger continued his father's plans. His developments included the novel King's Circus (1754–64), with a surrounding network of residential streets; and culminated in the majestic sweep of the much-admired Royal Crescent (1767–75).

Numerous other architects contributed to the building of Georgian Bath, amplifying and extending the fashionable classical style. They were attracted to Bath by the abundance of patrons, while their work – such as Baldwin's Bathwick Estate (1788–93) and Palmer's Lansdown Crescent (1789–92) – became talking points in urban design. A degree of visual unity was created by their collective use of local stone, much of it from the quarries at Combe Down owned by the entrepreneur and powerful city councillor, Ralph Allen. Not that the whole city was composed of modish residences: there were humbler areas; and fashions changed fast. Queen Square itself was considered somewhat *passé* by the early nineteenth century. But the general effect was grander than the individual details. Bath had thus obtained an expanded housing stock with a distinctive urban style.

Public venues for the congregation and entertainment of fashionable society were also furnished by private developers, sometimes with the encouragement and patronage of the Corporation. The first playhouse was opened in 1705 in the Borough Walls (demolished 1737); the first Pump Room, to accommodate and entertain those taking the waters, was opened in 1706 and extended in 1751; the first Assembly Rooms (known as Harrison's, after the local businessman who promoted them) were completed in 1708; and a Ballroom was opened in 1720 and remodelled in 1749. Wood himself promoted in 1728 the construction of the second Assembly Rooms (known at first as Lindsey's and later as Wiltshire's). Harrison's Walks were laid out for the fashionable promenade, as was the nearby gravel walk between the baths and the river, later known as the Orange Grove. The Bowling Green was another popular venue, as were, in the mid-century, the Spring Gardens, on the east bank of the river and reached at that time by ferry. A new theatre was erected in Orchard Street in 1750, substantially reconstructed in 1775. All these focused upon the environs of the baths and the Abbey in the lower town. But the growth of the upper town led to changes. A third assembly was started at the Upper Assembly Rooms, constructed on a sumptuous scale in 1769 by John Wood the Younger. They were immediately successful with the residents of the upper town, who no longer had to travel the steep and slippery hills of Bath to find entertainment. Such success rewarded the venture that Wiltshire's Rooms closed permanently, and great pressure was placed on Simpson's Rooms (formerly Harrison's, and thenceforth renamed the Lower Rooms). The rival assemblies continued in uneasy tandem, each with its own Master of Ceremonies and code of etiquette. Unavoidably, however, the growing physical dispersal and increasing scale of Bath's entertainments industry entailed some loss of consumer cohesion. As the social range of visitors widened, the number of private aristocratic parties and 'at homes' increased – a practice that had been severely frowned upon half a century earlier by Beau Nash.

In the later eighteenth century the Corporation itself was stimulated into a programme of renovation for the lower town, and its baths. A special Improvement Committee was established, with an Inspector of the Baths in 1787; and the Bath Improvement Act was sought in 1789. The baths themselves had changed relatively little in the course of the century, and were coming under increasing criticism for poor maintenance and insalubrity. Wealthier patrons preferred the private fee-paying baths erected by the Duke of Kingston in 1766. The Corporation therefore sponsored the building of a new Hot Bath (1773–7), built by the younger Wood, the New Private Baths (1788–9), a new Pump Room (1790), and the rebuilding of the Cross Baths, which were linked with the other main baths by the elegantly colonnaded Bath Street (1791). It took a constant effort to remain in fashion, particularly when Bath's social monopoly was challenged by the growth of rival places of resort in the later eighteenth century.

Much therefore turned upon the third factor in a resort's success: the nature of its patronage. Some of the initial social prestige of Bath stemmed from royal favour. Queen Anne visited the resort for two summers in succession in 1702 and 1703. In essence, however, the early support for Bath was drawn strongly from aristocratic and fashionable London society. The accession of the socially unpretentious Hanoverians therefore did not undermine the prestige of Bath, although neither of the first two Georges ever visited it. When the Princess Amelia visited in the 1730s, her request that dancing be prolonged beyond the customary closing hour of 11.00 p.m. was firmly refused. At the same time, Bath society was not exclusive. Awareness of social rank and distinction there undoubtedly was; but the public gatherings were open to all who had the money, status, or audacity to attend. As Master of Ceremonies Richard 'Beau' Nash, himself of modest social origins, was adept at making his displeasure felt at overt displays of snobbery. He publicly rebuked aristocrats who refused to dance with people they deemed to be social inferiors. He wished to preserve rank but not segregation.

Ultimately, however, the relative social openness of Bath contributed to the flight of the ultra-fashionable. The growth of population and the diffusion of wealth had created an even larger urban and middle-class clientele by the later eighteenth century, who were also anxious to join in the entertainment. It became impossible for the Master of Ceremonies to greet all visitors personally and for the traditional welcome of a peal of bells and musical serenade to be provided. Smollett satirized in *Humphry Clinker* (1771) these widening social horizons and gentry reaction to them. 'Every Upstart of Fortune, harnessed in the Trappings of the Mode, presents himself at Bath, as in the very Focus of Observation', grumbled Squire Bramble. He concluded that Bath contained nothing but 'a very inconsiderable Porportion of genteel People . . . lost in a Mob of impudent Plebeians'. These hostile strictures were exaggerated, but they did contain an element of accurate social observation. It was not true, as is often claimed, that Bath had simply effected a transition from an aristocratic to a middle-class resort in the course of the century. Part of its early success had been its admixture of town and country grandees, and it retained this capacity throughout the century. But it was true that the glamour began to fade. Increasingly, in the later eighteenth century,

Bath became a retirement as well as an entertainments centre. Rentiers, lesser gentry, absentee clergymen, retired military men, and numerous widows, settled in the city as permanent residents, finding, as did Jane Austen's spendthrift country gentleman, that they could 'there be important at comparatively little Expense'.

Lastly, a resort depended for its success upon the promotion of an attractive image. For this, early eighteenth-century Bath owed much to the achievement of its uncrowned king, Beau Nash, who fostered the image of the city as the natural home for elegant leisure. He encouraged the Corporation to cleanse the city and inspect lodgings; he insisted that the sedan chairmen should be licensed and fares regulated; he banned duelling and the wearing of swords; he promoted the provision of amenities. Certainly, Nash alone did not create Bath as a resort. It may well be argued that he fulfilled an obvious social need by acting, in his long regime as Master of Ceremonies from 1705–61, as the unofficial (and unpaid) host to the large and heterogeneous company attracted to Bath to 'take the cure'. Nash's importance, however, lay in his codification of social manners, and his organization of the daily social round. The Beau was a distinctive figure there, with his 'very agreeable oddness of appearance', marked by his white hat and flamboyant dress. In manners, he favoured a relaxed and witty good breeding. He himself cultivated a reputation as a wit. Goldsmith's *Life of Richard Nash* noted slyly: 'Once a week he might say a good thing, this the little ones about him took care to divulge; or, if they happened to forget the joke, he usually remembered to repeat it himself.' Nash's celebrated eleven rules of conduct, promulgated in 1742, towards the end of his regime, were intended initially as a joke, at least according to his biographer; and certainly some of them – such as the edict against gossiping – were unenforceable (see Appendix, p.64). Nonetheless they were taken very seriously, and posted in all places of public assembly. These rules, and other of Nash's *dicta* on apparel and etiquette, originally served the purpose of welding together a disparate company and providing a social code for the uninitiated. They also helped to give Bath its reputation for elegance as well as leisure. Anstey's mock-heroic stanza (1766) laughed gently at its claims:

> . . . the World to refine,
> In Manners, in Dress, in Politeness to shine,
> O *Bath!* – let the Art, let the Glory be thine.

To some extent, the tradition began to ossify in the later eighteenth century. Nash himself in old age lost much of his social sway, and died in penury in 1761. Successive and less imaginative Masters of Ceremonies issued very detailed and inflexible rules governing public conduct and the appropriate garb for attendance at balls and assemblies. In due course, the code became resented, although not jettisoned. Much the same fate eventually befell Nash's careful organization of the social round of the resort. Initially, the synchronization of a variegated programme was welcomed: the company proceeded from the baths or Pump Room in the early morning, to refreshments and music in the later morning (ladies in dishabille), to promenades, cards, and excursions in the afternoon, and to gaming, concerts, and dancing at the assemblies in the evening (full dress). 'The Course of Things is as mechanical as if it went by Clockwork', noted the *English Magazine* in 1737, in reluctant praise.

Yet gradually the routine lost some of its savour. One form of excitement was lost when public gaming was banned by laws of 1739 and 1745 (and Nash himself lost his chief source of income). Others found the way of life stultifying. Mrs Montagu complained, in a private letter of 1739, that the only conversation there was 'How d'ye do?' in the morning, and 'What's trumps?' in the afternoon. Too little change was introduced into the programme in the later eighteenth century, despite the fact that the smart 'season' became extended from a few months in the early summer into two seasons in spring (March–June) and autumn (September–December). 'The sameness of a Bath life is proverbial', noted a character in a novel set in Bath *c.* 1800. Nonetheless, despite the criticism and the satire that its claims attracted, the city's entertainment round had achieved and sustained a brilliant reputation. By 1801, with a population of virtually 35,000, it was one of the leading provincial towns – not challenging a Manchester or a Liverpool, but larger than places like Portsmouth, Hull, and Nottingham.

Another of the early spas to develop as a resort in the eighteenth century was Tunbridge Wells. Conveniently accessible from London, the Wells never attained the headiest social glamour, but some preferred its calmer ambiance to the bustle and worldliness of Bath. Situated in pleasant wooded countryside, it had a number of the attributes needed to sustain a fashionable resort. There were regular coach and post services to the capital city, and the London newspapers were delivered daily. Some imposing new housing developments were constructed, both near the wells and on Mount Sion, and further afield on Mount Ephraim. The place abounded with 'genteel lodging houses' for summer visitors. The wells themselves were improved and the famous colonnaded promenade, the Pantiles, was paved over in 1700. A cold bath (1708), an Assembly Room, two libraries, and a small theatre (1770), superseding a large inn room that was used for plays, were also provided. Royal patronage added social cachet and Queen Anne contributed to the funds for improving the

Pantiles. For a while, in the mid-eighteenth century, Tunbridge Wells was promoted as an outpost of Bath. A summer season from June to August at the Wells dovetailed with the shift to two seasons in spring and autumn at the premier resort. Nash himself became part-time Master of Ceremonies in 1732, and posted there in fine style each summer, travelling in a sumptuous equipage, heralded by two outriders with French horns. That marked its social apogee.

Nonetheless, Tunbridge Wells did not seriously challenge Bath. It remained small, lacking a marked urban focus. Fanny Burney was critical, when she stayed there in 1779 *en route* for Brighton. 'How such a place could first be made a fashionable pleasure-walk, every one must wonder,' she wrote dismissively of the Pantiles; adding: 'the houses, too, are scattered about in a strange wild manner, and look as if they had been dropt where they stand by accident, for they form neither streets nor squares, but seem strewed promiscuously.' Perhaps because it was a relatively small and intimate resort, it was famed for the virulence of its gossip and lampoons. By the later eighteenth century there were some signs that its fashionableness was ebbing. When Derrick visited the Wells in 1767, he was perturbed to be waylaid on the road by two horsemen riding furiously out from town, and surprised to discover that these were tradesmen touting for his custom during his stay. The practice of touting, or 'tooting' as it was called, was, of course, not uncommon at the resorts, but such enthusiasm was considered excessive. 'These Gentry are very troublesome, if not intimidating,' he concluded. A thoughtful local history, published in 1766, realized that Tunbridge Wells would need some alternative economic base if the springs were 'to fail, or, which is far more probable, become unfashionable'. It recommended that its amusements be diversified, its market developed, and its over-zealous 'touting' curtailed. In the event, however, the resort did not take this advice. Yet it retained successfully enough a role as a minor spa, and, increasingly in the later eighteenth century, as a retirement centre, with a permanent population in 1801 of from 4,000 to 5,000.

Scarborough, an 'exceeding romantick' spa, was in many ways a northern counterpart of Tunbridge Wells. But the fortunes of Scarborough described an even more distinct parabola in the course of the eighteenth century. Initially a small port and favoured place of residence for ship-owners, it blossomed in the early eighteenth century as a coastal resort. It combined the joint attractions of a spa with facilities for the newly popular recreation of sea-bathing. Scarborough, too, gained amenities: the cliffside spa house (built in 1698, and rebuilt in 1739 after a dramatic landslip two years earlier), two Assembly Rooms, a theatre, coffee-shops, and a circulating library. Extensive new building created the new or upper town on the cliffs. But again, Scarborough, even more obviously than the Wells, did not manage to achieve 'take-off' into the front ranks of the spas. Lacking a national appeal, its regular consumer hinterland was largely confined to families from the north of England. The eccentric Dicky Dickinson, who rented the spa from the Corporation (1698), was not such an inspired promoter as Beau Nash, although Charles Jones, appointed Scarborough's first Master of Ceremonies in 1740, had assisted Nash at Bath. *The Bath, Bristol, Tunbridge, and Epsom Miscellany* of 1735 satirized their northern rival:

> O *Scarb'rough*, say, how comes thy Pow'r so great,
> Thus to attract the Wealthy and the Great?
> What Pleasures can in unceil'd Rooms be found,
> Where buggy Beds with Fleas and Lice abound?

The 1720s and 1730s marked the peak of the spa's social success. In the summer season lists of 1733 were included two dukes, six earls, and one marquis. After the mid-century, however, the spa became superseded, partly as improving transport facilities made it easier for northern families to attend the southern resorts. Scarborough settled instead into a role as a small coastal garrison town (barracks were built in 1746) and as a minor seaside resort, catering chiefly for middle-class families from the north of England. The indomitable William Hutton holidayed there with his daughter in 1803 and enjoyed standing on the cliffs and watching a collier fleet of 200 sail pass by. He noted, however, that the great days of the spa were passed. Scarborough's population grew less rapidly in the later eighteenth century, although, with over 6,500 inhabitants in 1801, it remained larger than Tunbridge Wells.

The implications of these developments clearly suggest that there were limits to the number of large spas that the relatively restricted consumer market of eighteenth-century England could sustain. Few others of the country's many mineral springs attracted a resident population of any great size before 1801, although they were often visited. The hot springs at Matlock and Buxton, for example, were regularly included in the tour of the Peak District. Defoe thought that, were 'a City built here for the Entertainment of Company', Buxton would easily outdo the closer confines of Bath. But difficulties of access over the 'base, stony, mountainous' roads, and the paucity of good accommodation once arrived there, discouraged a long stay. Knaresborough and Harrogate were only tiny settlements in the eighteenth century. Similarly, Cheltenham, although rapidly gaining in popularity after a visit by George III in 1788, was still only small in 1801, with a population of just over 3,000. Its rapid growth, as spa and place for genteel retirement, was a phenomenon of the early nineteenth century. Indeed, in many ways the supply of spas ran ahead of demand. The many sponsors who 'discovered' new mineral springs – at least 225 were listed in 1740 – hoping to cash in on the success of Bath, were in most cases disappointed.

Another emergent specialism was the growth of the seaside resort. It reflected the growing scale and diversification of the leisure industry, and the discovery of a popular new source of entertainment. The gadarene 'rush into the sea', satirized by Cowper in 1782, did not happen overnight. Sea-bathing had been advocated on medicinal grounds by some doctors from the later seventeenth century; and bathing-machines were in use at Scarborough by the 1730s. But the practice was greatly encouraged by fresh medical endorsement. In 1750 Dr Richard Russell's influential tract advocated drinking and bathing in sea water for the treatment of glandular diseases. Russell himself settled in Brighton in 1754 and began an extensive promotion of the resort. He was later given the accolade of 'the inventor of the sea'; and swimming gradually became popular as a recreation in its own right.

A growing number of seaside resorts therefore began to emerge in the later eighteenth century, and attracted a wide social range of visitors. One of the earliest to expand was the south-coast resort of Brighthelmston, abbreviated in the early nineteenth century to Brighton. In 1722 it had been dismissed as 'a poor fishing Town', falling into the sea. But the determined medical patronage of Dr Russell, and the social approbation of the Prince of Wales (later George IV) from 1783 onwards, transformed the place. It was modelled on the older spa resorts, with its own Master of Ceremonies (*c.* 1770), and the same social round of entertainments. 'Morning Rides, Champagne, Dissipation, Noise and Nonsense, jumble these Phrases together, and you have a complete Account of all that's passing at Brighthelmston', recorded the *Morning Post* in 1785. Rows of smart terrace houses were erected hastily to accommodate the growing throng of visitors. The first sea-water baths were constructed in 1769; the Assembly Rooms were opened in 1776; and the Brighton races were first held in 1783. In 1784 the building of its famous Royal Pavilion was begun (completed in 1820) – to a mingled chorus of horror and enthusiasm. By 1801 Brighton was in fact larger than Tunbridge Wells or Scarborough, although still conspicuously smaller than Bath, which was not overtaken by the premier seaside resort before 1851.

Brighton derived much of its prominence from its relative proximity to London. Similarly, Margate had an early start as a popular seaside resort for Londoners, who journeyed there by sea to 'drink the sea water, as well as to bathe' (1754). The hoys, or sailing barges, took people there more cheaply than did the coaches (2s. 6d. compared with 16s.–19s. in the 1770s) and more rapidly (8–9 hours with a favourable wind, compared with 13–14 hours). Margate therefore became early on much more of a lower-class resort than other places. Without the same pretensions to gentility, it found the absence of royal patronage no handicap. It did, however, open an Assembly Room in 1769. But, where Brighton was compared with the West End of London, Margate in 1804 was compared with Cheapside and Wapping; and the resort was a pioneer in cheaper forms of mass entertainment – with, for example, donkey rides on the sands (1800), boat trips, bands, and walks along the pier (the old wooden pier was encased in stone in 1787 and rebuilt in 1808, after which an admission fee of one penny was charged).

Few other seaside towns had grown to any great size by 1801, although some signs of later patterns of resort development were already apparent. Weymouth, rendered modish by the summer visits of George III between 1789 and 1805, was sponsored as a summer outpost from Bath (ousting Tunbridge Wells from this role). Lyme Regis was also a small resort, but Bournemouth was still a sandy cove with no houses at all before 1812. In the north of England, Blackpool was also visited by the tireless William Hutton in 1789. It was then merely an 'expanded Hamlet', with no more than fifty houses scattered along the sea bank, although with commendable prescience Hutton suggested a number of improvements for 'this infant Commonwealth'. But the seaside resorts were as yet still out of reach – both in terms of travel time and cost – of the mass of the population of the northern industrial towns.

As in the case of the rush to discover spas, a number of promoters tried their hands at creating seaside resorts. One of the most ambitious schemes was the development of the hamlet of Bognor between 1784 and 1799, for an outlay of over £60,000, by a London hatter, Sir Richard Hotham. But his creation, launched as Hothampton, did not initially prosper. The ingredients of a fashionable success were as complex as the rewards were tempting.

The resorts displayed a number of distinctive characteristics as service economies. Employment there was highly seasonal, and geared to the demands of the tourist industry. There was a hidden but vital infrastructure of services. Criticized as a 'sharking people' in 1787, many inhabitants of the resorts made their living from these visitors. The ethos was one of an outward deference, counterpoised by the freemasonry of the servant network. Women made up a large proportion of the workforce there, either in service or as lodging-house keepers. Elizabeth Ham of Weymouth recorded in the later eighteenth century how her family were sucked into the tourist trade. All her little-known country cousins came to stay whenever the King visited the resort: 'This made my Mother desperate, and she thought she would try what effect letting two of her rooms would produce.' Cousins were thus turned into tourists and seaside landladies. Indeed, the abundant work for women at the resorts meant that the proportion of women in the urban population was exceptionally high, even allowing for the fact that almost all towns did in fact contain a majority of women. At the new resorts of Margate and Brighton in 1801 women constituted 54 per cent and 55 per cent of the population respectively, while at the older-established spas of Scarborough and Bath they accounted for fully 59 per cent and 61 per cent.

Furthermore, the resorts were also an important social as well as economic force. They were in a sense showcases for the urban way of life, and powerful propagandists for the consumer society. The stream of plays, poems, novels, and essays about the resorts – from Shadwell's *Epsom Wells* (1673) to Jane Austen's *Persuasion* (1818) – passed on this involuntary message, their own satire notwithstanding. The gesture of hanging the portrait of Nash between the busts of Pope and Newton in the Pump Room at Bath, although greeted with ridicule at the time, was not without point. The growth of the specialist entertainment industry was also a sign of the times. Consumer demand extended in the nineteenth century, with the gradual evolution of a mass market. Between 1801 and 1851 the English spas and resorts showed a faster rate of growth in aggregate than did the manufacturing towns and great ports, while the emergence of many continental resorts – notably Baden-Baden itself – drew from the English prototype as well as upon English custom.

Appendix *

'Nash's *Rules to be observ'd at Bath*, promulgated in 1742, stated as follows:

1. That a visit of ceremony at first coming and another at going away, are all that are expected or desired, by ladies of quality and fashion – except impertinents.
2. That ladies coming to the ball appoint a time for their footmen coming to wait on them home, to prevent disturbance and inconveniencies to themselves and others.
3. That gentlemen of fashion never appearing in a morning before the ladies in gowns and caps, show breeding and respect.
4. That no person take it ill that any one goes to another's play, or breakfast, and not theirs; – except captious by nature.
5. That no gentleman give his ticket for the balls to any but gentlewomen. – N.B. Unless he has none of his acquaintance.

6. That gentlemen crowding before the ladies at the ball, show ill manners; and that none do so for the future; – except such as respect nobody but themselves.

7. That no gentleman or lady takes it ill that another dances before them; – except such as have no pretence to dance at all.

8. That the elder ladies and children be content with a second bench at the ball, as being past or not come to perfection.

9. That the younger ladies take notice how many eyes observe them. N.B. This does not extend to the *Have-at-alls.*

10. That all whisperers of lies and scandal be taken for their authors.

11. That all repeaters of such lies, and scandal be shunn'd by all company; – except such as have been guilty of the same crime.

N.B. Several men of no character, old women and young ones, of question'd reputation, are great authors of lies in these places, being of the sect of levellers.'

Goldsmith added: 'These laws were written by Mr. *Nash* himself, and by the manner in which they are drawn up, he undoubtedly designed them for wit. The reader, however, it is feared, will think them dull. Poor *Nash* was not born a writer; for whatever humour he might have in conversation, he used to call a pen his torpedo, whenever he grasped it, it numbed all his faculties.'

* O. Goldsmith, *The Life of Richard Nash of Bath, Esq.* (1762), pp. 31–4.

5 The capital city

London was both the exemplar and the exception among English towns: exemplar, because its size and dominance made it the model for aspiring provincial towns, flattered to be described as 'London in miniature'; but an exception just because the capital city was so very much larger than any individual provincial centre in eighteenth-century England. It was a 'world city' by 1801, prompting in heightened form reactions of shock, doubt, and awe. "'Tis a Kind of large Forest of wild Beasts', warned *The Tricks of the Town laid open* (1699). But it was 'a colossal emporium of men, wealth, arts, and intellectual power', a place simultaneously full of 'mysterious grandeur' as well as 'Babylonian confusion', recorded the young De Quincey on a visit in 1800.

The capital was a very heterogeneous place. It did not fall into any one specialist category. The role of capital city has often proved a powerful motor for urban growth, as seen in the case of Madrid and other, later, capitals created *de novo*; but such a role did not preclude other economic functions. Indeed, in many cases political capitals were located historically in towns that were already large and powerful for other reasons. London had evolved in this manner, drawing upon multiple sources of growth. In the eighteenth century it was not only the seat of government in England, and the chief residence of the court: it was also the head of an expanding overseas empire; an international port and finance centre; an immense market and centre for inland trade; the location for a number of substantial manufacturing industries; and a social resort with a winter season of much magnificence. Even among other historic European capitals, London was outstanding for its size and diversity. Paris, for example, was only slightly its inferior in population at the start of the eighteenth century, but was rapidly outstripped by London in the following decades. By 1801, London with its 900,000 inhabitants was beginning to approach twice the size of Paris, housing approximately 550,000. And London presided over an England and Wales of only nine million people in 1801, while Paris was capital of a France of about twenty-seven million. Within the British Isles, too, the distinct acceleration in the growth of both the Scottish and Irish capitals still left them well behind London: Edinburgh (with Leith) housed some 83,000 residents in a national total of one and a half million, Dublin almost 170,000 in a country of over five million.

Yet even the huge London showed important signs of structural change in the course of the eighteenth century. Its own growth slackened in relative terms, and it ceased to grow much more rapidly than did the population of the country as a whole. London also displayed some signs of economic specialization within the different sectors of its already diverse economy. Adaptation came not so much as a result of provincial hostility to London, for merchants and manufacturers in the capital were often instrumental in promoting provincial industries, but in response to a growing integration of regional markets into a national – and international – economy. Partly resulting from those changes, the capital city in turn showed an intensified social and spatial polarization within its own confines. By the start of the eighteenth century its growth had already spread well beyond the boundaries of the medieval city, and in the course of the century its physical expansion continued markedly. With a population of almost one million by 1801, spread over approximately twelve square miles of densely packed housing and surrounded by suburban villages, it really constituted an immense urban region in its own right; and within that 'greater London' it increasingly displayed differential patterns of development in the component sub-regions.[1] 'When I consider this great City in its several Quarters and Divisions,' wrote the *Spectator* in 1712, 'I look upon it as an Aggregate of various Nations, distinguished from each other by their respective Customs, Manners and Interests.'

The population of London continued to expand, though less rapidly than in the previous two centuries. Its population had then increased from about 2 per cent of the total population of England and Wales in the 1520s to a little over 11 per cent by 1700. Many of the phrases expressing fears that London had become 'a head too big for the body', routinely reiterated in the eighteenth century, originated in the early seventeenth century, when it was first realized that London's headlong expansion was not going to come to an end, and when government policy had attempted (unsuccessfully) to stem its advance. In the eighteenth century, by contrast, London's rate of population growth virtually matched that of the population of the country as a whole. Overall, its population almost doubled, growing more rapidly in the later decades. Its share of the total population, however, remained constant, at just over 11 per cent in 1700 and 1750, falling fractionally to 10.7 per cent in 1801, as shown in Table II.[2]

The capital certainly retained immense powers of attraction. For most of the century its growth was fuelled by immigration from rural England. Urban mortality rates, everywhere high, were exceptionally savage in early eighteenth-century London; and even when, in the later decades, levels of mortality in towns began to fall slightly, London still needed a considerable net inflow of migrants to produce its substantial population gains. In the early eighteenth century the London conurbation was dependent for its growth upon a minimum annual recruitment rate of some 8,000 individuals, and, since the gross turnover of population was much greater than the net increase, literally tens of thousands of people must have entered and left London each year. In 1757 it was estimated that 'two Thirds of the grown Persons at any Time in *London* came from distant Parts.' Dr Bland's survey of the origins of several thousand adult patients at the Westminster General Dispensary between 1774 and 1781 showed that an even larger proportion, fully 75 per cent, had been born outside the capital (see Table VII). Those figures were not necessarily typical of the metropolitan population as a whole, but they constituted one of the very few detailed surveys of the subject in the eighteenth-century capital.

Table VII Origins of 3,236 patients at the Westminster General Dispensary, 1774–81*

Place of birth	Men		Women		Total	
	Total	Percentage	Total	Percentage	Total	Percentage
London	329	20.3	495	30.6	824	25.5
Elsewhere in England and Wales	952	58.8	917	56.7	1,869	57.8
Scotland	135	8.3	74	4.6	209	6.5
Ireland	162	10.0	119	7.4	281	8.7
'Foreign parts'	40	2.5	13	0.8	53	1.6
	1,618	99.9	1,618	100.1	3,236	100.1

  * From R. Bland, *Some Calculations... taken from the Midwifery Reports of the Westminster General Dispensary* (1781), pp. 18–19, also published in *Royal Society Philosophical Transactions*, LXX (1781), 355 ff.

London was a magnet for considerable Scottish and Irish migration in the course of the century: Dr Johnson waxed sarcastic about the Scots, while Adam Smith allowed himself a comment on the beauty of Irish prostitutes in London. There were about 14,000 Catholic households in the capital by the 1780s – mainly Irish in origin and settled chiefly in St.

Giles and Holborn. The Protestant Scots were fewer in number, and their residences dispersed. Other foreign communities settled in eighteenth-century London included some 20,000 Jews, chiefly resident in the East End. There was also a continuing small inflow of French migrants, joining the French Huguenots in Spitalfields. And a very small number of Negroes from North American shipping, and Lascar seamen employed by the East India Company, settled in the capital. Yet the bulk of London's new recruits came from within England and Wales. Tales of ambitious youngsters making their fortunes in a city whose streets were paved with gold were part of the national mythology, despite the fact that realities could often prove disillusioning. A London guide-book of 1776 admonished young girls against falling into the hands of a procuress immediately upon arrival in town; and *The Countryman's Guide to London, or, Villainy Detected* (1780) warned of the 'waggon-hunters' at the coaching inns, waiting for their incoming prey – Scene One of Hogarth's *Harlot's Progress*.

London's continued expansion in the eighteenth century was a sign of England's growing economic strength; but the diversification of the country's economy meant that the capital's proportionate size (already considerable by 1700, in the context of a non-industrialized economy) could not continue exponentially. Indeed, even in the later context of full industrialization in the nineteenth century, London's share of the total population of England and Wales did not again outmatch the collective strength of the provincial towns, although its proportionate size did subsequently continue to increase. In 1851 metropolitan London contained at least 13.2 per cent of the population of England and Wales, and in 1901 the county of London with Middlesex contained 16.4 per cent, excluding surrounding suburbia. Therefore its relative stability in the eighteenth century was unusual in the context of its long-term history – reflecting both its own very high mortality rates and the novel emergence of the provincial towns as rival magnets for recruits from the countryside.

Indeed, London's magnetic 'pull' over migrants became geographically more constricted in the later seventeenth and eighteenth centuries than it had been in the previous two hundred years. Analysis of the place of origin of apprentices to the London Weavers' Company has shown that, whereas in the years from 1655–64 only 41.8 per cent were drawn from London and the Home Counties, by 1736–45 90.6 per cent and by 1786–95 fully 95.5 per cent were drawn from that area (but the number of registered apprenticeships, it should be noted, was falling). Again, the evidence is imperfect, but it suggests a likely trend. In other words, rural migrants from the north and Midlands were now more likely to turn their eyes to nearby growth points, while London's recruits were drawn chiefly from the south. In a polycentric urban society total mobility was greater, while mean distance of migration into town was often shorter, than in countries with only one large 'magnet' city.

In the context of change, London's own economy showed signs of adaptation. It remained, of course, a huge and demanding market for the foodstuffs and raw materials necessary for its survival. As Defoe so vividly recounted in the 1720s, the economic tentacles of the capital city had spread through many parts of the country, encouraging local product specialization. North-country coals, Cheshire cheese and salt, Midlands cattle and grain, east coast malt and grains, Norfolk turkeys, Yarmouth herrings, Colchester oysters, Home Counties dairy produce, Kentish hops and apples, Portland stone, Cheddar cheese, and Devonshire cider were all brought into London by road, river, and sea. Close at hand, market-gardening flourished in the riverside parishes of Middlesex, Kent, and Surrey. 'This whole Kingdom, as well the People, as the Land, and even the Sea, in every Part of it, are employ'd to furnish Something, and I may add, the best of every Thing, to supply the City of London with Provisions', Defoe added, exaggerating somewhat to make his point.

That trade amplified and its organization became streamlined in the course of the eighteenth century. All the major wholesale produce markets in the capital – Billingsgate for fish, Bear Key and Queenhithe for grain (and from 1760 onwards the Corn Exchange in Mark Lane), Smithfield for cattle and sheep, Covent Garden for fruit and vegetables – were experiencing severe congestion by the 1790s. In the long-distance trades business became increasingly monopolized by a relatively small number of leading merchants and factors. London's grain trade was concentrated in the hands of as few as fourteen leading factors (dealers) by the end of the eighteenth century, selling on commission for farmers or country suppliers of corn, although the number of jobbers, speculating in the wholesale market, was much greater. The Smithfield livestock market was similarly dominated, at least by the mid-eighteenth century, by a relatively small number of dealers and jobbers, who bought in stock wholesale from country farmers and graziers. In other wholesale trades, by contrast, the concentration of control was much less marked, and the organization of the market much more variegated. In general, however, there was a tendency for the number of middlemen and intermediaries between producer and consumer to increase. The attraction of London's market and the scale of its trading network certainly brought it regular supplies. Unlike the experience in many smaller towns, there were virtually no major riots there that were prompted by food shortages as such, even in riotous eighteenth-century London.

The capital city was also a major nerve centre of international trade. A large proportion of all English imports and exports was conveyed through London. In 1700 fully one quarter of the capital's workforce was said to be employed on trades connected with the port. Shipping of all sizes crowded into the Pool of London. 'The whole river, from the bridge, for a vast way, is covered with a double forest of masts, with a narrow avenue in mid-channel,' it was reported in 1790. Indeed, by that date the joint problems posed by expanding trade and an increase in the size of ships had produced major difficulties from congestion, pilferage, and delays at the 'legal quays' and the supplementary 'sufferance wharfs' (where dutiable goods had to be landed). A parliamentary committee was established in 1796 to investigate remedies. After intensive lobbying and debates, a further spate of dock-building ensued, constructed by chartered companies under special Acts of Parliament: the West India Dock on the Isle of Dogs (opened 1802), the London Dock at Wapping (1805), the East India Dock at Blackwall (1806), and the Surrey Docks on the south bank (1807).

At the same time London's share of England's overseas trade declined somewhat in relative terms; and its role became more specialized. Its strengths lay in its trade with mainland Europe, and in the East and West India trades. That meant that London was especially dominant in the lucrative re-export trades, whereby colonial goods were resold to European markets. It became a great clearing-house. Warehouses for silks, tea, sugar, and tobacco lined the Pool of London; and a number of important commodity exchanges sprang up – such as the tea exchange near the old East India House in Leadenhall Street. By contrast, London had little part in the expanding Anglo-Irish trade; and none in the bulky coal-export business. The changing pattern can be seen in the figures in Table VIII. London's direct share of England's overseas trade fell gradually from 75.8 per cent in 1699–1701, to 69.8 per cent in 1752–4, and to 63.4 per cent in 1790. Its share of the country's registered shipping tonnage was already smaller than its share of total trade at the start of the century; and that further declined from 43.8 per cent in 1709, to 28.4 per cent in 1751, steadying at 31.5 per cent by 1792. The process of specialization provoked some complaints and uncertainties from London merchants in the 1730s and 1740s. But they were too envious of the provincial ports and insufficiently aware of London's built-in advantages, warned an essayist on trade in 1749: '*The Fluctuation* of some Branches of it, from one Port to another, ought *not* to give... any *Umbrage*', he concluded.

London's economic importance, on the contrary, was confirmed by its growing specialization as an international banking and financial centre.

Table VIII London's changing share of England's overseas trade and shipping in the eighteenth century

(a) Goods cleared through the Port of London*	Annual average for 1699–1701	Annual average for 1752–4	Single year 1790
	(At official valuation, in £ million)		
Imports	£4.6	£6.0	£12.3
(Percentage of all English imports)	(79.7)	(72.7)	(70.7)
Re-exports	£1.7	£2.6	N/a
(Percentage of all English re-exports)	(84.4)	(75.4)	
Exports	£3.6	£5.4	N/a
(Percentage of all English exports)	(68.1)	(64.6)	
Total export trade	£5.3	£8.0	£10.7
(Percentage of all English export trade)	(72.6)	(67.8)	(56.6)
Total overseas trade	£9.9	£14.0	£23.0
(Percentage of all English overseas trade)	(75.8)	(69.8)	(63.4)

(b) London-owned shipping**	1709	1751	1792
Shipping in '000 tons burden	c. 140.0	119.4†	347.2
(Percentage of all English shipping)	(43.8)	(28.4)	(31.5)

* Figures for 1699–1701 and 1752–4 from Inspector General's Ledgers of Imports and Exports in PRO Customs 3/3–5, 52–4; and for 1790 from Report on the Port of London in *House of Commons Sessional Papers*, XII (1796) and from E. B. Schumpeter, *English Overseas Trade Statistics, 1697–1808* (Oxford, 1960), pp. 15–16.

** As Table V.

† This figure may be unduly low. W. Maitland, *History of London* (1739), p. 621, thought London's shipping totalled 178.6 thousand tons in 1732.

There was a rapid growth of 'Agents, Factors, Brokers, Insurers, Bankers, Negotiators, Discounters, Subscribers, Contractors, Remitters, Ticket-Mongers, Stock-Jobbers, and of a great Variety of other Dealers in Money, the Names of whose Employments were wholly unknown to our

Forefathers,' wrote the same essayist in 1749. Its marine insurance business was institutionalized around Lloyd's coffee-house; its stockbrokers met informally in the Exchange coffee-house in Sweeting's Alley (the first Stock Exchange building being opened in 1802); its growing banking sector established a central clearing house in Lombard Street in 1775; and the Bank of England presided majestically over London's financial world. In these activities, London was certainly not in competition with the outports, but was the purveyor of specialized commercial services for the provincial and metropolitan business communities alike. Its growth contributed to the growth of the outports' trade, and vice versa. Far from being in decline, London was adapting to England's new strength in world trade – ousting Amsterdam from its earlier supremacy as Europe's premier money market and attracting an inflow of foreign investment. To London's trading account should therefore be added the city's substantial, if incalculable, 'invisible' earnings.

Some specialization was also seen among London's multifarious industries. These covered an immense array of trades, producing goods for the huge consumer markets within the metropolitan region – and also some products for national and international consumption. Most permanent were those that were associated with London's role as a port and entrepôt. The refining and processing of colonial raw materials employed numerous people – chiefly in the East End around the port, and on the south bank. Shipbuilding also continued as a substantial industry, although it was now complemented by the shipyards of the north-east ports. London chiefly specialized in the construction of the larger ocean-going vessels, particularly for the East Indies trade. These commerce-linked industries expanded solidly, with the general growth of trade. London also developed wholesale production in brewing and distilling, taking advantage of economies of scale for the mass market. A handful of major breweries, for example, including celebrated businesses such as Whitbread, Meux, Truman, Perkins, and Thrale's, sprang up in the eighteenth-century metropolis and increasingly dominated the market for beer. 'The sight of a great *London* brewhouse exhibits a magnificence unspeakable,' enthused Pennant in 1790. A few large distilleries also produced a sizeable proportion of the great quantities of English gin consumed in the eighteenth century.

Equally successful were the multitude of skilled crafts to be found in the capital city. A list of London trades noted 215 different occupations in 1747; by 1792 its *Directory* named 492. Many of them were also connected indirectly with the success of the port. For example, London was a major centre of nautical instrument-making and cartography, producing maps, globes, telescopes, barometers, and compasses. Its craftsmen also manufactured high-quality cutlery, scientific and surgical instruments, clocks and watches, plate, jewellery, furniture, and coaches. And London housed a large proportion of the country's printers and engravers. These were all specialist industries, dependent both upon supplies of skilled labour and upon ready access to affluent consumer markets at home and abroad. The capital's skilled craftsmen were famed throughout Europe. The German collector, Von Uffenbach, toured the leading London 'Mechanicians' in 1710 to view clocks and scientific instruments as eagerly as he visited the rest of the tourist sights. Later, visitors flocked to see public experiments with electricity, 'a thing its Impossable to describe', as a Somerset yeoman gasped in 1774.

Many of the production processes became more intricate and subdivided into their component parts. In watch-making, for example, a considerable degree of division of labour had come into operation by the mid-century. Each intricate stage in production was carried out by a different journeyman, working for a master craftsman who, according to an account in 1747, 'put his Name on the Plate, and is esteemed the Maker, though he has not made in his Shop the smallest Wheel belonging to it'. With growing division of labour it became possible also to contract work out to provincial workmen. In clock-making, some of the routine parts were made outside London, and only carried there for assembly. The capital also began to lose some mass-production industries entirely to the provinces. 'A Practice hath lately prevailed', wrote a witness in 1751, 'of working, in the Country, Manufactures for Sale in *London,* which formerly employed great Numbers of Journeyman in this City.' Its two major industrial 'exports' in the eighteenth century were shoe-making (moving to Northampton and its region) and the manufacture of hosiery (moving to Nottingham and Leicester). The process was lengthy but inexorable. London manufacturers were reported to be contracting out work to the Midlands in the early eighteenth century, in pursuit of greater profitability through lowered production costs; and eventually a number of masters and men themselves followed in the wake of the industry.

One large-scale industry that did remain in London, despite provincial competition, was its long-established silk-weaving industry, which had been powerfully reinvigorated in the 1680s with the settlement of a number of Huguenot refugees in the Spitalfields area of east London (once a fashionable suburb). Despite its precarious dependence on volatile fashion markets, the industry expanded behind protective tariffs against imported silks, employing some ten or twelve thousand men and women weavers at the height of its success in the 1740s and 1750s. Later in the century, however, the industry faced severe difficulties, and well-organized industrial militancy in response, from its weaving workforce. Special protective legislation, in the form of the Spitalfields Act of 1773 (repealed 1824), attempted to salvage the industry by simultaneously curtailing the recruitment of apprentices, regulating pay, and forbidding weavers' combinations to raise piece-work rates. But problems continued in the later decades of the century, and the less skilled branches of the industry (unable to carry the capital's high production costs) were moved to the provinces. The survival even of a 'fashion-plate' industry in eighteenth-century London was, therefore, far from unchequered.

While its commercial and industrial life adapted to other changes in England's economy, the service economy of the capital was greatly strengthened. The early size of its consumer market and its diversity of function, as centre of government and court life as well as of trade and industry, consolidated a role as purveyor of specialist services. Among them were those of the legal profession. The law-courts brought many litigants to town and supported an extensive legal fraternity. They maintained 'so vast a Multitude of Attorneys, Petty-foggers and Understrappers of the Law, as must necessarily embroil the Spirits and devour the Substance, of the Inhabitants', snorted Sir John Fielding in 1776. It was also a major education centre, although Defoe's ambitious proposal for a University of London in *Augusta Triumphans; Or, the Way to make London the Most Flourishing City in the Universe* (1728) was not adopted. It housed many schools (including four of the country's nine major public schools) and Gresham College, somewhat fallen off from its greatest days in the early seventeenth century but still offering public lectures on a range of scientific and mathematical subjects. The medical profession was also to be found in great numbers in the capital, either in private practice or attached to one of the large London hospitals: the ancient foundations of St. Bartholomew's in Smithfield and St. Thomas's (then in Southwark) were augmented by five new hospitals, founded in the early eighteenth century, as well as numerous dispensaries.

To that galaxy were added the multifarious entertainment industries of London, arising from its role as social capital. The presence of the court at St. James's, and from the 1760s at Buckingham House (later rebuilt and renamed Palace) helped to make the metropolis a magnet for polite society. The social prestige of royalty outweighed the prosaic and quarrelsome reality of court life under the Hanoverians. Many great landowners also maintained smart London houses – some on a palatial scale – and helped to confirm the capital's pivotal role in the social life of landed society. The lengthy London winter and spring seasons dovetailed with the summer popularity of Bath and the resorts. The metropolitan social round was both variegated and eclectic. There was no Beau Nash here but social leadership went, as it were, into commission, organized around the clubs, salons, and great houses. In such a context, the entertainment industry, in all its prolific branches, flourished mightily. Actors, authors, poets, musicians, artists, all flocked to town in search of an audience, patrons, and fame. The vitality of London's artistic and literary life added lustre to its reputation. The intensity of artistic rivalries testified to the extent of competition for its valuable prizes. Patronage was drawn both from the 'court' and 'city' interests, the most skilled performers managing to appeal to a wide audience. That was said to be part of the secret of David Garrick's outstanding success both as actor and theatre manager.

In addition to the more respectable entertainments, the huge and poorly policed capital city also had an extensive semi-licit market in sexual services, for which consumer demand was clearly much stronger than official disapproval. This trade drew much custom from the 'night life' associated with the theatre world. Covent Garden, the home of the most fashionable 'bagnios', was said to contain 'lewd Women in sufficient Number to people a mighty Colony' (1766). Later, in 1796, Colquhoun estimated that there were over 55,000 prostitutes in the capital as a whole – a much inflated figure (it amounted to approximately one in every four adult women in the whole of greater London) but indicative of magistrates' anxieties. Indeed, a French visitor in 1772 had commented on the scale and commercial organization of the business, which was 'so far from being considered as unlawful, that the list of those [women of the town] who are any way eminent is publicly cried about the streets'.

Just as the complexity of London's economy prompted the publication of a host of specialist directories and trade handbooks, so the physical expansion of the conurbation encouraged production of numerous maps and guides in the course of the century. In 1700 London was still a tolerably compact urban entity, hugging the great bend of the Thames from Westminster to Wapping. People travelled across town by river ('it is especially difficult to boat on the Thames, because men's Wigs look so frightful', worried Von Uffenbach) and by sedan chair. By the end of the century, however, the city had begun to sprawl northwards and away from the river. The building of further bridges across the Thames (Westminster Bridge was the second in 1750, Blackfriars the third in 1769) eased access to Lambeth and the south bank; but most of the new development lay on the gravelly terrain to the north. Only about 14–15 per cent of the population of 'greater London' in 1801 actually lived in the industrial suburbs south of the river. Pleas from advocates of 'improvement' that the visual amenities of the Thames be opened up in the course of development were not answered.

As the conurbation expanded, hackney coaches were increasingly used for longer journeys across town, the distance defeating the sedan-chair bearers. There were worries in 1789 that transport within the city would be arrested by a shortage of hay and straw: 'London is so overgrown, and so crowded by Horses, that the Consumption of Straw is, within these few Years, doubled . . . . This devilish Increase of London will in time cause a Famine, because it cannot be supply'd.' By 1800 the built-up area stretched from Hyde Park to Limehouse, and from Southwark to Hoxton, with fingers of further ribbon development stretching out, along the main routes from the city, to Kensington, Camden Town, Islington, Mile End, and Camberwell. A ring of suburban villages provided further evidence of London's outward push. At the same time the older housing, particularly in the City and East End, remained tightly packed into a maze of courtyards and alleys, threaded by 'such sphinx's riddles of streets, without obvious outlets or thoroughfares, as must baffle the audacity of porters, and confound the intellects of hackney coachmen', recalled De Quincey, claiming that one footpath in Holborn actually ran through a man's kitchen. The urban fabric was meanwhile undergoing considerable building and rebuilding – so that, at the periphery, the town appeared ringed with smoking brick kilns, and, at the centre, under constant renovation and extension, full of half-built housing.

Within the vast urban region a degree of *de facto* zoning became increasingly manifest. Different sections of the town catered for different specialisms; and these distinctions were visible in terms of housing and topography, as well as in economic and social structure. Addison in 1712 had remarked upon the different terrains of the court, city, law courts, and markets: 'The Inhabitants of *St. James's*, notwithstanding they live under the same Laws, and speak the same Language, are a distinct People from those of *Cheapside*, who are likewise removed from those of the *Temple* on the one side, and those of *Smithfield* on the other, by several Climates and Degrees in their Way of Thinking and Conversing together.' Others were content with the more traditional and stereotyped distinction between the West and East Ends. 'The Contrast betwixt that and the western Parts of the Metropolis is astonishing,' wrote the German traveller Von Archenholz after a visit to the City of London in the late 1780s, while Dr Johnson, wishing to educate Boswell, who lodged in Westminster, advised him to '*explore Wapping*'. In fact, when Boswell eventually did so in 1792 (thirty years after his first visit to town), he was rather disappointed. Nonetheless, whether astonishing or disillusioning,

London's internal diversity certainly did exist, in an interwoven pattern of some complexity.

Polite society or 'the People of Fascination', as Henry Fielding termed them kindly in 1755, focused upon the West End of London, which was itself moving west and north. At the start of the century Covent Garden and the parish of St. Giles were fashionable places of residence, but gradually the upper classes moved further from the old urban centre, as the workaday city advanced upon them. Fielding did indeed describe the process as a social battle, but the conflict was subtle and imperceptible. Leicester Square – home of the Prince of Wales and the Leicester House Whigs in the 1740s – was modish for a while, followed later in the century by Grosvenor Square and the environs of Hyde Park. It was in the West End particularly that were concentrated most of the great estate developments of eighteenth-century London. Aristocratic landowners put extensive properties on to the market on long leases; and speculative builders and developers laid out new streets and fashionable squares for the social parade.

The social composition of the West End was not, however, as monolithic as its image might suggest. Here dwelt a multitude of servants, tradespeople, innkeepers, specialist craftsmen, and service workers, catering for the upper-class clientele in their midst. When developing housing for the rich, the architect and planner John Gwynn noted, with unconscious snobbery, that 'it will be found Necessary to allot smaller Places contiguous, for the Habitations of the useful and laborious People, whose dependence upon their Superiors requires such a Distribution.' Examination of the Westminster Poll books for the 1730s and 1740s has, in fact, shown how numerous were the trades plied in the area, how independent the tradespeople were from any one source of patronage, and how difficult therefore they were to organize into a pro-government or 'court' interest. With its extensive franchise and lively political awareness, the Westminster constituency became one of the most independent in the country.

The need for supplies of labour also helps to explain the location, close to the respectable West End, of one of the most populous, poverty-stricken, and notorious areas of eighteenth-century London. This was the area around Seven Dials in the parish of St. Giles, spreading east to Bow Street and Drury Lane. Considered to be one of the most dangerous of London's 'rookeries' or criminal quarters, it was also said, with some exaggeration, to contain a third of the capital's beggars. In the later eighteenth century it was 'to the Timid and Respectable, very properly a perfect *Terra Incognita*'. It was, however, a huge reservoir of labour for many of the capital's less glamorous services – inhabited by labourers, porters, servants, as well as tradesmen and artisans. The boundaries of the area were fluid. As the West End itself moved west, Soho began to acquire more markedly raffish characteristics. Many of the institutions of the city's labour-intensive entertainment industry were located here. Covent Garden and Drury Lane theatres, in its heartland, constituted meeting grounds for courtier and citizen. As *The Art of Living in London* (1768) declared:

> From either End, from City and from Court,
> In thronging Multitudes they here resort;
> Shower'd o'er with Powder, and bedaub'd with Lace,
> My Lord just issues from St. *James's Place* ... ;
> Here too the Cit – to calm domestic Strife
> Smirks in the Chariot by his half-pleas'd Wife ....

The old centre in the City of London was less preoccupied with fashionableness – and was less admired by canons of eighteenth-century taste. All that was to be seen was a 'confused *Babel* ... with the *Hotch-Potch* of half-moon and serpentine narrow Streets, close, dismal, long Lanes, stinking Allies, dark, gloomy Courts and suffocating Yards', complained an observer in 1748. 'Here lives a Personage of high Distinction; next Door, a Butcher with his stinking Shambles.' Nonetheless, the City also made some efforts towards the quest for urban 'improvement' in the later part of the century. It decided to pull down all its brightly coloured but overhanging street signs in the 1760s, although 'our neighbours in the City' were teased by a West End observer for their reluctance in doing so. The area of the old centre within the walls, in fact, began to lose its resident population, properties being turned over to office and mercantile uses. Within the walls, the population of the City, estimated by Gregory King in 1695 to number approximately 80,000, had risen to an estimated 87,000 by mid-century, but had declined to 78,000 by 1801. Much of its conspicuous building activity was institutional in origin: the City of London's bulky Mansion House, built by Dance, the Corporation's 'clerk of works', between 1739 and 1753; the repair of London Bridge, which lost the last of its houses and shops, in 1757–9; the gothic refronting of the Guildhall in 1789. Such changes confirmed the City's increasing specialization as a financial and business centre, and its differentiation from other parts of London, despite the pulling down of most of the old city walls and gates.

Meanwhile, spreading out to the north, east, and south of the old centre lay a large and fast-expanding industrial and commercial zone. As many trades were still domestic in their organization, these were also among London's most densely populated residential areas. The poorest parishes were to be found here, with some of the flimsiest and cheapest housing. Crowded tenements, shops, warehouses, workshops, and the ubiquitous alehouses and gin-shops abounded. These parishes, too, were not without some large-scale development in the course of the century. The area north of the City around Finsbury Square, for example, was developed for the City of London between 1777 and 1791 by Dance's assistant, James Peacock. But in general the industrial areas failed to attract 'prestige' developments and did not contain much upper-class housing. The meagreness of their rating income accentuated the problems of poverty in the poorest parishes. As the reforming magistrate, Patrick Colquhoun, pointed out in 1797, in Tower Hamlets 'the lower classes ... are compelled to contribute largely to the fund for supporting the poor from the daily pittance which arises from labour ... , while, in almost every other part of the metropolis, as the rich form a considerable proportion of the inhabitants, the [same] burden does not attach.'

The whole metropolitan complex was completed by a loosely articulated outer ring of suburban villages within a few miles of the centre, where City merchants and West End grandees retreated to escape the crowds and smog of town. Some maintained summer residences only, others moved out permanently. The migration was particularly marked to the west and south-west, the haunts favoured by the aristocracy: Horace Walpole's 'Gothic Mouse-trap' at Strawberry Hill caused an architectural sensation in the mid-century. To a lesser extent the process also occurred in the north and north-east: Hampstead, Highgate, Epping, and Stratford attracting the affluent City gentry.

The three great amusement parks of eighteenth-century London were also sited on the outskirts of town, all in the fashionable west and south-west. These were Hyde Park, where the citizenry paraded on Sundays in emulation of the weekday show of fashionable society; Ranelagh Gardens, opened in 1742, next to Chelsea Hospital and adorned with its famous concourse hall, the Rotunda; and the Spring Gardens at Vauxhall, with their intricate ornamental walks and brilliant lighting. Their fame was created by their fashionable clientele, but their boast was their universality. 'Everybody goes there,' claimed Horace Walpole in 1744, speaking of Ranelagh at the height of its early summer season, '... from his Grace of Grafton down to children out of the Foundling Hospital.' In fact, as both the formal Gardens charged entrance fees (Ranelagh was the more expensive at 2s. 6d. a head, while Vauxhall cost 1s., up to 1792) their accessibility was limited; but the illusion of unfettered opportunity was particularly metropolitan. Social differentiation was counterpointed by the relative openness of urban society.

Although apparently inchoate, therefore, and often described as such, the growth of London had a form and logic of its own. The great corpus of literature – both serious and playful – devoted to surveying its diversity and immensity, in fact served to render it intelligible. London certainly had its share of noise, dirt, stench, disorder, brutality, danger, and crime. It was, after all, a huge metropolitan region with nearly one million inhabitants by 1800. Yet it manifestly functioned and survived, displaying as it did so differentiation and specialization within its confines – and putting into kaleidoscopic context the often conflicting reports of social conditions. Both Gin Lanes and Beer Streets were to be found there.

This complex regional economy and society evolved across and around a great number of local authorities. Its political and administrative structures were accordingly highly diversified – from the politically powerful Corporation of London, to the humbler Borough of Southwark, through to the many parish vestries, upon whom local authority – and quarrels – devolved. The parishes outside the City were governed in the eighteenth century by over 300 local bodies, all with differing authorities and constitutions. Difficulties in providing basic urban services – water supply, sanitation, refuse clearance, road maintenance, regulation of building standards, policing, poor relief – were compounded by the confusing patchwork of many different authorities. Defoe's proposal for a unitary local government for the whole of the then 'greater' London, however, found no favour.

Yet if it was the exemplar of many classic urban problems, the capital city also indicated the durability of its social fabric. Some steps, furthermore, were taken towards 'improvement' – in the piecemeal fashion characteristic of eighteenth-century reform. In many ways, for a sprawling metropolitan city-region, London functioned relatively smoothly. The many social tensions of the capital city were, for the most part, contained within its great diversity. A German traveller commented: 'It appears to me wonderful, that the crowds of poor wretches who continually fill the streets of the metropolis, excited by the luxurious and effeminate life of the great, have not some time or another, entered into a general conspiracy to plunder them.' But, while he observed the extremes of wealth and poverty, he underestimated both the normalcy of social divisions, and conversely the persistence of popular traditions of radicalism in eighteenth-century London.

6 Towns and the economy

The substantial growth of towns in eighteenth-century England meant that the urban economy had come of age; town life had become normalized. Problems were there in plenty, but magistrates no longer feared the imminent collapse of the urban economy with each downturn in trade, or shortage in the food market. The 1790s were perhaps the most difficult decade in eighteenth-century urban economic life, and even then problems were not uniformly shared by all towns. The resilience of urban economies is indeed often remarkable. The fears of collapse are real but the recovery from even the most terrible crises produced by dearth, pestilence, or war, is often surprisingly rapid; and eighteenth-century English towns certainly experienced nothing as drastic as wholesale devastation from either famine, Black Death, or sacking by enemy forces. The nearest thing there was to a hostile invasion was the Young Pretender's march through northern England to Derby in 1745; but the impact of this adventure was very limited, apart from presenting magistrates with the quandary of whether formally to recognize the claimant or not. Manchester welcomed him with illuminations, Derby with half-hearted bonfires – and complaints at the disruption to trade. Rarely were towns at the margins of sheer survival. The promptitude of urban crowds in the eighteenth century to demonstrate against food shortages or high unemployment marked their sense of outrage at these exceptional crises rather than a chronic state of urban malfunction. Indeed, much of the contemporary writing about the differential economic performances of English towns in the eighteenth century was concerned to identify and propagate the secret of urban growth rather than to warn of its perils and fragility.

The general vitality of urban economic life in the eighteenth century was, however, a compound of many diverse experiences. There is no simple index of urban economic performance in aggregate. Just as towns had many different economic specialisms, so their economic fortunes varied. A foreign war that damaged markets served by one town could stimulate the trade and industries of another. Some urban industries – in textiles for example – were in competition with each other. Most towns saw an overall expansion in their output of goods and services in the course of the eighteenth century – but not in equal measure.

The causes of popular discontents provide some guide to urban economic difficulties. For example, many provincial towns faced problems from grain shortages and heightened social tensions in years of harvest failure – such as 1709–10, the 'hard winter' of 1739–40, 1756–7, 1766, 1781–3, and the troubled later years of the 1790s. Urban industries catering for domestic markets were simultaneously depressed when consumers' pockets were pinched by high food prices. There were, however, regional divergencies in response to harvest failures. Even in 1766, one of the worst single years for grain shortages in the whole of the century, the gravity of the situation varied considerably across the country. Market riots and affrays, expressing, in varying degrees of intensity, resentment at high prices and the export of grain, were reported from towns and market villages across a broad swathe of England from the south-west, through the Midlands, and into East Anglia. There was, on the other hand, remarkably little protest or recrimination at high prices in the large urban centres of northern England. Above all, London itself remained quiet in 1766, although it saw extensive riots on industrial issues in 1768. Regional fluctuations in grain prices were becoming synchronized as regional markets were integrated into one national economy, but the local impact of food shortages was variable. It was often the conjunction of dearth with high levels of local unemployment that created the greatest hardship and ferocity of protest, especially when those problems occurred in arable regions that were net exporters of grain. There were also numerous disputes over industrial grievances in the eighteenth-century towns that provide evidence for the state of urban economic activity. In general, economic diversity tended to provide a cushion against economic crisis, while single-industry towns showed greater vulnerability.

One of the general characteristics of urban economic life was its flexibility and adaptability. Collectively, the towns constituted an immense reservoir of labour, both skilled and unskilled. The larger the town, the more diverse its population's array of skills. Little is known in detail about the patterns of work in these eighteenth-century towns. E. P. Thompson's luminous essay on 'Time, Work-Discipline, and Industrial Capitalism' stands virtually alone.[1] It seems probable, however, that, as was usual in a developing economy, a large proportion of the population was drawn into the workforce. In the expanding towns, men, women, and young children, in all but affluent families, worked for a living. The sudden numbers thrown out of work in urban economic depressions indicated the usual extent of the working population. Many were in regular employment, others were engaged in the multitude of semi-permanent and casual occupations characteristically found in large towns. Jobs were generated within the towns by the economic interaction of a sheer mass of people. The relative abundance of employment opportunities, plus the competitive ambiance of an urban society, produced an economically active population; and high levels of immigration into the expanding towns meant that they contained an unusually large proportion of young adults, at the height of their earning capacities.

The towns' relative productivity was matched by wages that were generally higher than those earned in the countryside. Additional labour in the towns was channelled into new employments rather than, as in traditional agrarian economies, sharing in existing tasks on the land. Not all urban occupations were equally productive, of course. But the growth of towns in eighteenth-century England encouraged a gradual shift away from the backward-sloping supply curve for labour that was often found in pre-industrial economies, where the hours worked varied inversely with real wages (so that the value of per capita output in terms of current prices remained fairly static). Instead, they tended to attract people into the labour market.

Many eighteenth-century travellers commented on the industriousness of the workforce, especially in the manufacturing regions. Dr Pococke in his *Travels through England* in 1750, for example, waxed lyrical about the Potteries: 'There is such a Face of Industry in all Ages and Degrees of People, and so much Civility and obliging Behaviour, as they look on all that come among them as Customers, that it makes it one of the most agreeable Scenes I ever saw.' Arthur Young wrote in 1770 of 'a new race of the industrious' in the manufacturing towns. Such comments were often made about the fast-growing towns in particular; but Adam Smith in 1776 thought it a fairly general phenomenon. A few workmen, he conceded, showed a marked leisure preference in good times, but in many instances quite the reverse was the case. 'Workmen, on the contrary, when they are liberally paid by the piece, are very apt to over-work themselves, and to ruin their health and constitution in a few years,' he argued, instancing the London craftsmen as a case in point. Urban productivity was increasingly constrained as much by overwork and industrial illness as by underwork and preference for intermittent leisure.

The towns, therefore, were among the notably productive areas in the contemporary economy, although the portents of economic change were not confined to them. Some towns did contain a degree of chronic unemployment, especially among the elderly or disabled; and those with seasonal economies had much occasional unemployment. In slumps, furthermore, levels of those out of work or on short time in most places could rise to alarming heights. Urban unemployment has always been much more visible than rural underemployment; and the urban workforces quick to react to threats to their livelihood. The political militancy of radical artisans in many towns in the 1790s, for example, derived added fuel from their resentment at economic hardships.

Hours of work for those in employment were long. The urban working day did not cease with sunset, but continued by candle- and lamp-light. Campbell's *London Tradesman* (1747) carefully listed variations in hours of work, as well as in earnings and in the demand for labour. He found that many indoor businesses worked for twelve or thirteen hours, from six in the morning to eight or nine at night, with one and a half or two hours off for rest and meals. Building workers, however, worked in the daylight hours, and those engaged in river trades 'by Tydes'. In the emergent factory industries very long hours were instituted, for adult and child labour alike. Twelve working hours were common in a number of northern spinning mills, and thirteen and a half hours were worked in some factories in Preston, Ashton, and Bury, according to a report of 1816. The impact of growth was first to lengthen but then to standardize working hours. In some skilled crafts in London, in the course of the eighteenth century, there was intermittent pressure for a reduction of working hours without detriment to earnings. The hours worked by journeymen tailors, for example, were codified by Act of Parliament at thirteen in 1721, and reduced to twelve hours daily in 1768. Some other London crafts also faced demands for reduced working hours from their journeymen: in 1761 the cabinet-makers were indicted for combining to raise wages and to shorten their hours of work. Concessions made after disputes were not always sustained. Gradually, however, the concept of a standard ten-hour working day, from six to six with a two-hour break for meals, evolved, although many worked for longer than that in practice, especially in the factories. There, the first cautious reforms in 1802 and 1819 did no more than limit the working hours of children to twelve a day, and both Acts lacked provision for enforcement.

At the same time the organization of work became increasingly formalized and disciplined. Jobs became more specialized, and the division of labour more pronounced. In some industries work patterns were intensively organized. By 1750 some London bookbinders, for example, employed two complete shifts of labour, 'Day-men or Night-men, each Party working from Six to Six'. Many heavy industries traditionally also worked two long shifts, while the management at the Dowlais ironworks in 1785 instituted a novel experiment of three eight-hour stints. In a number of domestic industries, on the other hand, the routine was less strictly defined, much work being crammed into the end of the week, after a leisurely start celebrating 'Saint Monday'. But even these work patterns were becoming standardized by local custom. In Sheffield, for example, the cutlers' Monday rest-day was a well-established collective tradition, transmuted into the later practice of closing the steel mills on Mondays for repairs and overhaul.

Town societies were particularly conscious of measured time. Theirs was an urban and commercialized world, marked out in the eighteenth century by the multiplication of municipal clocks and private timepieces. In place of the daily and seasonal rhythms of work on the land came the complex orchestration of urban employments, varying according to the nature of each job and the seasonality of each urban economy. In the same way, it was then business fluctuations rather than the state of the harvest that came increasingly to determine aggregate levels of urban economic activity. Urban work-patterns gradually constituted a new norm, divorced from the traditional routines of the countryside.

With growth, certain of the traditional regulations and controls upon urban trade and industry began to be relaxed or bypassed. Restrictions on recruitment of labour in many industries were gradually eroded. The trade guilds or companies which had been the local agents of regulation in many incorporated towns either withered away or transformed themselves into social clubs or property-owning trusts. The process of change was erratic and far from uniform.

One of the most notable features of the guilds had always been their great diversity and adaptability to local conditions. Even in their heyday their powers had never all been systematically enforced. The same diversity obtained in their demise. They were never abolished *en masse*, just as they had never been so created. Although subsequently much derided and resented, the guilds had emerged initially in response to genuine economic needs. Sustained by the force of municipal by-laws, or fortified by the full majesty of royal charter (and, very rarely, by parliamentary statute), the guilds were trade associations that were designed to protect their membership in a hostile and uncertain economic world. Typically, they controlled admissions and apprenticeship to the trade; sometimes they regulated conditions of work and trade; and, in theory at least, they supervised the standard of goods produced or vended by all members of the guild, to prevent fraud and to protect their collective reputation. All practitioners of a trade or industry within a given locality (usually the incorporated town, but sometimes including its economic hinterland) were expected to join the guild and to share in its activities, although the unpaid offices usually fell to the wealthiest members who could afford the expense and time.

Essentially defensive and protective, the guilds had evolved in the context of a relatively static and backward economy. Their authority was usually more strongly endorsed in times of economic difficulty, and relaxed in times of expansion. That also made practical sense, for it was much more difficult for the busy, unpaid, and part-time guild officials to supervise a rapidly growing trade or industry than to control their sometimes recalcitrant membership in hard times. In other words, the power of the guilds waxed and waned in response to local circumstances and local needs – and had done so long before the onset of the eighteenth century.

The gradual demise of the guilds took many forms. In some cases they simply stopped making their annual election of officials, and all their functions lapsed forthwith. In other cases they faded away slowly, shedding their powers one by one. The annual appointment of officials often continued but active supervision was abandoned or invoked only intermittently, leaving the guild with a more nebulous role as representative of the industry's interests. For example, the once-powerful Norwich Weavers' Company (incorporated by Parliament in 1650, with officials drawn equally from the ranks of the city and country industry) fell into gradual oblivion in the later seventeenth and early eighteenth centuries. The cumbersome system of searching and sealing all worsted stuffs was increasingly evaded by merchants who were anxious to get wares speedily to London markets. The search was abandoned finally in 1705. The last recorded annual election of company officials occurred in 1727. After that, references to the Company simply cease. Within only a few years, in 1736, a separate manufacturers' association, the Committee of Trade, was active in Norwich. It marked a shift from the old vertical organization of interest groups by trade to a new horizontally structured division between employers and employees. In this particular instance, however, the new manufacturers' Committee proved short-lived.

Some guilds collapsed with greater contumely and dispute. The London Framework Knitters' Company (incorporated in 1657) had nominal jurisdiction also over the provincial industry. Long-range supervision, even with locally appointed deputies, meant that the Company's powers were unpopular and easily evaded. Fines and fees were paid intermittently until the later 1720s, but their attempted revival in 1752 led to an appeal from the Midlands industry to Parliament. 'He never heard that the Company endeavoured to prevent Frauds in the Manufacture; and believed the sole Reason of putting their Bye-laws into Execution was to raise Money', was the damaging testimony of the Nottingham framework knitters' spokesman. In April 1753 the House of Commons resolved that the London Company's powers did 'tend to a monopoly' and were 'injurious and vexatious to the manufacturers'. The force of their resolution, limited as it was, sufficed to halt the Company's claims. Indeed, there was in general a growing uncertainty about the legal status of guild powers that both inhibited guild officials and encouraged their critics.

On the other hand, a small number of the myriad of early guilds did not die away but mutated. Shedding any serious attempt at supervision, some became vehicles for ceremonial and festivities. A handful of the eighteen guilds created in Leeds, when the city was incorporated in 1626, survived into the eighteenth century as 'Convivial Societies'. The Preston guilds had evolved an elaborate month-long celebration, with feasting, entertainments, and a grand procession, held, according to the town's charter, every twenty years. By the eighteenth century these occasions were only vestigially concerned with the regulation of trade: they had become important social events in their own right, attracting much business to the place. An onlooker at the guild in 1822 concluded that it was 'a sort of public carnival or jubilee. . . . The sports and revelry, which are inseparable companions of the guild, and the processions of the various trades and occupations of the inhabitants, draw together on this occasion, immense multitudes of people.' This was the apotheosis of the social dimension of guild life, no longer regulating trade but generating it, in a municipal festival.

The greatest longevity was conferred upon those few guilds that owned sizeable amounts of property. These were often the wealthy merchant guilds rather than the less affluent craft companies. Although shedding their claims to regulate trade, a few guilds survived as independent property trusts, often with a developing role as educational and/or charitable institutions. They usually retained an interest in their original trade affiliation (although not all members were practitioners) and apprenticeship schemes were a favoured form of educational endowment. The most successful examples of survival through such adaptation were the London Companies, headed by the twelve great Livery Companies. These developed into powerful City institutions, with ample funds to invest and with considerable status to confer upon their membership. The eighteenth century was something of a watershed in their history, when the emphasis among their many functions shifted decisively away from trade regulation to a new concentration upon a role as a charitable and educational trust. The increasing importance of the Merchant Taylors' School to the functions of the parent Company was a case in point. In reflection of these changes, membership of the surviving London Companies, which was declining in the early eighteenth century, began to recover subsequently, but now on a different basis, and for different purposes.

A number of other forms of economic regulation were also slowly adapted to the changing economic environment. For example, the old apprenticeship laws relating to the training of young craftsmen (which did not apply exclusively to the workforce in corporate towns, as is sometimes wrongly assumed) were not stringently enforced; much untrained, so-called 'colt', labour found its way into many urban employments. It became an optional rather than an automatic procedure, although in a number of cases a formal apprenticeship was still valued: large premiums were paid to apprentice young men to skilled craftsmen or lucrative businesses. The apprenticeship clauses of the Statute of Artificers were repealed in 1814 after years of administrative leniency and legal uncertainty; it was the artisan workforce not the employers that had attempted to secure their enforcement.

Similarly, in many incorporated towns the traditional obligation upon all craftsmen and traders to apply for the freedom of the city was enforced only haphazardly. It became an optional privilege rather than a compulsory duty. Where the freemen retained little political independence their numbers dropped sharply; while those towns with 'open' constitutions (see ch.9) attracted a larger number of applicants. In many cases, therefore, an increase in admissions to the freedom was more likely to signal the imminence of a disputed election, or a drive to replenish corporate finances, than a commercial or industrial boom. In Carlisle in 1786 the sudden creation of many new freemen, or 'mushrooms' as they were termed, before a disputed parliamentary by-election, was a matter for much satirical comment.

A number of other economic regulations were also ignored or circumvented. At Reading in 1722–3 the Mayor attempted to declare the formal Assize of Bread, that regulated the marketing of the standard wheaten loaf. But, as he recorded in his Memorandum Book, he 'did not meet with suitable Encouragement from some of my Brethren, who said it would be hard to alter an old Custom in the Town, and so the Thing was not taken notice of further for this Year.' The Assize was still formally declared in some places, but its impact was patchy. Urban officials and magistrates operated with considerable independence in the eighteenth century; and the patterns of market tolls, fees, dues, supervisions, and local regulation of all forms was very diverse. Nor did such codification, in any case, amount to anything like a modern 'managed' economy.

Gradually, therefore, the major constraints upon economic activity became those of the market and not those of municipal or guild regulation. Change did not come about systematically in response to a sudden application of principles of *laissez-faire*. Eighteenth-century economic policies and their administration were eclectic, old paternalism dying slowly. By the time that Adam Smith came to synthesize the new economic liberalism, however, many of the traditional regulations that were targets of his criticism had already been abandoned.

Guild and corporation controls and regulations were therefore essentially adaptive forces, rather than formative agents in the differential processes of urban growth. This subject has, however, been a matter for long-running debate. The presence or absence of municipal and guild powers has been invoked to explain the variegated economic performance of eighteenth-century towns. Economic 'freedom' promoted growth, the argument runs; regulation retarded it. 'New' unfettered towns surged past 'traditional' incorporated centres, encrusted with obsolete regulations and expensive municipal government. Such a distinction appeared to provide a clue to the diverse experiences of towns. Certainly, there was a wide variety of urban growth rates in the eighteenth century. Some long-established, incorporated towns were not growing rapidly. Conversely, some of the towns that were expanding briskly were not incorporated municipalities but were constitutionally 'mere villages', under the nominal suzerainty of a lord of the manor and without an elaborate superstructure of municipal and guild authority.

In fact, as already noted, effective guild regulations were generally in decay. But constitutional differences between towns provided a peg for debate. Defoe, for example, on his *Tour*, noted that a number of incorporated boroughs were in reality tiny and unimportant. Queenborough in Kent was a 'miserable, dirty, decay'd, poor, pitiful, fishing Town', yet it had a Mayor and Corporation, while Manchester had none: it was 'an open Village, which is greater and more populous than many, nay, than most Cities in England'. In the case of Bristol, Defoe took the equation further and denounced all corporation powers as obfuscatory: 'the general Infatuation, the Pretence of Freedoms and Priviledges, that Corporation-Tyranny, which prevents the Flourishing and Encrease of many a good Town in England.' It was a surprising example to take, for Bristol was then emerging in the very front rank of England's provincial towns and, incidentally, was not enforcing the traditional requirements for merchants to be freemen of the city; but a suspicious attitude towards corporation powers was becoming increasingly common.

In York, for example, the local historian, Francis Drake, anxious about the city's economic stagnation, decided (in 1736) that: 'Our Magistrates have been too tenacious of their Privileges, and have for many Years last past, by Vertue of their Charters, as it were locked themselves up from the World, and wholly prevented any Foreigner from settling any Manufacture amongst them; unless under such Restrictions they [i.e.

outsiders] were not likely to accept of.' In fact, the Corporation had earlier, in 1713, tried to advertise for merchants and manufacturers who would be allowed 'free Liberty to trade and traffic'. But the failure of that and a similar venture in the 1740s discouraged further initiatives, making the city a target for criticism in the emergent climate of economic liberalism. A pamphleteer in 1752 developed the general argument even more sweepingly: 'Corporation-Laws are trifling Restraints in Appearance, yet trifling Restraints retard the Growth of Cities: And that so effectually and certainly, that there is not a single City in *England* at this Day on the Increase; whilst most of our free Towns, tho' with manifest local Disadvantages, get all the Trade from them, and daily advance in Wealth and Numbers.' The assertion, penned in the context of the pamphleteer's fluent advocacy of naturalization for foreign workers in England, was not literally true; but it shows that the allegation had a long intellectual ancestry, well before it became a commonplace of liberal thought in the nineteenth century.

Does the detailed evidence in fact sustain the view that constitutional differences caused the differential economic performance of eighteenth-century English towns? The question in fact falls into two parts: was there a positive correlation between 'new', 'free' towns and growth, 'old' incorporated towns and stagnation? And, if so, was it a causal correlation?

The answer to both parts of the question seems to be simply, No. In the first place, there are problems of nomenclature. Very few expanding towns in the eighteenth century were completely 'new' settlements, springing up from less-than-village origins. Whitehaven in the later seventeenth century provides one of the few examples (and its growth was promoted, if not planned, by the intervention of the Lowther family). On the contrary, quite a number of the non-incorporated towns that were growing rapidly in the eighteenth century had already grown into sizeable places by 1700. Manchester and Birmingham, for example, were hardly newcomers, being then among the dozen largest English towns. Manchester had already been (briefly) enfranchised by Oliver Cromwell in 1654. But even if the designation 'new' is accepted as signifying constitutional rather than chronological novelty, the equation still does not work. Rapid growth was, indeed, observed in a number of 'new' or non-incorporated towns: Manchester, Oldham, Birmingham, Wolverhampton, Halifax, Bradford, Stoke, Merthyr Tydfil, were some of the leading exemplars. But, equally, it was found among many 'old' or incorporated towns, such as Liverpool, Preston, Wigan, Hull, Leeds (incorporated in 1626), Newcastle upon Tyne, Leicester, Bath, Plymouth, and Portsmouth. One exception might prove the rule; so many disprove it. All that the case history shows is that incorporation was not in itself an essential ingredient of urban growth. It was the eighteenth-century reluctance to create new corporations that allowed constitutional recognition to lag behind the shifting regional balance within the English economy – most of the fast-expanding 'new' towns being found in the industrial north and Midlands. Furthermore, the 'old' or incorporated towns were themselves extremely diverse in their constitutions as well as in their powers and policies.

Nor were the non-incorporated urban centres without their own elements of economic regulation and constraints on trade. Manorial custom was by no means always libertarian. In the case of two leading manufacturing towns, Manchester and Bradford, manorial custom sustained the controversial Soke-Mills, which had, in theory at least, monopoly rights over the grinding of corn within the extent of the manor. Such claims were greatly resented, especially when wheatflour began to replace oatmeal as a staple dietary ingredient in the north of England. In Bradford the soke-rights lapsed gradually through consumer evasion, despite being upheld legally in a test case at the York Assizes in 1781 (and not finally extinguished by purchase until 1871). In Manchester, by contrast, the Soke-Mills, owned by the trustees of Manchester Grammar School, came under literal attack at the Shude Hill market riots in November 1757. After that the corn soke was repealed in 1758, leaving only the less contentious malt monopoly, which survived, at least in theory, until 1884. These examples show that manorial custom could enshrine constraints on trade that equally had to be adapted to the changing economic environment. Similarly, market fees and tolls continued to be levied by some manorial lords, so that, paradoxically, relief from such irritant costs became a major policy of the newly incorporated large towns in the nineteenth century. In 1845 the new Manchester Borough Council had to pay the sum of £200,000 to Sir Oswald Mosley to purchase all manorial rights, including control over town markets. Reference to urban constitutional format does not therefore afford a satisfactory guide either to the state of the town's economy or to its degree of regulation.[2]

Secondly, and more fundamentally, even assuming that the structure of local government did correlate closely with the pattern of urban economic change, there are still analytical difficulties in explaining the chain of causation that linked one to the other. The argument has to show not only that restrictions hampered, but also that 'freedom' caused growth. Obscurantist regulations and costly municipal government might arguably have retarded expansion in some cases. But was the converse necessarily true? Was the absence of these constraints in itself sufficient to cause economic growth? Does taking off the brakes cause a train to move? Only if it has some motive power, or is already on a slope; and provided that there are no other obstacles. Opportunity and outcome are not the same things. Feedom to take up new trades will not necessarily cause new trades to spring up. Low levels of investment in municipal ceremonial will not necessarily cause large investment in trade and industry. In fact, the absence of municipal and guild regulations on trade can have been permissive at best – but not causative. After all, literally thousands of towns and villages up and down the country were not ancient corporations. They, too, experienced constitutional 'freedom' but without becoming another Manchester, another Birmingham. Even in the most rapidly developing regions of the country, many non-corporate villages remained exactly that. Nor, conversely, did the eventual incorporation of both Manchester and Birmingham in 1838 actually have a deleterious impact upon their later growth in the nineteenth century.

Individual towns grew in response to a variety of factors. Important among these were location, resource endowment, communications (whether natural or 'improved'), labour supply (both in terms of quantity and quality), and business enterprise. Some of these factors fell within the scope of policy-making, others did not. Certainly, a number of towns not among the urban leaders made efforts to introduce new trades and industries: attempts at establishing a cloth manufacture in York in 1698 and in the 1740s, or the production of Norwich stuffs at Tiverton in the 1750s, are examples. It was easier, however, to import a new line of business than to make it thrive. 'Any village in this country might by an increasing employment be presently raised to a Sheffield or a Birmingham,' wrote Arthur Young in optimistic mood in 1770. What any place might do in certain circumstances, however, all places, by the nature of things, could not do. Economic growth has never promoted all towns equally; nor was there any reason why it should, despite the disappointed grumbles of towns that were overtaken by faster-growing rivals.

The largest concentrations of population were to be found in towns carrying out an array of labour-intensive activities. Some of these towns were spatially dispersed, according to the location, accessibility, and development of certain key natural resources (the ports, dockyard towns, resorts). Others were grouped together in urbanizing regions, influenced by the location of raw materials and access to markets, labour supply, and traditional craft skills (the manufacturing towns). In an era of developing use of coal, the fastest-growing urban-industrial regions were those on the most accessible coalfields. Lastly, underpinning the whole urban network and providing a basic infrastructure of urban services, there was a mesh of smaller market and commercial centres, distributed across the countryside in response to population density and patterns of communications and trade.

The principle underlying these developments was that of specialization. 'We are a City of Philosophers: we work with our Heads, and make the Boobies of Birmingham work for us with their Hands,' asserted Dr Johnson in 1776, invoking the concept to defend his birthplace, Lichfield, from an accusation of idleness. By implication, consumer demand for Birmingham's guns and buttons was much greater than the demand for philosophers – a not uncommon state of affairs. Specialization refers, therefore, to the differentiation and consolidation of a leading economic role, or combination of roles. The growth patterns of towns were correlated in the long term with the growth and labour requirements of their leading function or functions, with all their attendant employment ramifications. For example, the sluggish expansion of the ancient universities in eighteenth-century England was closely matched by the slow population growth of the cities of Oxford and Cambridge. Towns therefore did not grow at uniform rates; nor was growth necessarily continuous, if the basis of any particular urban economy was liable to erosion or undercutting. Above all, specialization did not mean that expanding towns became monochrome in their social and economic configuration; on the contrary, they varied considerably. Coketown was one exemplar of specialized development, not its universal model.

In the same way, the general process of urbanization accorded with the degree of specialization in the economy as a whole. As the proportion of the total population engaged in agrarian activities declined, so the urban population engaged in full-time manufacturing and service employment increased. Such non-agrarian occupations do not absolutely demand location in an urban environment but they certainly favour it, as offering prompt access to concentrations of producers, distributors, and consumers. Even the speedier transport technology of the twentieth century has not diminished the force of the proposition that manufacturing and service occupations tend to cluster in towns – even though it has encouraged the internal topography of the towns themselves to become much more spatially diffused. Viewed in the long term, therefore, the degree of urbanization in an economy has tended to reflect the nature of its economic development. The highest levels of urbanization today are correlated closely with industrialization or a non-agrarian specialism, the lowest with what are termed undeveloped agrarian economies. Between those extremes there are many variations. More than 25 per cent of the population living in towns argues a degree of commercial development; more than 50 per cent marks an industrial or specialist economy. The urbanization of England in the eighteenth century, therefore, mirrored its eventual transformation from an affluent commercial economy into the world's first industrial nation.

Nonetheless, the relationships are complex. Urban growth has not by any means had a universally good press; nor has its impact been self-evidently conducive to a wider economic growth in all circumstances. Currently, the debate over urbanization in the Third World has highlighted fears that growing towns, particularly those with a high natural birthrate and economies based on service rather than manufacturing activities, may prove harmful rather than beneficial, 'parasitical' rather than 'generative'. Similar concern was expressed by some onlookers in eighteenth-century England, as it had been in the sixteenth and seventeenth centuries. The huge capital city in particular had long been a target for criticism, allegedly draining revenues away from the countryside to be dissipated unproductively in town. Fielding depicted an aspect of this attitude when teasing the squirearchy by pointing to the economic self-interest behind village enthusiasm for their return from town. The disagreeable Lady Booby was welcomed home by 'the Ringing of Bells and the Acclamations of the Poor, who were rejoiced to see their Patroness returned after so long an Absence, during which Time all her Rents had been drafted to London, without a Shilling being spent among them, which tended not a little to their utter Impoverishing.' But analysis must also take into account the return economic linkages in the form of the towns' provision of markets, communications, goods, services, and investment. In other words, the impact of towns and their growth cannot be analysed in isolation from the wider economies and societies in which they are found; just as economic policies directed at the towns alone are unlikely to prove either feasible or efficacious. Towns cannot usurp the stage as the unique 'villains' of backwardness, and certainly not as the sole 'heroes' of growth.

The mythology – or demonology – of urban development does nonetheless make one important point. While it is unrealistic to claim causal primacy for the towns, it is equally mistaken to assume that their growth had no impact at all. On the contrary, urbanization in the long term has had major economic, social, cultural, and ultimately political, implications, for all countries in which it has occurred. It has influenced the process of change, as well as itself being influenced by it. Analytically, the problem is to identify one strand in a complex of interrelated changes, without claiming either too much for it, or too little.

The collective dynamism of urban growth in eighteenth-century England certainly had important ramifications for the economy as a whole. But statistical measurement is not a simple matter. It has been suggested that the relative economic importance of the towns can be established by comparing the growth rates of the towns collectively with that of the index of real industrial and commercial output, which is taken to stand proxy for industrialization.[3] That exercise suggests that the growth of industrial output was more rapid than the increase in the country's total urban population; and, since much industry was rural rather than urban in location, it could be argued therefore that urbanization was not central to industrialization – and indeed had lagged behind industrial development elsewhere in the economy. But the comparison cannot really stand. Apart from the fact that the index might more properly be compared to that of the growth of the commercial and manufacturing towns, there are analytical problems in such an approach. It takes no account of all the linkages and feedbacks – whether positive or negative – between urban growth and the industrial countryside. And does the fact that indices of very different things proceed at different rates disprove any relationship between them? Urbanization was a long-drawn-out but finite process, whereas industrial and commercial growth can proceed exponentially. In fact, industrial and commercial output in eighteenth-century England grew at a sustainedly faster rate than the expansion of the population as a whole, whether resident in the towns or the countryside. That is, indeed, what is meant by the onset of industrialization. The growth in per capita productivity was at least as likely to have been nurtured by specialization in the towns as by the development of the rural economy. Both changes were different sides of the same coin.

What then did urbanization in eighteenth-century England contribute to the complex process of economic change? The streamlining and adaptation of the towns in fact had extensive impact. Firstly, the expansion of an urban population, dependent upon non-urban resources for foodstuffs and raw materials, had in itself a stimulant effect upon the commercialization and development of the agrarian economy, although by no means all supplies were furnished from English resources alone.

Secondly, the towns were crucial nodal points on the network of exchange and distribution, servicing every aspect of the growing economy, increasing the efficiency of networks of inland and overseas trade, and generating pressure for improvements in the system of transport and communications. For example, urban growth was often a stimulus to river and road improvements; and docks and canals were built in response to the need to expedite the movement of goods to and from the growing towns.

Thirdly, the towns themselves played an important role in the development of industry, whether as finishing, marketing, or production centres in their own right. Among other things, they themselves created a huge building industry. And external economies for industrial growth were provided by the towns' reservoirs of labour, their provision of specialist services, and their access to the communications network. There was also some spin-off from the diffusion of urban work discipline, craft skills, scientific enquiry, and technological knowhow.

Fourthly, the towns were the locations of an extensive and broadening range of tertiary-sector service specialisms, including those of banking, insurance, law, medicine, education, entertainment, even government. Their role was particularly visible in the case of London's economy, but was pervasive also among the provincial towns. The economic impact of such services was very varied; but the diversification of these labour-intensive services collectively oiled the wheels of change on both the supply and demand sides of the economy. They also absorbed much urban labour into the active economy.

Fifthly, as noted by Adam Smith, the towns were accumulators and circulators of investment capital. As accumulators, the developing towns themselves constituted an immense stock of investment in 'social overhead' capital, in the form of the urban fabric and its eighteenth-century 'improvements'; while as circulators, the towns not only housed the growing number of banks and agencies of exchange but also furnished a pool of middle-class investors, with relatively fluid assets and a propensity to invest. (It is pointless, however, to try to draw too rigid a distinction between 'urban' and 'rural' sources of capital, as many town-dwellers owned rural properties, and vice versa.)

Lastly, the towns, with their relatively open, fluid, competitive, and acquisitive societies, were important purveyors of the new consumer ethos. That was indeed the essence of the moralists' critique of the towns: that they encouraged worldliness, dissatisfaction, emulation, and desire for luxury. Such aspirations, whatever their moral worth, were clearly of importance in generating the emergence of a consumerist, market-oriented society and economy. In fact, the highest concentrations of 'luxury' in eighteenth-century England were probably to be found in the great aristocratic country houses; but they seemed to represent timeless inequalities. In fast-changing urban societies, on the other hand, such matters appeared mutable, and therefore open to challenge.

The growth of towns, even on a small scale, is therefore likely to have some economic impact, however minor; and when both the scale and the continued pace of urbanization become substantial, there is a good case for pointing to this as one of the key 'disequilibria', promoting, as well as responding to, fundamental economic mutation. Urbanization was emphatically not, however, the long-sought but ever-elusive 'first cause' of England's Industrial Revolution. Most historians and development economists have now rightly abandoned the quest for single-cause explanations of very complex structural economic and social transformations. But if, on the other hand, the genesis of industrialization is regarded as a series of simultaneous equations, that is to say, many variable forces interacting at the same time – when changes in the conditions and technology of supply intersected with changes in the nature and extent of effective demand in the Atlantic economies of both England and North America – then the gradual and eventually irreversible shift from a rural to an urban population can be seen to have had numerous implications for many, if not all, the components of these changes. Urbanization represented, but also helped to foster, structural transformation.

The radical nature of these changes in industry, towns, and countryside was not lost on contemporaries. In 1788 Arthur Young was impressed to see that the new technology of mechanized spinning was rapidly spreading from the cotton to the woollen industries. So successful was it that it had created a relative shortage of combers to prepare the wool for the machines. Northern industrialists were advertising in the East Anglian press:

Wool-Combers wanted.

Constant Work for all good Hands that apply, with Blanks [i.e. tickets] from their [journeymen's] Society, to William Toplis and Co. of Mansfield, in Nottinghamshire.

N.B. Any tolerable Hand may earn 3s. per day, and a very good one 3s. 6d.

When he reprinted this, in the *Annals of Agriculture,* Young commented quietly, 'A revolution is making'.

7 Urban demography

Much of the growth of towns in eighteenth-century England was fuelled by a persistent flow of migrants from the countryside. It is true that, later in the century, the balance of fertility and mortality within the towns itself began to change; but urban mortality rates were still very high. Therefore, as in earlier times, the towns depended upon rural recruits for an above-average rate of population growth. Even those towns that were not expanding dramatically in the long term saw a constant turnover of population. All places had some immigration. The larger and more rapidly growing a town, the greater its proportion of recruits from the countryside, and the larger the number of newcomers to assimilate into urban society. Indeed, it is noticeable that in this period the application of the term 'foreigner' to those coming from out of town gradually lapsed, while it was retained, of course, for those coming from outside national boundaries.

Young single people were especially prominent in the move from the English countryside into the towns, in search of apprenticeship, employment, education, and the casual pickings of urban life. The growing towns thus contained an above-average proportion of young people, at the height of their working and reproductive capacities. Hence the unofficial role of the town as a marriage mart, as well as an employment bureau. In particular, there was a constant stream of young country girls – the Sally Bashfuls and Margery Mushrooms of journalistic satire – entering into domestic service in urban households. Virtually all towns contained a majority of women, reflecting the relatively greater range of job opportunities for them in the towns as compared with the countryside, as well as female longevity. At the end of the century Oxford was the only large town in England and Wales not to house a majority of women. Literary jests about the enthusiasm of women to get to town were accurate reflections of contemporary reality.

Eighteenth-century English society was very much one on the move. Formal constraints upon the free movement of poor families still remained on the statute books, in the form of the notorious Settlement Laws. Their provisions were extensively but not intensively or uniformly invoked. In theory, under the law of 1662, a poor settler (defined as one renting a tenement worth less than £10 per annum) could, upon complaint made within forty days of arrival that he or she was likely to become a burden upon the poor rates, be sent back to the parish of original settlement. Enforcement was left to the discretion of parish officials, under warrant from local JPs. But it often proved difficult to detect candidates for removal, or, having detected and removed them, to make them stay away. In the large towns, where the population could and did move easily from parish to parish, problems of enforcement were particularly acute. 'The great Numbers, already there, screen those that creep in,' commented Roger North in the early years of the century.

Already in 1697 Parliament had recognized that the letter of the law hampered the recruitment of labour in places 'where the increase of Manufactures would employ more Hands'. The law was therefore substantially amended to license mobility. Poor settlers were permitted to establish a new residence upon the production of a certificate from their parish of legal settlement, accepting responsibility for their relief. But even this attempt to reconcile free movement of labour with parish parsimony was only partially enforced, especially in the towns. There were a number of practical problems. Not all churchwardens would issue certificates. Many did not bother to inspect them. In some towns, such as Leeds for example, they were completely ignored by the end of the eighteenth century. Furthermore, it proved very difficult, in a mobile society, to define precisely what constituted and established legal rights of settlement. Which parish was responsible for the children of migrants, born after the parents had moved? And for the children of those children? Which parish was responsible for those with dual residences, such as the family of an impoverished Leeds coachmaker, whose wife and daughters lived on a small property that he rented in Blackfordby, Leicestershire? The determination of these and other issues made the case-law of settlement exceedingly complicated.

In fact, many families did arm themselves with a certificate or 'testimonial' before moving (a few municipal listings of certificate-holders still survive), but the scale of population movement made it quite unrealistic for urban officials to remove impoverished settlers every time they needed poor relief. Up to a third of the population in some large towns in the later eighteenth century were known to be without a settlement there. In those circumstances relief was usually given, however grudgingly, locally and on an *ad hoc* basis, by private charity if not by parish grant. The number of people actually removed under the Settlement Laws in the eighteenth century was very small indeed; and the rising levels of urban rents in the later decades removed increasing numbers of artisans from the shadow of the law. The most frequently threatened were the socially most defenceless: unattached women and children, and pregnant single girls. In practice, however, the Settlement Laws, offensive and cumbersome as they were, had little direct effect on the substantial movement of population into the towns. It was noted in 1758 that 'the general Course of Migration in *England*, is, from *Rural Parishes* to *Market-Towns*, and from *both of them* to the *Capital City*; so that great Multitudes of People, who were born in *Rural Parishes*, are continually *acquiring* SETTLEMENTS in *Cities* or *Towns*, more especially in those Towns where considerable Manufacturies are carried on.' That description over-simplified the cross-currents of migration patterns and the state of the law; but its general testimony was emphatic.

Migration on a large scale into the towns of eighteenth-century England occurred in response to two related forces. One was an element of 'push' from the countryside. It was not true, as the old myth used to claim, that the English poor were collectively forced off the land and into the towns, for the rural population actually continued to grow in numbers throughout the eighteenth and early nineteenth centuries. But the streamlining of the agrarian economy did mean that it was able to function successfully without pressing into service the labour of all those who were born in the countryside, who were thereby released to move into the towns – or indeed to move to other rural parishes or even to other countries. That is not the same as saying that all migrants moved willingly. The impact of agrarian change was sometimes highly controversial. For example, the operation of some forms of enclosure and the engrossment of farms in Warwickshire propelled people from those parishes. In 1794 John Wedge decided that, 'from these causes, the hardy yeomanry of the country villages have been driven for employment into Birmingham, Coventry, and other manufacturing towns, whose flourishing trade has sometimes found them profitable employment.'

Yet his analysis clearly pointed to a complex of factors at work: the level of earnings was greater in the vicinity of Birmingham and Coventry than in the countryside, providing an attraction to labour. The 'push' from the villages did not operate as an indiscriminate, blind force, shunting countryfolk willy-nilly into every nearby town. The counties with the greatest amounts of enclosure and engrossing were by no means automatically those with the most substantial levels of urban growth in the eighteenth century. Nor did all innovation in the rural economy work to reduce local demand for labour. The cultivation of some new root crops, for example, was very labour-intensive. In other words, there was also a distinctive 'pull' emanating from the towns. Their allure was in part a product of a general urban mythology of opportunity, advancement, riches, and glamour. At the same time it was also compounded of highly specific and practical considerations, that operated with a differential force from town to town. Prominent among these were the demand for labour in the towns, and levels of earnings to be gained there. The fluctuations in the fortunes of different urban economies, therefore, help to explain the marked variations in the pace and pattern of rural–urban migration over time.

Sustained urbanization was more than an accidental by-product of rural change. It depended both upon the ability of the towns to absorb a disproportionately fast-growing share of the population, and upon that of the agrarian economy to release it. The traditional inertia and conservatism of the English rural population (itself something of an urban myth) proved, in fact, no barrier to a prompt response to a changing economic environment. The growth of towns, therefore, itself stimulated the processes of commercialization in the countryside, which in turn helped to fuel urbanization.

Much of this migration took place over relatively short distances, often following trading and transportation routes. Expanding towns drew many recruits from country villages within their own immediate orbit, although the scale and direction of these local flows varied with the balance of 'push' and 'pull' factors. In general, the larger the town, the stronger its powers of attraction over a long distance; but there was still an unmistakable regional basis to migration patterns, notably in the case of large towns in relatively remote parts of the country. Even London, whose reputation was nationwide, probably drew the majority of its recruits in the eighteenth century from the rural south and east (see ch. 5 above).

Patterns of migration varied from town to town, industry to industry. But even in the case of, for example, the successful Sheffield metal-manufacturing trades, growth did not greatly widen the area of recruitment. In the early eighteenth century the immediate origin (as denoted by father's place of residence) of approximately 85 per cent of the indentured apprentices enrolled before the Hallamshire Cutlers' Company derived from Sheffield itself and its immediate vicinity (within five miles as the crow flies); in the later eighteenth century the proportion remained high, at 75 per cent. Of the other, 'immigrant', apprentices to Sheffield, the great majority throughout the century had come from places no more than twenty miles from the town: in the years from 1700 to 1749 only 5.4 per cent and, from 1750 to 1799, only 7.5 per cent, had travelled further than forty miles.[1] These details, of course, merely recorded one move in an apprentice's career. It may well be that his family had already migrated before that, or that he himself moved again subsequently. Migration to town was not a once-and-for-all event; but individual changes of residence often took place over relatively short distances.

The recruitment of young single men into formal urban apprenticeship was not necessarily typical of all immigration into town, which embraced a much wider spectrum of age, sex, and social composition. Other sources, however, tend to suggest a similar picture of predominantly short-distance movement. In Birmingham, for example, 76.7 per cent of the 617 people with settlement certificates recorded between 1698 and 1726 had been recruited from villages in Warwickshire and the counties immediately adjoining. And in the smaller but prosperous county town of Maidstone, between 1691 and 1740, over half of the 592 men and women with settlement certificates had travelled fewer than ten miles from their legal parish of settlement, while only about 15 per cent had come further than forty miles, and only 7 per cent more than one hundred miles. This eighteenth-century recruitment by towns from within their own regional hinterlands contrasted with the experience of the sixteenth and early seventeenth centuries, when there had been a relatively greater proportion of long-distance migration, particularly among the new-comers to London, but the growing number of expanding provincial towns extended the range of local options to would-be migrants.

Some social groups were more mobile than others. At one end of the scale, professional men were prepared to move long distances, in order to match scarce skills with specialized demand. Other migrants also moved across country in response to commercial and industrial, rather than geographical, contacts; but the extent of occupationally directed migration seems to have been relatively small.

Some of the country's vagrant population had also tramped many miles from town to town in search of shelter and succour. A few contemporary observers, indeed, claimed that the administrative rigidities of the Settlement Laws tended to increase the numbers forced to move on from parish to parish. Even so, the number of long-distance migrants among the 'rogues, vagabonds, sturdy beggars, and vagrants' who fell foul of the law was still relatively low. A survey of 2,000 adult beggars (most of them women) in London in the 1790s revealed that 37.5 per cent had been attracted from parishes that were within ten miles of the capital. Of the 55.5 per cent that had come from further afield, only 16.8 per cent had travelled from elsewhere in England, while 33.95 per cent came from Ireland, 3.25 per cent from Scotland, and 1.5 per cent from outside the British Isles (leaving 7.0 per cent who were uncertain as to their place of settlement). That was, however, only a very imperfect survey, conducted by a few private individuals concerned at the disarray of the law. It is extremely difficult therefore to establish the full scale of vagrancy in eighteenth-century towns. Parliament had experienced continuous problems in devising stringent punishments for beggars and vagrants that did not simultaneously penalize genuine supplicants and bona fide travellers. As a result, the Vagrancy Laws were, if anything, even more confusing and less systematically enforced than were those relating to settlement.

A few urban authorities in the later eighteenth century themselves attempted to promote long-distance migration into areas where labour was in demand, by the apprenticing of pauper children. The parish of St. Clement Danes, London, for example, advertised 'several stout boys' for apprenticeship in the *Manchester Mercury* in January 1787. The seven-year-old Robert Blincoe, whose memoirs later helped to stop the practice, was apprenticed by St. Pancras Workhouse, London, into a cotton-mill near Nottingham in 1799. Take-up in the towns was, however, relatively small. It was chiefly the early factories in the countryside, experiencing exceptional difficulties in recruiting labour, that drew upon this source. The enforced migration of youthful paupers to places far distant from their friends and families was from the start a highly controversial policy, which was gradually abandoned in the early nineteenth century. In 1816 the movement of parish apprentices from London was legally restricted to forty miles; while in the mills, the parish recruits were superseded by the 'free hands'.

Perhaps the greatest amount of long-distance movement into eighteenth-century towns was that of Irish and Scottish emigrants, who were not subject to the English Settlement Laws and whose own economies were not urbanizing so rapidly. There was a steady influx of Scots, including many professional men, throughout the century. Scottish migrants were concentrated especially in London, and on a lesser scale in Norwich, as well as in Carlisle and the Lancashire cotton towns. Irish immigration, on the other hand, continued throughout the century but expanded considerably in volume in the later decades. These migrants also settled chiefly in Lancashire and London. As poor Catholic immigrants in an officially Protestant country, they tended to congregate together, for protection and communal assistance, in areas of low-cost housing. The most celebrated Irish territory in London lay in the parish of St. Giles, while in Manchester, where the first Catholic Chapel was opened in Rook Street in 1774, they settled in the areas later known as 'little Ireland' and 'Irish Town'. Other than that, immigration from overseas was very small in scale in the eighteenth century, and almost entirely to the cosmopolitan capital city, whose established foreign communities readily absorbed the continuing trickle of newcomers.

The fact that much migration took place over relatively short distances, and usually in a familiar regional context, did much to ease the shock of transition to an urban society. Hutton observed on his travels in the Midlands that the populous places were more tolerant than the remoter villages, where 'the inhabitants set their dogs at me merely because I was a stranger.' No doubt the help of family and friends was invoked by many settlers, as well as contacts with previous migrants from the same area. Hutton again recorded an instructive episode when, as a runaway apprentice, he was seeking work in a new town:

The first question usually put was, 'Where do you come from?' My constant answer was, 'Derby'. 'There is a country-man of yours', said the person, 'in such a street....' I applied, and found I had been a neighbour to his family. He also knew something of mine.... He set me to work till night, about two hours, in which time I earned two-pence.

On that occasion the young Hutton was eventually persuaded to return to his family; but the assumption was plainly that assistance could be expected from a fellow countryman, who had already made the move.

Often, too, the coaching inns and the nearby taverns acted as clearing houses for regional flows of migration into the towns, as did the artisans' unofficial employment exchanges: many trades designated a favoured alehouse as a 'house of call' for news and information. Some social clubs, benevolent societies, and even churches were organized on a regional basis, and also provided institutional buffers for newcomers in a strange urban environment. A Scots Society was founded in Norwich in 1775, a Salopian Amicable Society was projected in Manchester in 1785, a Norwich Society (a Whig social and political club) was formed in London in 1808, and congregations of Welsh Calvinistic Methodists were active in both Manchester and Birmingham in the early nineteenth century. The private chapels of the Roman Catholic church also played a similar role for the Irish communities in English towns.

The aggregate volume of immigration into the towns from all sources was considerable. 'The great Multitudes of People requisite for Manufactories, Sea-Ports, etc. proves the Necessity of In-comers,' decided Dr Short in 1750. Most towns contained many recent arrivals, and in the most rapidly growing centres their numbers may have amounted to well over half the adult population. In London, Dr Burrington claimed in 1757 that fully two-thirds of the adults there had been born outside the capital. That would have amounted to at least 270,000 migrants out of an estimated 405,000 adult inhabitants at mid-century. Yet even that huge total represented only a minimum figure. Gross turnover was even more substantial, as there was also a smaller but not insignificant reverse flow of people from the metropolis into the countryside.

Comparisons of a town's actual growth rate with that suggested by the balance of baptisms and burials (where the records survive) go some way to suggest the scale of the immigration that must have taken place, but cannot yield precise figures because the subsequent offspring (and indeed the eventual mortality) of the migrants themselves are counted as part of the urban vital statistics. At all events, it seems clear that in the course of the century literally thousands of country people made their way into the towns. Hence it was that they acquired their traditional reputation as 'the *Graves* of Mankind'. Yet the relatively worse health record of the urban environment proved no deterrent to migrants. Indeed, a spate of epidemic mortality in the towns was not uncommonly followed by a surge of replenishment migration from the rural villages around. 'A lodger fresh from the country often lies down in a bed, filled with infection by its last tenant, or from which the corpse of a victim to fever has only been removed a few hours before,' protested Dr Ferriar in Manchester in 1795.

At the same time there were some key changes in the urban birth and death rates themselves during the course of the century. The demography of towns was a matter of much contemporary debate and analysis. A great corpus of rather disparate data was amassed and scrutinized – prompted in part by the mid-century controversy as to whether the national population was rising or declining, and in part by a growing concern for the environmental implications of large-scale urban growth. Some towns themselves collated records of baptisms and burials from Anglican parish registers and published them in the local press, in the form of weekly, monthly, and annual Bills of Mortality. The best-known compilation was that for the City of London and a swathe of parishes to the north and east, which thus gave its name to the extensive area of the metropolis that lay 'within the Bills'. Unfortunately the records were collected very imperfectly and are difficult to interpret, especially as they excluded, for the most part, the demographic record of the Dissenters. Information about baptisms and burials therefore can do no more than suggest the real picture of births and deaths. 'One of our great Misfortunes in [the] Cities, is, that we affect to despise our Bills of Mortality,' sighed the reformer Hanway in 1767, perplexed at the difficulties in establishing accurate information about child mortality in the towns.

Parish-register evidence for urban baptisms and burials must there fore be used with great caution. The more comprehensive the coverage, the better. Partial surveys of one parish, or even group of parishes within a town, are of limited value, as there is no guarantee of their typicality. Similarly, analysis of figures for individual years in isolation may prove very misleading as a guide to normal levels of baptisms and burials, as annual totals were liable to fluctuate dramatically in the short term.[2]

Some surviving evidence does, however, suggest that the towns were not exclusively dependent upon recruitment of country migrants for all their growth, at least by the end of the eighteenth century. The balance of baptisms to burials began to change. In earlier decades the annual total of burials in many large towns had often surpassed the number of baptisms. By the end of the century that pattern was no longer so clear-cut, in an increasing number of large and small urban centres. Certainly, when civil registration began later in the 1840s, urban birth rates were found to be universally higher than urban death rates. Growth from the 'natural' increase of population within the towns had been added to growth swelled by the continuing stream of immigration. In the long term, such a change was crucial to the sustaining of urbanization. The gradual shift from a rural to an urban population could not continue indefinitely. A highly urbanized society, with few rural recruits to draw upon, could not afford to lose its population at continuously profligate levels, and survive. In modern times both towns and countryside have seen a marked decline in the death rate, followed, at varying speeds in different parts of the world, by a long-term reduction in the birth rate. In the later eighteenth-century towns, by contrast, when the great modern rise in population was only just beginning, the changing balance between fertility and mortality was prompted both by a rising birth rate in the towns as well as by a slight but significant diminution in the death rate.

Variations in the balance of births and deaths in eighteenth-century England are difficult to establish with precision, because the basic data are so imperfect. Indeed, not only the causation but even the chronology of population growth in the country as a whole have generated considerable controversy. Much urban evidence has been invoked in the course of that debate. However, as the bulk of the population still lived in the countryside, changes in urban birth and death rates do not have to account for the general growth of population throughout England and Wales. The health record of the towns attracted much contemporary attention in the eighteenth century, precisely because it was generally worse than that of the countryside. Urban demographic change was but one factor in a complex of interrelated developments. Far from exclusively creating the modern rise in England's population, therefore, the towns found themselves in the midst of that process.

As far as the crude birth rate was concerned, the propensity of the growing towns to attract disproportionate numbers of young adult migrants to their ranks tended to push up the rate of reproduction. That is to say, even without any variations in the fertility of young couples in the towns, the age-structure of a fast-expanding population in itself promoted a relatively high birth rate, in terms of the number of children produced for every thousand inhabitants. Young couples and their offspring constituted a large proportion of the urban populations. Rapid growth became cumulative, as long as the towns' attraction for young migrants continued. Conversely, declining towns that were not attracting or retaining many young migrants showed lowered or even falling birth rates.

At the same time, it is likely that age-specific fertility in many towns also increased in the course of the century, hence pushing up urban birth rates still further. A rise in fertility was probably encouraged by a combination of a slight fall in the mean age at first marriage, from the very late first marriages of people in their mid-20s recorded in the later seventeenth and early eighteenth centuries, and by an increase in the incidence of marriage in the urban populations as a whole. Urban societies, in fact, as well as in their own mythologies, offered ample opportunities for meeting people of the opposite sex, and social constraints against setting up a new household were relatively weak. It was true, as some contemporaries in the mid-eighteenth century pointed out, that numerous living-in servants and apprentices were prevented from marrying. But turnover of the youthful servant population was rapid, and the extent of formal apprenticeship was steadily diminishing.

Also important in influencing the urban birth rate was the high proportion of young women in the towns who were 'at risk' of pregnancy. By reputation, urban societies in eighteenth-century England were famed for their sexual licence and laxity, and for their high incidence of illegitimacy. No doubt much of the contemporary torrent of moralizing on the subject was exaggerated. Yet it was probably easier, if not obligatory, to flout traditional morality in the relative anonymity of the towns. Indeed, Dr Short decided sadly that their whole way of life was liable to lead urban residents astray, 'From the Peoples more plentiful Eating and Drinking, greater Idleness, Immodesty, Intemperance, and other Incitements and Opportunities for Wantonness'. In fact, the history of recorded illegitimacy as such is very complex, and does not correlate simply with social and economic indices, such as urbanization. From the point of view of the demography of the towns, however, the important factor was that a relatively high proportion of young women living there were liable to reproduce, whether before, during, or outside matrimony.

Other contemporaries also argued that economic considerations, especially in places where there was a heavy demand for child labour, encouraged the poor to marry young, and to produce large families.

There is no need, however, to postulate too rational a calculus. Youthful labour was clearly not everywhere in demand. The opening in 1745 of the London Foundling Hospital as a refuge for children abandoned in the streets of the capital city testified to that. But most couples had little effective choice in the number of their offspring. Artificial means of inhibiting conception were certainly known in the towns: Boswell's London Journal recorded references to his sexual encounters 'in armour', although his own concern was rather to avoid venereal disease than to safeguard the woman from pregnancy. However, male condoms, usually made of sheep's gut, and the various traditional devices, such as herbal abortifacients, were highly unreliable. Even infanticide, as a desperate remedy for the problem of unwanted children, occurred only rarely in eighteenth-century England – rendered otiose, among other things, by the prevailingly high levels of infant mortality. Without any systematic and reliable means of contraception, therefore, the youthful and migratory populations in the growing towns tended to produce high birth rates – as the 'frontier' populations of the English economy.

The detailed records of four towns, selected merely by virtue of the survival of long runs of baptismal and burial data, demonstrate the process of change, and also its complexities. All four places were textile centres, but with very different growth rates and economic fortunes. Their statistics are unlikely to be accurate in themselves, and they give a lower estimate of the total number of births and deaths than must actually have occurred. Fastest-growing of the four was Leeds, where the annual average of baptisms already outnumbered that of burials for most of the five-year periods between 1740 and 1770, and pulled away even more markedly thereafter (see Graph 1). In the smaller Nottingham, the annual average of baptisms lagged behind the average of burials in the early eighteenth century; but again the position was consistently reversed from the mid-1740s onwards, when the city's population began to grow briskly (see Graph 2). Both Norwich and Exeter, by contrast, were initially larger centres, but experienced subsequent periods of economic stagnation and possibly some outright population loss. In the case of Exeter, the annual average of baptisms in every ten-year period continued to lag behind that of burials until the 1770s, after which they moved ahead – at a time when other sources confirm that the city had recovered from its mid-century economic depression (Graph 3). Slowest to show the changeover was the city of Norwich, whose annual Bills of Mortality demonstrate, incidentally, how markedly the totals fluctuated from year to year. Norwich experienced economic problems in the later eighteenth century, and probably a net emigration from the city in the 1790s, when totals of both baptisms and burials showed a decline. There, the annual level of baptisms did not exceed burials consistently until after the turn of the century (Graph 4).

Translated into very notional baptismal and burial rates (by comparison with independent estimates of these towns' total populations), the figures displayed in Table IX suggest that baptismal rates of at least 30 per thousand (1 in 33) were to be found in all the expansive urban centres. Since the Anglican registers under-registered the real demographic experience, the actual birth rates must have been much higher in all cases.[3]

At the same time, the estimates in Table IX also direct attention towards changes in levels of mortality in the towns. There is indeed some statistical evidence to support the contemporary view that crude urban death rates fell, at least to some extent, in the later eighteenth century. The trend, incidentally, was not irreversible. There is also valid evidence for a later worsening of some urban death rates in the 1820s and 1830s, particularly in the larger conurbations. It was not until the mid- and later nineteenth century that the death rate in even the largest towns assumed its unbroken and substantial downward movement. Change was neither simple nor linear. There were many factors in play, efforts at improvement on the one hand being set against the continuingly hectic pace of urban expansion on the other.

For much of the eighteenth century, therefore, death rates remained relatively high. The populous towns were hosts to a great range of contagious diseases, whose devastation was difficult to combat. Death rates were certainly higher in the towns than in the countryside, and tended furthermore to be higher in the larger towns than in the smaller ones. Dr Percival in 1773 considered the death rate in London to be 1 in 21 (47.6 per thousand), compared with 1 in 27 or 28 (35.7 per thousand) in Liverpool and Manchester, and only 1 in 35 (28.5 per thousand) in rural Eastham, in the Wirral. Levels of mortality also varied between, and within, towns according to the density of habitation. Already Dr Short's comparative survey of urban and rural bills of mortality – modelled on Graunt's pioneering work in the 1660s – had convinced him, in 1750, that traditional explanations of the incidence of disease solely in terms of differences in soil and climate were inadequate: 'The closer Towns and Villages stand, the more pent-up the Houses, the lower and closer the Rooms, the narrower the Streets, the smaller the Windows, the more numerous the Inhabitants, the unhealthier the Place.'

Yet other differences in the health of towns were produced by variations in the nature of the local economy. The resorts had a reputation for salubriousness, but therefore attracted invalids as well as pleasure seekers. In 1690, for example, Sir John Sudbury was given a

Table IX Notional baptismal and burial rates for four textile towns in the eighteenth century (Anglican registers only)*

	1700	1710	1739	1750	1775	1786	1801
Leeds							
Baptisms per '000					32		32
Burials per '000					27		26
Total population	7,000?				29,941		53,162
Nottingham							
Baptisms per '000	31		36		35		36
Burials per '000	30		39		29		28
Total population	7,000?		9,900		17,771		28,861
*Exeter***							
Baptisms per '000	30						33
Burials per '000	29						28
Total population	14,000?						17,418
Norwich							
Baptisms per '000		30		32		28	26
Burials per '000		34		33		28	28
Total population	29,000	31,000?		36,169		41,051	36,854

* As notes to Graphs 1–4.
** Exeter figures include returns from three Nonconformist registers.

choice by his doctors between Tunbridge Wells or death. He chose the former, but under protest (he preferred Epsom). By contrast, the metalware and refinery towns were grimy and smoky, and had a tendency to show an above-average incidence of chest and lung diseases. In fact, it took the debate over the impact of the factories to stimulate in 1831 the first official enquiries into comparative urban environments and mortality; but the problems were by no means confined to places whose industries were early to mechanize. Increasing job specialization in the

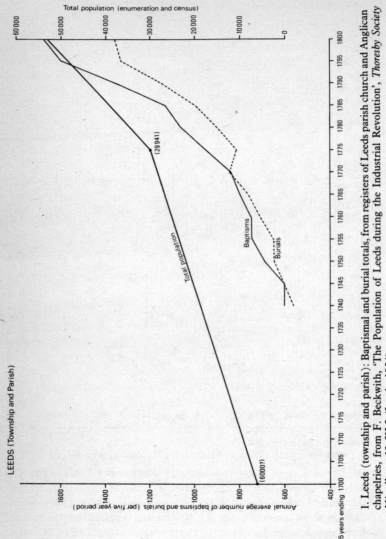

1. Leeds (township and parish): Baptismal and burial totals, from registers of Leeds parish church and Anglican chapelries, from F. Beckwith, 'The Population of Leeds during the Industrial Revolution', *Thoresby Society Miscellany*, 12, XLI (Leeds, 1954).

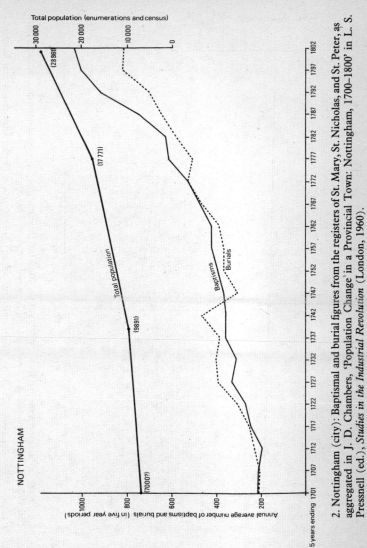

2. Nottingham (city): Baptismal and burial figures from the registers of St. Mary, St. Nicholas, and St. Peter, as aggregated in J. D. Chambers, 'Population Change' in a Provincial Town: Nottingham, 1700–1800' in L. S. Pressnell (ed.), *Studies in the Industrial Revolution* (London, 1960).

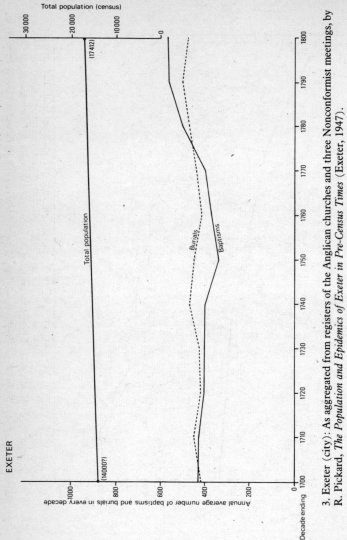

EXETER

Total population (census)

Total population

Burials

Baptisms

Annual average number of baptisms and burials in every decade

Decade ending

3. Exeter (city): As aggregated from registers of the Anglican churches and three Nonconformist meetings, by R. Pickard, *The Population and Epidemics of Exeter in Pre-Census Times* (Exeter, 1947).

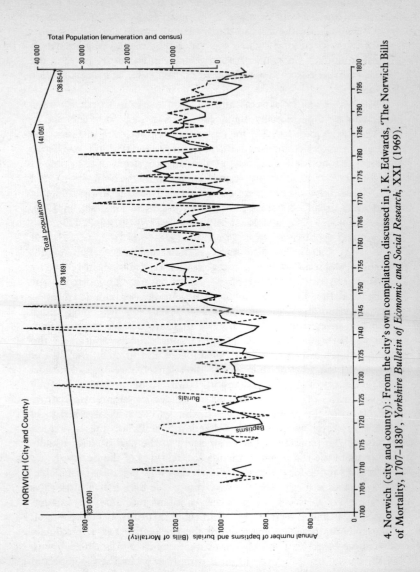

4. Norwich (city and county): From the city's own compilation, discussed in J. K. Edwards, 'The Norwich Bills of Mortality, 1707–1830', *Yorkshire Bulletin of Economic and Social Research*, XXI (1969).

towns encouraged the growth of many occupationally related health hazards. In Sheffield, for example, it was noted as early as 1767 that there were many male deaths from phthisis, the pulmonary complaint known locally as 'grinder's lung', which was fostered by the daylong inhalation of dust from dry-stone work. An early nineteenth-century poem to the *Sheffield Grinder* observed him, bleakly, as 'Coughing, at his deadly trade he bends'.

These variations in patterns and levels of mortality between towns persisted over time. Equally, many infectious diseases were common to all. Among the most lethal in the eighteenth century were smallpox, the scourge of the very young, and influenza (agues) and typhus fever. These diseases were not only endemic but also flared up from time to time in epidemics of great intensity. Some swept through both towns and countryside; other attacks were confined chiefly to the towns. Notably widespread urban epidemics included outbreaks of smallpox in 1710, 1722–3, 1740–2, 1747, and 1781; influenza in 1729–30, 1743, 1775, and 1781–2; and typhus and 'fevers' in 1710, 1728–9, 1741–2, 1772–3, and 1799–1800. There were also many regional epidemics. Portsmouth, Plymouth, and south-west England generally were ravaged in 1735–6 by 'a malignant spotted Fever' (typhus), said to have been imported by the return of the fleet. Other perennially infectious diseases included measles, thrush, consumption, diphtheria, scarlet fever, and whooping cough (then known as chincough). Many of these were liable to strike with great virulence and to spread rapidly through the population of the towns. Numerous other causes of death were also listed in the Bills of Mortality, from 'feasting to excess' to the relatively rare cases of suicide. The evidence of the Bills cannot, however, be accepted as fully comprehensive or reliable, except as guides to eighteenth-century perceptions of the problems. Many fatalities ('old age', 'weaknesses of infancy') clearly perplexed the diagnostic skills of the appointed searchers, who reported the cause of death to the parish clerk, usually relying upon the testimony of friends and relatives of the deceased.

The risks to life for townspeople of all ages were certainly formidable. Most vulnerable of all were the very young, the high urban birth rates producing an answering crop of heavy infant mortality. In London between 1730 and 1749 it has been estimated that fully 75 per cent of all children born there had died before the age of five (an approximate calculation, based on a comparison of the number of infant burials with the number of baptisms over the same period but excluding the impact of migration). A similar calculation for the smaller Manchester in 1773 put the figure there at 50 per cent.

It is probable, nevertheless, that the very high urban death rates of the early eighteenth century showed some diminution in subsequent decades, as many contemporaries indeed suggested. The partial data from many Bills and registers confirm that the worst peaks in epidemic mortality, between the 1720s and 1740s, did not recur thereafter, even when allowance is made for the under-registration of burials in the later period. In the case of Nottingham, for example, it has been observed that, after the mid-1740s, the 'age of massacre by epidemic was over'. Indeed, the notional burial rates for all four textile towns studied in detail (Table IX) show a broad similarity in their general downward trend from the mid-eighteenth century, despite other differences in urban size and economic fortunes. Little precise reliance can be put upon the figures, which are no more than minimum estimates. It is highly probable that the under-registration of burials increased considerably in the later eighteenth century, as new burial grounds away from the city centres began to take business from the overcrowded parish churchyards. An Anglican clergyman was moved to publish in 1800 an appeal for cremation, as a means of ending the scandal of bodies piled into 'open graves for indiscriminate and plebeian putrefaction *en masse*'. To an extent, then, the estimates in Table IX record also the declining efficacy of burial registration. The burial rates for later eighteenth-century Leeds, in particular, look suspiciously low, especially as the pressure on parish churchyards was greatest in the largest towns. As minimum estimates, however, the figures at least suggest that some general forces were at work to reduce burial (and therefore probably also death) rates from the very high levels that had obtained in the period between 1720 and 1750.[4]

The fall in levels of mortality seems to have been spread fairly evenly among all age groups, though some have argued that the change was accomplished chiefly by a substantial reduction in infant and child mortality. But that view is not upheld by the detailed records, which show that the burials of young people continued to make up a very high proportion of all interments throughout the century; they had only fallen in so far as the number of burials generally had diminished in per capita terms. For example, in Nottingham, 'child' burials (i.e. of those aged under 20 years) were never less than 40 per cent or more than 55 per cent of the total in every five-year period between 1701 and 1750. In 1736, a year of smallpox 'distemper', they had actually soared to a devastating 72.9 per cent of all burials. But in the later eighteenth century they continued to constitute over 52 per cent of all burials in every five-year period between 1750 and 1801.

Even in the huge metropolis the Bills of Mortality showed that, in every twenty-year period between 1730 and 1810, 'child' burials amounted to virtually 50 per cent of the total. Specifically, they made up

51.7 per cent between 1730 and 1749, 50.9 per cent between 1750 and 1769, 51.2 per cent between 1770 and 1789, and 49.2 per cent between 1790 and 1809. Figures are sometimes cited to show a dramatic improvement in youthful life expectancy in eighteenth-century London, but they cannot be substantiated. First presented in the *Lancet* in 1835–6, they were estimates based on a comparison of the rising absolute total of baptisms in the London Bills of Mortality between 1730 and 1810, with the falling total of young burials.[5] Yet, since the number of interments recorded for all age groups fell absolutely over the same period, such calculations merely highlight in a particularly dramatic way the growing deficiency of registration of burials within the Bills as compared with baptisms. In other words, burials were taking place outside the central parishes, while baptisms were still recorded there. There is indeed plenty of circumstantial evidence that Londoners 'within the Bills' did take corpses for burial to non-parochial graveyards, or even, as Maitland noted in 1756, to burial grounds completely outside the metropolitan area. Among the total of all burials that were in fact registered in the Bills, those of the young continued to constitute 50 per cent. Indeed, doctors and reformers did not cease to warn of the dramatic losses of young lives in the capital – from Hanway's *Letters on the Importance of the Rising Generation* (1767), on the scandalous loss of lives among infant paupers, to Garnett's *Lectures on the Preservation of Health* (1797), which reiterated that 'it is a melancholy fact that above half the children born in London die before they are two years old.' To the extent that mortality did fall in the later eighteenth century, therefore, it was a change shared generally by all age groups, including the very vulnerable young. The really marked reduction in infant mortality did not follow until the mid-nineteenth century and after.

Many suggestions were put forward in the later eighteenth century to explain the changing urban death rates. They were not, of course, equally authoritative; but the very range of ideas implies that there was more than one factor at work. The diversity of infections and their modes of transmission meant that medical and environmental 'improvements' were needed on a broad front. Sweeping single-cause explanations underestimate the complexity of the long-term onslaught upon infectious diseases. Part of the change may, in fact, have stemmed from relatively autonomous fluctuations in the virulence of various strains of the infective organisms that cause disease. Some of the major 'killer' diseases may have waned slightly in ferocity in the later eighteenth century. It is known that bacteria and viruses have their own life cycles of growth, mutation, and decline. For example, some doctors thought that the virulence of smallpox had lessened in the later decades of the century, although the first medical campaigns of inoculation against that disease may also have served to propagate milder strains. At the same time it is unlikely that all infective organisms were waning in intensity simultaneously. There was in the later eighteenth century, however, no new pandemic 'killer'. 'King Cholera' had not yet arrived, to frighten even more by reputation than in action. Nor was there any return of the bubonic plague, although the old scourge still retained its power to terrify. The Corporation of Newcastle found it necessary to advertise in the *Gazette* in 1710 that the city was free of the disease, then rampant in the Baltic ports; while the Corporation of Nottingham in June 1781 had rushed out 'a thousand Handbills on fine paper about the plague reported', before an erroneous rumour was contradicted. But none of the epidemics that struck the eighteenth-century towns created quite the sort of panic reaction that the plague had done, or that cholera was to do later.

If infective viruses and bacteria have their own histories, so too changes in the life styles of their human hosts crucially affect the impact and diffusion of disease. In the course of the century a number of developments began to weaken its force, although the pace and, above all, the uniformity, of improvements should not be exaggerated. In the first place, the steady supply of foodstuffs to the towns began to guarantee basic nutritional standards and hence to increase resistance to some chronic and epidemic infections. As the towns were able to rely upon fairly regular provisioning, from a variety of sources, there was a weakening in the age-old connection between local harvest failure and an outbreak of epidemic disease among under-nourished and susceptible inhabitants in the towns. By the later eighteenth century crop failures in the countryside no longer filled the urban graveyards, as they had often done in the past (although patterns and causes of urban epidemics had never been simple). The notoriously bad harvests of the mid- and later 1790s certainly promoted attendant epidemics of typhus and influenza in many towns. But the attacks were by no means as devastating (even allowing for defective burial registration) as had been, for example, the outbreaks following the dearths of 1709–10, or of 1739–40.

Above all, the medical reports suggest that mortality from these epidemics was increasingly confined to the ranks of the urban poor. They had always suffered disproportionately from such attacks, it is true, but that contrast was heightened, in the later eighteenth century, by the growing immunity of the urban upper and middle classes. Typhus became known as the 'poor man's disease'; and Dr Currie decided that it was typically fostered by 'damp, fatigue, sorrow, and hunger'. As he could not remedy all of these problems, he added that the poor should at least be offered appropriate advice on diet and nutrition (he thought they drank too much tea). Some earlier reformers had also believed that excessive gin-drinking fostered low fertility and high mortality in the early eighteenth century; but no substantial medical evidence has ever been adduced to support this, and the significance of the 'gin mania' is rather social than demographic (see discussion on p. 144).

The towns certainly incubated and diffused many contagions on their own account. Even though the surviving residents began to build up collective immunities against some diseases, there was always a fresh batch of vulnerable migrants entering the towns from the countryside. Without fully understanding the nature and transmission of infection, many contemporary observers of town life were nonetheless worried by the manifest risks to health among numerous, crowded, and migratory populations. A number of civic 'improvements' were canvassed on grounds that were not only aesthetic and utilitarian but also, increasingly, medical. Proposed reforms included, among other things, attention to street cleansing and paving, and better ventilation for crowded streets and housing. These ideas reflected a growing urban self-consciousness, as well as an awareness of the fact that the scale of some problems required communal responses.

The practical effects of these initial reforms were by no means negligible; but they were highly selective and partial in their impact. Had they been completely inefficacious, the eventual pressure for continued and extended reforms would have been easier to resist. Yet, in an era of continuing urbanization, the problems were also growing rapidly; and the implementation of improvement greatly tested the fiscal and administrative machinery of eighteenth-century local government. In practice, therefore, the earliest improvements were very much area- and class-selective. They tended to service the more affluent and prosperous areas of town, and the wealthier citizens, who also campaigned most actively for these improvements. For example, the provision of fresh water supplies was usually made only to those private houses that could afford the costs of connection and rental. The poor still relied on public pumps or supplies from potentially contaminated rivers, wells, and springs, although they avoided some problems by not drinking much fresh water. Similarly, the street cleansing schemes that were adopted in many towns were not carried out at all systematically. Main thoroughfares, public places, and smarter residential areas received some attention; but most side roads, and all yards, courts, and alleys, were left untended, and domestic refuse was often left to rot for long periods. Many towns showed startling contrasts between areas of relative cleanliness and areas of deep squalor. Sometimes the latter were found uncomfortably close to the former, which caused later heart-searchings when the dangers of contagion were more fully understood.

The contrasts between different classes of society also extended to standards of housing, living and working conditions, and personal hygiene, although naturally there were many gradations and individual variations. Writing in 1801, Dr Willan implied that the affluent citizenry, at least, did not itch, washed themselves daily, changed their bedclothes frequently, and lived in habitations whose privies were cleansed regularly, even if the poor did not. That puts in context the divergent contemporary assessments of the effects of improvement in the eighteenth century. Some waxed eulogistic; others were more cautious. No doubt all reforms contributed in reducing to some extent the risk of air- and water-borne contagions; but the benefits had not yet substantially reached all sections of the urban community. Dr Moss's *Familiar Medical Report of Liverpool* (1784) could report in good faith on the city's relative healthiness and claim that 'There has been but one instance of a truly malignant infectious fever, happening in the Town for many years'; while Dr Currie's *Medical Reports* (1797) riposted that 'The typhus, or low contagious fever, prevails in all large Cities and Towns to a degree that those are not aware of, who have not turned their attention to the subject, or whose occupations do not lead them to mix with the labouring poor', adding that in Liverpool itself, 'among the inhabitants of the cellars and these back houses [i.e. back-to-backs] the typhus is constantly present.' Similarly, when conducting an enumeration of the very much smaller but densely inhabited town of Carlisle in 1779, Dr Heysham was surprised to discover 'scenes of poverty and filth and nastiness'. That the health hazards of the towns came increasingly to be discussed in terms of the problems of the poor indicated therefore something of the scale of social differentials. Little is yet known about the details of these changes, but some research suggests that the broad trends of change were similar in the long term though at different levels of expectation between the different social classes.

The medical profession, expanding in numbers as it was in the eighteenth century, certainly contributed to the growing concern with medical improvements. Health care became an increasingly specialized – and urbanized – occupation. The numbers, training, expertise, and professional self-confidence of the doctors were also augmented. Although it was not a period of major developments in theoretical medicine, there was a great expansion of empirical study and experimentation – for example, in techniques of surgery and midwifery. Similarly, although epidemiology had not yet deciphered the nature of infection, the eighteenth century produced a voluminous literature on the history, incidence, nature, classification, and treatment of disease. Doctors could no longer simply be caricatured (as in 1741) as 'ignorant conceited Coxcombs', whose remedy for every malady was to cry 'Egad! Sir, I must have some of your Blood!' There was a growing and keen interest in evironmental medicine, and in the prevention as well as treatment of disease. In the industrial and commercial centres in particular, doctors, such as Ferriar and Percival in Manchester, Currie in Liverpool, Clark in Newcastle, Lucas in Leeds, Heysham in Carlisle, and many others, were prominent in pressing for medical and sanitary reforms; while the spa doctors, by contrast, who tended to specialize in non-infectious diseases, played a much lesser part. The first local Board of Health was established by a group of volunteers in 1794–6 in Manchester.

There was furthermore a growing institutionalization of health care in the course of the century. The number of hospitals (the term now acquires its modern meaning) and dispensaries multiplied. Between 1720 and 1801 five new general hospitals and three specialist centres were founded in London, plus 31 in the provinces. There were also at least 17 medical dispensaries in the capital city by 1800, as well as 13 in the provincial towns. Their direct impact in reducing mortality as opposed to professionalizing health care was, however, marginal. The number of such institutions was still very small in comparison with the fast-growing population; and the treatment that hospitals could offer was limited. Many institutions also had restrictive admissions policies. They did not admit cases of, for example, incurable illness, the visibly dying, or children under seven. Their own statistics of the number of patients 'cured' do not, therefore, necessarily indicate the arrest of an otherwise fatal malady, as has sometimes been assumed. In fact Dr Champney was able to write quite casually in 1797 that 'Public Hospitals . . . it is well known, are not favourable to the cure of diseases', although he agreed that they did have beneficial functions. Their importance lay rather in the stimulation of a consumer market for professional medical attention; and indirectly in their advocacy of the merits of cleanliness and fresh air.

Highly controversial, both in its own day and subsequently, was the first medical development of preventive immunization, in the form of inoculation. Sometimes termed 'buying the smallpox', it involved inducing a mild attack to secure subsequent immunity. The treatment was first introduced to England in the 1720s but then fell out of favour. Later, however, it was adopted, in both town and countryside, on quite a sizeable scale from the 1760s onwards, using improved methods that involved injecting a minimal amount of attenuated virus. Some doctors carried out mass inoculations of a town's poor, waiving the usual fee. Dr Haygarth in Chester founded a Small-pox Society (1778) to combat the disease and promote inoculation. The treatment began to gain in popularity, although it was often most eagerly sought in the smaller towns and villages, where smallpox epidemics were relatively infrequent and hence very damaging when they did occur. On the other hand it was slower to make headway in the very large towns, although becoming more common there by the 1790s, partly through the work of the dispensaries.

Inoculation may therefore have contributed to the reduction in mortality from smallpox that was noted in many places in the later eighteenth century. Fears that the controversial treatment would actually exacerbate the disease were confounded. But immunization was far from thoroughly or systematically carried out; and the relative attenuation of smallpox was also observed in places where inoculation was little practised, as Dr Percival noted in Manchester in 1773. The demographic significance of inoculation should not therefore be over-stated. In particular, it cannot be held responsible for a steep decline in infant mortality in the towns, for that did not occur. Many other contagions awaited the vulnerable young. But both the theory and practice of inoculation signified a growing interest in preventive medicine, and held out the hope that a particularly virulent and disfiguring disease could be actively combated. When Jenner published his pioneering paper on vaccination in 1798, the new treatment was eagerly taken up by the medical profession, despite the many flaws in Jenner's original research data. Smallpox must 'necessarily decline, and soon become extinct', an enthusiast for vaccination prophesied in 1815.

The growing towns, then, had slowly begun to challenge their traditional unhealthiness, and the 'silent mortality' that daily purged their ranks. A town was like a huge army encampment, decided Dr Bateman in 1819, but 'so constructed, as to be destitute of the means of changing its situation'. In that case, sanitary and medical reforms had to be effected within the towns. Eighteenth-century improvements were only partial, and socially selective. Yet they had indicated at least that the devastating effects of huge concentrations of population could eventually be resisted and reduced.

8 Urban society

In general terms, the urban societies of eighteenth-century England were relatively open, fluid, and competitive. They offered many avenues of advancement for the ambitious, even though aspirations to upward social mobility were sometimes hard to realize. Parentage and wealth were still highly important assets in the scramble for status, but ambition, abilities, perseverance, and luck, in various combinations, could also make an impact. Townspeople were taken to be what they appeared to be. They were 'valued . . . by their clothes', as Moll Flanders was told by a countrywoman. And garb and appearance, if not accent and mannerisms, could be relatively easily adapted. Fashions of wigs, patches, masks, and powders presented an outward show that assumed the presence of onlookers. Social transformation was further eased when accompanied by a change of address. Indeed, the physical mobility of the urban populations was even greater than their social adaptability. Many moved frequently, not only between town and countryside but also within the confines of the towns themselves. Listings of urban residents over successive years in the eighteenth century are very scarce, but sources that do survive, such as the names of freemen voters in urban poll-books, suggest a very rapid turnover of population within any given parish. No doubt death or disinclination to vote accounted for some of the absentees, but others had simply moved. Not that change was by any means solely for the sake of advancement: the towns were not only showcases for the successful and places of work for many, but places of concealment for the unfortunate or nefarious. Disguise and evasion were easier among crowds, as countless literary heroes and heroines attested.

At the same time, however, there were intricate variations between town and town despite their common urban characteristics. Indeed, the proliferation of towns tended to promote diversity within the species. One variation was related to size. There were differences between the social milieux of the small town and the great cities. Residents in the smaller places were often particularly sensitive about the modesty of their municipal status, and equally anxious to assert their claims to urban ranking.

There were similar differences of scale between the capital city on the one hand and all the provincial towns on the other, although their growth was being matched by an increasing prestige in the course of the century. Manchester 'has now excited the attention and curiosity of Strangers', it was noted by 1783, and the town was later given the title of 'metropolis of manufactures'; Liverpool was saluted poetically as 'the Darling Child of Fate' (1706) and as the 'emporium of the Western World' (1773); Bath was designated the 'Province of Pleasure' (1761); while the Birmingham patriot affirmed confidently in 1781 that 'when the word Birmingham occurs, a superb picture instantly expands in the mind, which is best explained by the other words grand, populous, extensive, active, commercial, and humane.'

More complex and subtle, but also important, were the variations in social atmosphere between different towns according to their predominant social and economic roles. Actual case histories were more variegated than the stereotypes; yet there was enough verisimilitude in the imagery for it to persist. The naval dockyard towns, for example, produced relatively bustling but inward-looking and disciplined societies. The visitor to Chatham was 'dazed by the beating of drums and the marching of troops...on every side', as Dickens, himself the son of a minor clerk in the Naval Pay Office, later recorded. Many of the smaller cathedral cities, by contrast, wore an air of outward calm and torpor. In 1776 Boswell found little sign of 'the busy hand of industry' at Lichfield and thought its inhabitants 'an idle set of people'. The wife of the Dean of Lincoln, on her arrival there in 1758, complained that the city was '*never* remarkable for furnishing Anecdotes' – although she later found the assessment premature. Elsewhere, the residents of the spas and resorts cultivated a blend of outward deference combined with social opportunism. 'There is no Place in the World, where a Person may introduce himself, on such easy Terms, to the first People in Europe, as in the Rooms at Bath,' declared the Master of Ceremonies in 1767. The ethos of the great commercial and manufacturing towns, again, was more robustly utilitarian and independent. Trade and advancement were common topics of conversation. 'In their own Phrase, [they] look upon themselves to be as good as the Best, that is, deserve to be treated with Respect', reported a scandalized visitor to the 'populous, trading Towns' in 1731.

If their competitiveness in some ways sharpened a sense of the different interests of individuals and classes within the towns, yet urban societies were also knitted together by a variety of social bonds and networks. The loneliness of the stranger in town was not the typical urban experience, but was the more striking precisely because everyone else seemed to have something to do. But urban social contacts were typically heterogeneous

Table X Age, sex, and status in Gloucester, 1696, and Leeds township, 1775*

Gloucester, 1696			*Leeds township, 1775*		
Population as listed	Total	Percentage of total	Population as listed	Total	Percentage of total
Husbands	770	16.2	Husbands	3,122	18.2
Wives	771	16.2	Wives	3,187	18.6
Widowers	112	2.4	Widowers	417	2.4
Widows	335	7.0	Widows	724	4.2
Bachelors	100	2.1	Men over 20	861	5.0
Maids	52	1.1	Women over 20	1,333	7.8
Children: M	889	18.7	Men under 20	3,712	21.7
Children: F	1,060	22.3	Women under 20	3,765	22.0
**Servants: M	194	4.1			
**Servants: F	279	5.9			
Sojourners: M	64	1.3			
Sojourners: F	130	2.7			
Total men	2,129	44.8	Total men	8,112	47.4
Total women	2,627	55.2	Total women	9,009	52.6
Total	4,756	100.0	Total	17,121	100.0

* For Gloucester, see King's papers printed in G. Chalmers, *An Estimate of the Comparative Strength of Great Britain* (1804), Appendix, pp. 70–1; for the Leeds enumeration see British Library, Add. MSS. 33,770.

** Indicated at that date not only domestic servants but also living-in apprentices.

in their nature, and of diverse strengths and importance. There were close contacts made through work and social life, through religious and group affiliations, and through residence in distinctive localities within the town. Yet there were, too, the more impersonal, fleeting, and casual encounters with strangers, or semi-strangers, in the daily bustle of life in the crowd. Gay's *Trivia; Or, the Art of Walking the Streets of London* (1716) offered light-hearted advice on the skills of survival in the rush:

> ... nor struggle thro' the Crowd in Vain,
> But watch with careful Eye the Passing Train.

With much going on, people began to search for ways of classifying and filtering so multifarious an experience. Human societies, even in single-industry towns, were variegated and complex. Among the major networks – sometimes overlapping, sometimes in conflict – were those of family and kinship, those of social groups and class, and those of church and chapel.

In the towns of eighteenth-century England, as indeed in the countryside, people commonly lived in fairly small household units, centred upon one nuclear family. Extensive groupings of related kin did not normally live together, although relatives might live close at hand in the same part of town. According to an unusually detailed local enumeration of Leeds township in 1775, as shown in Table X, fully 80 per cent of the inhabitants there fell into the simple descriptive categories of 'husband' (18.2 per cent), 'wife' (18.6 per cent), and young people under the age of 20 (43.7 per cent), although that latter designation also included youthful servants and apprentices as well as dependent children. An earlier and still more detailed enumeration of Gloucester in 1696 had also delineated 73.4 per cent of the population as 'husbands', 'wives', and dependent children – excluding servants of whatever age. In a period when much work was still carried out in the home, these small domestic groups often constituted economic as well as social units: many urban families were also working teams. That conferred on urban women in particular economic importance and a relatively independent status. Interest in relationships between the sexes – never negligible – was a matter for keen speculation; and the changing roles of women in eighteenth-century society became a special topic for uneasy satire.

Household units, in great towns as in lesser places, remained relatively small on average, not only because of the very high levels of mortality, especially among urban children, but because many families sent their adolescent offspring away from home – to boarding-school in the case of some middle-class sons, or into domestic service in the case of the poor. There was, nonetheless, a considerable range of household sizes in the towns: from the very largest units of up to twenty or more co-residents, generally comprising the wealthiest families with their large numbers of surviving children and their retinues of servants, through to the smallest units of single people, such as widows, who lived on their own. Small households were, however, much more common than very large ones. The evidence of those local enumerations that recorded information on that point was strikingly uniform, as shown in Table XI. The mean household size from 27 listings, taken in 21 different towns in the hundred years after 1695, lay consistently between four and five individuals – with the solitary exception of thrice-enumerated Carlisle, whose households on average contained just under four inhabitants on each occasion, and whose small households were crammed with unusual density into the individual units of housing (see p. 181).

In detailed composition, household groups were certainly far from uniform. While many contained one couple and their children, there was also a sizeable number of one-parent families. Other households consisted not only of one nuclear family but also of their servants, apprentices, relatives, lodgers, and boarders. In fact, relatively few people were described as falling into the latter two categories, implying that long-term visitors to town were able to stay with relatives, or to rent rooms in inns, as Misson noted was the custom in early eighteenth-century London. In Gloucester, too, in 1696, only 4.0 per cent of the population were named as 'sojourners' (see Table X). Furthermore, the number of apprentices living in the household was tending to decline, while, by contrast, the number of resident servants was rising. The urban middle classes were eager to stress their claims to gentility by the conspicuous deployment of labour. 'There is scarce a Mechanic in Town who does not keep a Servant in Livery,' grumbled the *Craftsman* in the 1730s, in exaggerated outrage. Already by the 1740s familiar-sounding worries were being expressed that the growing service sector was not contributing productively to the country's economy but was merely creating 'Drones in the Hive'. 'It really is a Shame to see a strong, able, lusty Fellow spending the Prime of his Life in curling his own Hair, and that of his Master's,' sniffed the *Champion* in 1743.

In many ways, however, the living-in domestic servants played a significant part in spreading the influence of the towns. They were important social intermediaries between rich and poor and between town and countryside. They conveyed not only second-hand clothing and money back to their own families, but also more general news and information about urban consumerism and life styles. Town servants were notorious for the avidity with which they copied their employers' dress and mannerisms; though, as terms of employment became more

Table XI Mean household size from eighteenth-century urban enumerations*

Date	Town	Enumerated Population	Mean Size of Household ('Family')
1695	Gloucester	4,756	4.2
	Lichfield (City+close)	3,038	4.7
	Tiverton	7,351	4.5
1696	Norwich (City+county)	28,546	4.2
1736	Sheffield (township)	9,695	4.5
1740	Chichester	3,711	4.7
1743	Gloucester	5,585	4.2
1755	Sheffield	12,983	4.9
1763	Carlisle	4,158	3.9
1773	Liverpool	34,407	4.3
	Manchester and Salford	27,246	4.2
1774	Chester	14,713	4.3
1775	Ashton-under-Lyne (town)	2,859	4.8
	Leeds (township only)	17,121	4.2
1779	Nottingham	17,584	4.9
1780	Carlisle	6,299	3.9
1781	Maidstone	5,650	4.4
1784	Cockermouth	2,652	4.0
	Kendal	6,775	4.2
	Lancaster	8,584	4.8
1785	Frome	6,342	4.7
	Leicester	12,784	4.7
1788	Manchester (excl. Salford)	42,821	5.0
1790	Taunton	5,472	4.6
1792	Hull	22,286	4.2
1793	Kendal	7,154	4.2
1796	Carlisle	8,716	3.8

* From eighteenth-century local enumerations. And see R. Wall, 'Mean Household Size in England from Printed Sources' in P. Laslett and R. Wall (eds.), *Household and Society in Past Time* (Cambridge, 1972).

overtly contractual, servants became more assertive and less deferential. Many changed their jobs frequently; and specialized employment agencies, or register offices, sprang up in the largest towns to match supply with demand. If the masters campaigned with eventual success to prevent their staffs from levying the lucrative and time-honoured 'vails' (tips) from departing guests of the household, the servants were ruthless in extracting all possible fees and other perquisites to supplement their board and wages. Indeed, in 1764 Horace Walpole feared that servant discontent at the suppression of vails might exacerbate 'civil commotions', after a number of London footmen had 'mobbed and ill-treated some Gentlemen' at Ranelagh Gardens. Earlier, in 1724, Defoe had detected, in the generally 'Unsufferable Behaviour' of domestic servants in town, his own jaunty variant of the world-turned-upside-down: 'Order is inverted, Subordination ceases, and the World seems to stand with the Bottom upward.'

At the same time, there were marked distinctions and tensions between wealth and poverty in the towns. In Lincoln, social differences were literally demarcated by residence in the fashionable 'upper town' on the hill by the Cathedral and the 'lower town' at its foot. Conspicuous social display was juxtaposed with chronic poverty and indigence – and social distress in the towns was much less easily concealed than was, for example, rural under-employment. Eighteenth-century urban societies were therefore very conscious of income and status differentials, even while they were aware of their mutability – not, of course, that everyone wished to know: particularly in the larger cities, the growing residential segregation between areas of wealth and poverty facilitated a degree of social ignorance. 'One Half of the World knows not how the Other Half live,' announced a satirical guide to *Low-Life* in 1751. But the fast-increasing corpus of literature of social exploration was, equally, designed to end such a state of affairs. 'Great cities are like painted sepulchres, their public avenues, and stately edifices, seem to preclude the very possibility of distress and poverty,' wrote a medical reformer in 1774; 'but, if we pass beyond this superficial veil, the scene will be reversed; the pleasing lights and shades of the picture will be blended with, and lost in a dark background.'

In all towns an apex of wealth rested on a broad base of relative poverty. The absolute difference between the smallest annual incomes and the greatest had probably widened in the course of the century as the scale of the largest urban fortunes expanded. There were, however, many intermediate stages. The towns were noted for the size of their middle-income groups – and these were growing in numbers and relative affluence in the course of the century. Gross inequalities of fortunes between rich and poor were disguised by the thickening of the middle strata within these urban societies.

The 'big bourgeoisie' were powerfully buttressed by the collective economic and social strength of urban society in general. Their own wealth, status, and confidence increased accordingly. Already, by the early eighteenth century, it was a matter of note that the leading 'City' families in London moved on relatively easy social terms with – and married into – the ranks of English landed society, while landowners' younger sons not infrequently went into trade or the professions. By the end of the century such two-way relationships were very much a matter of course; and that applied not only to leading Londoners but also to prominent citizens in the great provincial towns. The collusion of interests marked as much a success for the dynamism of the towns as a capitulation to the prestige of land. Indeed, the landowners' own way of life was itself becoming increasingly urbanized – just as many of the great landed fortunes drew sustenance from urban rents, urban property developments, and urban investments. Because many incomes at all levels of society were in fact drawn from a variety of sources, it is not possible to distinguish readily between the urban and rural components of the national income estimates, made by Gregory King for 1688 and updated by Patrick Colquhoun in 1803. But if the great merchants are taken to stand proxy for leading non-agrarian economic interests, their relative success in comparison both with titled landowners and with lesser townsmen becomes apparent. Whereas King considered that an eminent merchant received annually an income that was only one-seventh that of a temporal peer but almost nine times that of an ordinary shopkeeper, Colquhoun felt emboldened to inflate the great merchant's income to one-third of the temporal peer's and fully seventeen times that of the rank-and-file shopkeeper, who was also given a fractionally improved income *vis-à-vis* that of the temporal peer by Colquhoun in 1803 as compared with King for 1688.[1]

Great merchants and wholesale dealers were often prominent among the social élites of eighteenth-century English towns – particularly in the ports but also in some inland manufacturing and commercial centres. In Leeds, for example, there were thirteen great merchant houses that held unrivalled sway in the early and mid-eighteenth century. 'They were the legends of Leeds,' remarks their historian.[2] At the very end of the century some leading industrial capitalists also began to join the ranks of the urban élites; but the eighteenth century as a whole was predominantly the century of the great urban merchants – and with them a host of urban professional men. Lawyers and doctors headed their ranks, both in terms of status and wealth, although the clergy enjoyed a social hegemony, buttressed by status, if not much wealth, in the smaller cathedral cities.

In the largest places, in fact, the great families were often relatively numerous. Their social hegemony was powerful but pluralist. It was in the smaller centres – and particularly in manufacturing towns with one intensively capitalized industry – that social influence and economic power could become highly concentrated. At Bury in the later eighteenth century the Peels' cotton-manufacturing and calico-printing works provided the major single source of employment in the town, while the family, who acquired 'princely fortunes' and a noted role in national politics, then lived locally 'at a short distance from Bury and the works'.

Similarly, the Wedgwoods' thriving potteries made them major employers in that area, while Josiah lived close at hand in Etruria Hall. Writing in 1769 of his plans, 'in the pursuit of *Fortune, Fame* & the *Public Good*', to sell his wares in French markets, he added with gusto: 'Conquer France in Burslem? – My Blood moves quicker, I feel my Strength increase for the Contest.'

Turnover among individual families within the urban élites was often, however, relatively rapid. The very speed with which large fortunes could be accumulated or lost in the towns accentuated the habitual processes of demographic renewal. The continuity of an urban élite was thus one of image and ethos rather than of sheer dynastic longevity. Some families certainly remained in their greatness for two or more generations; others moved quickly on. Failure was not unknown – whether demographic or economic. Yet others were translated by success. They joined the ranks of landed society – or they moved on to another town, perhaps to live at Bath or London as *rentiers*. The process of turnover was well exemplified in the case of Leeds, where much of the great wealth of its merchant community went into land, government stocks, or local transport securities, while notably little went into the mechanization of the wool textile industry at the end of the century, as new manufacturing entrepreneurs began to make their way to the fore.

But urban success was no longer simply a prelude to flight into the countryside. Some families who had made fortunes in trade or manufactures shifted into other urban occupations, such as banking or the professions: the Barings of Exeter constituted a pre-eminent example of a move from textiles into banking. English social and economic life was rapidly becoming diversified. The towns could now provide their own social rewards. Many palatial suburban villas were as grand as country mansions. And the accolade of 'gentleman' – never a precise term – was commonly, by the eighteenth century, conferred upon owners of urban and non-landed fortunes.

In a similar way the urban middle class was also growing considerably in the course of the century – in terms of numbers, relative affluence, and social esteem. Always less conspicuous than the great families, the urban middle class was nonetheless increasingly praised as the backbone of English society – in terms not unlike those formerly used of the yeomanry. To the Revd Joshua Larwood in 1800 the middle strata of town society were 'the middling, comfortable, modest and moderate, sober and satisfied, industrious and intelligent Classes'. The London politician William Beckford had declared, with a hint of political motive, in 1761 that it was not 'the Mob, nor two hundred great Lords' that buttressed the nation, but 'the middling Rank of Men it was, in which our Strength consisted'. Foreign visitors to England – or English travellers returning from overseas – were often particularly struck with the size and relative prosperity of this section of English society. Horace Walpole, who 'had before discovered that there was Nowhere but in England the distinction of *Middling People*', was confirmed in his impression by a visit in 1740–1 to the classic cities of Italy, which gave him a fresh appreciation of the 'snugness' of the middle-class world, in even the smallest of the English provincial towns.

This was a society of shopkeepers, small businessmen, minor merchants, traders and dealers, builders, small master craftsmen, lesser professional men, authors, journalists, clerks, clergymen, and government officials. Their interests and work experiences were variegated and far from homogeneous. Their social standing was particularly fluid and competitive. They were prey to social pressures from above and below. But both King and Colquhoun expected them to earn more – though not necessarily much more – than ordinary artisans; and normally to be able to live comfortably within their incomes. They valued sobriety, frugality, respectability, and savings. James Lackington, who built up a great fortune from his bookshop within twenty years of an impecunious arrival in London, had achieved it all on the basis of 'SMALL PROFITS, *bound* by INDUSTRY, and *clasped* by *ECONOMY*', as he explained with cheerful self-confidence in his memoirs in 1791. The urban middle-class families thus had a degree of economic independence in good times; and their savings gave them a small ballast against immediate difficulties. These men and women were notable among the investors in urban property and housing; and they also lent out money on mortgage. It was not surprising, however, that, in prolonged depressions, it was often the small masters who were the first to cut piece rates and against whom the wrath of the journeymen was first turned. Similarly, the small shopkeepers and traders were not immune when serious financial pressures beset their customers; and, in single-industry towns, a protracted slump in the staple business often meant that many ratepayers were unable to pay the poor rate, at just the time that demand for relief was greatest.

If the relative affluence of the urban middle class was therefore often tinged with uneasiness, the way of life of the urban masses was much less secure. They too were growing in numbers and social visibility in the course of the century; and they were gaining in confidence and social assertiveness. At the same time, they did not share so unambiguously or so rapidly in the material affluence of an industrializing economy, while their sense of the inequalities of wealth and status was greatly sharpened by the conspicuous consumption and social mobility in the towns.

Expectations were raised, and fatalistic acceptance of the status quo discouraged.

Lower-class families were often termed simply 'the poor', although, as noted below, social terminology began to change in the course of the eighteenth century. To all those of more elevated social status, the lives of 'the poor' did seem uniformly mean and impoverished. Yet such a description revealed as much about the onlooker's perspective as it did about social realities. There were among the lower strata of society many distinct gradations in income levels that made all the difference between relative solvency and the most dire poverty. Indeed, the smaller the margin between the two, the more vivid the appreciation of minor fluctuations in living standards. To themselves, therefore, the experiences of those known as 'the poor' were much more variegated and complex than they seemed to outsiders. Above all, 'the poor' were by no means all paupers, unable to subsist without poor relief or charity, as is sometimes mistakenly assumed. The scale of parochial assistance provided by eighteenth-century urban ratepayers was determinedly frugal; and the meagre poor relief was devised as a last resort for cases of hardship rather than as a general supplement to the chronically low earnings of the urban masses. Considerably more was paid out by private charity, in fact, than by parochial assistance.

That is not to say there was no great substratum of pauperism in the towns. There certainly was – especially in the capital city and, so contemporaries claimed, in the low-paid 'service' towns. But, in normal times, the paupers on poor relief did not include the ordinary artisans and labourers. Many, even of the very poor, supported themselves by casual labour or semi-licit dealings. The full dimensions of actual poverty were often therefore concealed from local ratepayers until sudden slumps and depressions placed immense strain on traditional systems of poor relief, which were supplemented by extensive, if sometimes unsystematic, private charity. Little new thought, however, went into overhauling poor-relief systems in the eighteenth-century towns – indicative both of administrative torpor and of artisan self-help. The uncertainty of the total scale of poor-relief problems, and the differing experiences of different areas, also tended to encourage a local and *ad hoc* response.

In fact, the range of occupations, skills, and earnings within the lower strata of urban society may well have widened in the course of the eighteenth century, as occupations specialized and the economy itself diversified. Not only did many journeymen artisans earn more than did day labourers in the towns, but the earnings of the artisans themselves covered a wide spectrum. The national income estimates furnished by King and Colquhoun are uninformative on this point, as they did not attempt to go beyond generalized averages for all 'artisans' and 'labourers'. Other detailed reports, however, indicated marked variations in weekly earnings, particularly among the artisan population. Some workmen were additionally paid with traditional but unquantifiable perquisites. Information collected by Arthur Young in 1770 and Sir Frederic Eden in 1797, for example, showed that a craftsman in a skilled or dangerous occupation might earn up to two or three times more per week than an unskilled artisan, whose income might differ little from that of a 'common labourer'. Case-histories from two manufacturing towns are shown in Table XII. In Manchester many weavers earned less than 12s. weekly, but the skilled men could earn considerably more than that; while the Sheffield razor polishers, whose work was both skilled and dangerous, were paid as much daily as were many weekly. Theirs were 'Surprizing wages for any manual performances!' Young commented respectfully; and, indeed, at 10s. 6d. a day, a polisher who worked a six-day week solidly throughout the year would have received more than many a shopkeeper, clerk, or lesser clergyman. However, in practice very few workmen were in continuous employment throughout the year, so that calculations of annual incomes from daily and weekly earnings are no more than notional estimates. Similarly, it is apparent that family incomes cannot be deduced solely from the occupation of the head of the household, because earnings were contributed from other members of the family.

Whereas the urban élite and middle class were, so to speak, self-selected by success, the urban lower class was by contrast relatively heterogeneous, and open-ended – rather than exclusive – in its composition and fortunes. Nonetheless, lower-class families had a number of things in common. They shared the need for often long hours of arduous work, in order to generate modest and mutable incomes. Family budgets frequently had to be boosted by the labour of all adults and children who could find work. Savings were generally small; and living standards were therefore quickly vulnerable to pressure. Families could certainly aggravate their own problems by injudicious expenditure, as wealthier onlookers sometimes pointed out: Clayton's *Friendly Advice to the Poor* (Manchester, 1755) was kind enough to advise restraint in the consumption of drink and advocated the 'Art of frugal Cookery'. But, for many, the problems were caused by general factors, quite outside their own control: a rise in food prices, a fall in piece-work rates, a reduction in demand for labour, structural unemployment, or a combination of all of those. An urban workforce was almost wholly dependent upon the market economy for the sale of its labour and the purchase of its provisions. Maintenance of smallholdings and livestock in the towns to

Table XII Variations in earnings in two manufacturing towns, 1770 and 1797*

(a) *Manchester (Textiles)*

Occupation		Range of earnings
1770	Fustian weavers (13 branches)	
	Men	3s. to 12s. per week
	Women	3s. to 10s. per week
	Children	1s.6d. to 3s.6d. per week
	Check weavers (9 branches)	
	Men	6s. to 10s. per week
	Women	6s. to 9s. per week
	Children	2s. to 5s. per week
	Hat makers (5 branches)	
	Men	7s.6d. to 12s. per week
	Women	3s.6d. to 7s. per week
	Children	2s.6d. to 7s.6d. per week
	Worsted small wares	
	Men	5s. to 12s. per week
	Women	2s.6d. to 7s. per week
	Children	1s.6d. to 6s. per week
	Cotton spinners Women	2s. to 5s. per week
	Girls (aged 6–12)	1s. to 1s.6d. per week
	Dyers, bleachers, finishers	6s.6d. to 7s.6d. per week
1797	'Manufacturing labourers'	
	Men	approx. 16s. per week but 'wages vary much'
	Women	6s. to 12s. per week
	Children	2s. to 4s. per week (by age)
	Printers	21s. to 40s. per week
	'Common labourers'	2s. to 2s.6d. per day (= 12s. to 15s. for six-day week)

continued opposite

supplement earnings was becoming less and less usual. The urban lower class had therefore some obvious communal interests, which they protected on occasion by collective action.

Popular willingness to give expression to their grievances, then, prompted much interest in the course of the century in lower-class living standards. The convergences and divergences of lower-class experiences, however, made the enquiry both important and difficult. Pointed disagreements among historians have continued the debate. Further

(b) *Sheffield (Metalwares)*

Occupation			Range of earnings
1770	Plated wares (silver)		
		Men	9s. to 23s. per week
		Girls	4s.6d. 'even to 9s.' per week
	Cutlery	Grinders	18s. to 20s. per week
		Others	1s.6d. to 10s.6d. per day (=9s. to 63s. for six-day week)
	'In general'	Men	9s. to 20s. per week
		Women and children	'earn very good wages'
1797	Cutlers		10s to 30s. per week
	Masons		2s.8d. per day (=16s. for six-day week)
	'Common labourers'		2s. per day+victuals (=12s.+ victuals for six-day week)
	Washerwomen		1s. per day+victuals (=6s.+ victuals for six-day week)

* Summarized from information in A. Young, *A Six Months Tour through the North of England* (1770), I, 132–5; III, 242–8; and F. M. Eden, *The State of the Poor* (1797), II, 357; III, 874.

detailed case studies are clearly needed – especially for the eighteenth century, which recent research has tended to neglect. In general terms, however, it seems that living standards were not only higher in eighteenth-century towns than in the countryside but were also rising in the long term. Spontaneous industrialization implied an ability to create and tap growing consumer markets at home as well as overseas. Yet the long-term diffusion of affluence was uneven and slow. Relative – and visible – inequalities of income and social status became even more sharply pronounced and resented as consumer expectations were raised. Lower-class living standards in the market economy were manifestly unstable, on a roller-coaster of dramatic fluctuations in trade and buffeted by the shock impact of technological and social changes. The urban lower classes therefore showed extensive signs of local organization to protect their common interests. Journeymen's organizations, 'box' clubs to assist savings, building societies, all signified some degree of organized labour – as did their militancy and activism at times of strikes and industrial disputes. The provision of strike pay, for instance, indicated an element of organization. That was by no means exclusively an urban process; nor were clubs and associations confined to the employees; but equally the town workforce was well to the fore in the creation of a conscious working-class tradition.

In those circumstances it was not surprising that gradually the old language of landed hierarchy, with its shadings of rank and degrees, mutated into an urban-industrial vocabulary of class. Terms of social description, indeed, showed a great fluidity and uncertainty throughout the eighteenth century, and became socially highly sensitive – as they have remained in mutable urban societies. The 'middle ranks' or 'middling people' made the transition into the quintessentially urban 'middle class' with relative ease. In 1767 Hanway could refer to the 'higher and middle Classes' in the towns; and by the 1790s Gisborne's *Enquiry into the Duties of Men in the Higher and Middle Classes* (1794) was not intended to be controversial.

There was, however, greater uncertainty *vis-à-vis* those of lower social status. The 'meaner sort', the 'lower orders', the 'common people', the 'poor', let alone the 'mob', the 'rabble', and the 'vulgar', all began to acquire a dated and partisan tone, losing descriptive neutrality. There was something of a hunt for an acceptable classification that would indicate economic role as well as collective status. It pointed to the common bond of labour, whether in traditional craft workshop or in new factory. Many people used a variety of terms interchangeably, from Fielding's 'lower Kind' (1751) and Earl Waldegrave's 'lower class' (1758), to Clayton's 'working People' (1755), Norwich Corporation's 'industrious class' (1763), Hanway's 'labouring part of the population' (1767) and 'lower classes' (1772), Adam Smith's 'workmen' and 'labouring poor' (1776), William Hutton's 'laborious class' (1781), through to Eden's 'labouring classes' (1797) and the eventually predominant 'working class', which was used to describe the population of Bolton in 1795, and first used ideologically by Robert Owen in 1815. The new vocabulary crystallized, although it did not create, the conscious self-examination of urban-industrial societies.

In pluralist and divided societies, as were the towns of eighteenth-century England, many institutions in their midst began to take on the same characteristics. That was abundantly so in the case of organized religion – and its absence. The churches played an important role in the history of towns, as institutions that could mediate the shock of urban society and, indeed, transcend the class and social barriers that existed. Yet the churches, too, showed a subtle adaptation to the transformation of the towns. In particular, they had to come to terms with the realities of consumer choice in religion. The often-repeated accusation, in the eighteenth century, that English towns were centres of the 'Torrent of Atheism, Deism, Irreligion, and Contempt of all Duties, human and divine', as a horrified clergyman put it, was only partially justified. The towns did offer variety in religious affiliation, including the popular options of a *de facto* irreligion or a minimal conformity to the Established Church. Attendance at regular services was therefore often very poor, although funerals (rather than, as now, weddings) attracted much public attention. Yet if the churches did not bond together the whole civic community, they continued to play partial and social roles of some importance. Church and chapel could, for example, play a part in the assimilation of new arrivals in town, the still-small Catholic communities among Irish immigrants proving particularly cohesive. At the same time, disputes over religious issues could still prove sources of strong feeling and heated controversy, especially where they dovetailed with other political or social grievances.

So though variety in religious affiliation did not mean that organized religion in the towns was dead, there was, nevertheless, a tendency for the social attributes of faith to become stereotyped. The Church of England was very much the church of the municipal establishments, especially in the traditional corporations and in the cathedral cities. It was, for much of the century, a calm and complacent church, especially as the heated competition with Old Dissent in the reign of Queen Anne gradually cooled into a *modus vivendi*. It also expected, as the Established Church, the adherence of the majority of the urban population. For that reason it was the most afflicted with problems of absenteeism among its flock, especially in places where rapid urban growth placed great strain upon the traditional parochial organization.

Some attempts were made to match church provision with urban growth. A number of very striking new churches were built by public subscription or under special Act of Parliament in the course of the century, notably the magnificent Hawksmoor churches in London. All expanding towns included some new Anglican churches. Yet these churches were often built for fashionable congregations in what were originally the fashionable quarters of town; and many ministers encouraged the practice of renting out private or proprietary pews, leaving little space for ordinary members of the public. 'Each Sitting is a private Freehold,' scolded a Dissenter sharply, 'and is farther disgraced, like the Coffin of a Pauper, with the paltry Initials of the owner's Name. These divine Abodes are secured with the coarse Padlocks of a Field Gate.' Although its actual membership was much wider, the Church of England in the towns thus acquired a distinctly middle-class gloss. A very few Anglican clergymen, concerned at the spread of militant secularism among the poor in the 1790s, had begun to press for a thorough overhaul of the finance and administration of the Church.

They suggested the construction of accessible churches in the poorer quarters of town, and an adequate funding for a resident minister in every parish. However, despite an incipient realization that the Church of England would have to adapt to an urban future, as little was done about the 'rotten parishes' in the eighteenth century as was done about the 'rotten boroughs'.

Reinforcing the relative complacency of the Established Church was the undoubted loss of momentum experienced by the rival tradition of Protestant Dissent. English Puritanism had always had a strong urban component, particularly among the commercial and manufacturing communities, where the work ethic and pride in one's calling were stressed. With freedom of worship after 1689, the Dissenters, however, lost much of their old evangelical fervour, especially by the mid-eighteenth century. In contrast to their very restricted role in the Anglican countryside, they remained an influential force in the towns, especially in some old-established commercial and manufacturing centres as opposed to the service centres and resorts. They were estimated to have constituted over a quarter of the population of early eighteenth-century Exeter, for example. And in many towns existing Dissenting congregations built, or rebuilt, in the course of the century their soberly elegant chapels and meeting-houses.

Yet for much of the century they ceased to recruit new members at the same pace as the growth of the urban populations. Their social composition tended to become insensibly ossified. The Presbyterian and Unitarian Churches were the most socially respectable, with much support among the merchant community; their membership was therefore the most susceptible to the lure of the Church of England. Some Unitarians also seemed to verge upon non-denominational deism. The Baptists and Congregationalists, by contrast, drew their strength chiefly from artisan society; while the Quakers, once the most plebeian of the nonconformist churches, began to move up the social scale, with the economic success of their membership. The Dissenting tradition tended therefore to become rather inward-looking, absorbed in its own debates. There were, for example, particularly heated controversies within the Presbyterian Church, between the rational calculus of the Unitarians (including many merchants among their number, some of whom eventually broke away to form their own congregations) and the orthodoxy of the Trinitarians.

The eventual renewal of revivalist and evangelical reform came in fact from within the Church of England, although subsequently it fostered a renewed zeal in some of the older Dissenting churches. The development of the early Methodist movement from the 1740s onwards had a considerable impact in revitalizing a degree of popular religious faith in the towns. The crusading zeal of Wesley and Whitefield was certainly not directed exclusively towards the urban lower classes; but their mission led them predominantly in the first instance to those towns and industrial regions of the country whose growing populations were least well served by the existing organization of the Church of England. The towns were used as headquarters in their evangelical campaigns. 'How swiftly does the word of God spread among those who earn their Bread by the Sweat of their Brow,' observed Wesley cheerfully in Sheffield in 1784, although he did not always get such a good reception. Especially in the early days, the itinerant Methodist preachers often found themselves in trouble with local magistrates, who connived at, or sometimes instigated, hostile crowd riots and demonstrations. And plainly the size of the large open-air gatherings attracted by John Wesley and George Whitefield was sufficient to trouble some nervous magistrates. At Halifax in 1748, for example, Wesley recorded that he spoke to 'an immense Number of People, roaring like the Waves of the Sea'.

Both Wesleyan teaching and church organization constituted a specific response to the new social order of eighteenth-century England. Wesley's preaching was simple, direct, and evangelical. He shocked people out of their sense of personal insignificance, as many spiritual autobiographies attested.

Gradually, however, in the later eighteenth century, Methodism, too, institutionalized itself. The Wesleyan Connection had effectively separated from the Church of England by 1795, and the New Connection broke away in 1797. They had already built huge auditoriums in popular venues, such as Whitefield's London Tabernacle in the Tottenham Court Road (1756) or Wesley's porticoed Foundry Chapel in the City Road (1777–8). As they did so, the new churches subtly lost some of their earlier radical momentum, although the Methodist Church remained (with some of the reactivated Baptist and Congregationalist Churches) much the most influential evangelical force among the urban masses. The social teachings of this 'new Dissent' had much of the ambiguity of impact that had earlier characterized those of 'old Dissent'. Their pastoral ministry and ardent revivalism was directed towards the poor, but their ethos of thrift, hard work, sobriety, and obedience fostered a personal faith in work discipline that gave a gradual accession of worldly success and social respectability to the movement. Even more than the older churches, then, Methodism had a dualism in its social message: at once a religion of emotion and drama, in consolation of the poor, and an ethos of social respectability and 'getting ahead'.

Hence, indeed, much of the drama and excitement of the towns. Their social configurations were complex, diverse, fast-changing. Hence, too, some of the difficulties in isolating their particular social experience.

The social impact of the towns can therefore be identified both in terms of 'opportunity' and of 'problems'. In terms of opportunities, it was their role as mediating centres of education, information, culture, that impressed. They provided that 'town education that dispelled diffidence', in Fielding's words. From the new Dissenting Academies in unfashionable environments such as Warrington, Whitehaven, and Stoke Newington, where modern languages, sciences, and mathematics were added to the traditional curriculum, to the old grammar schools, through to the many 'Dame' and junior schools, the towns were education markets. A large centre like later eighteenth-century Birmingham contained a great range of schools, boarding and non-residential, with daytime and evening classes, for both boys and girls. In the years 1780–93 at least 40 schools advertised their existence in the local press, as did a further 11 in the near vicinity, at very approximately 1 school per 750 young people under the age of twenty (although very far from all children would have been either free to attend or able to pay).

Adult literacy levels, which constituted very rough-and-ready guides to the general extent of educational attainment, were usually higher in the towns than in the countryside; and they were also tending to rise in the long term. In the later decades of the century adult male literacy levels in six towns (based on studies of marriage-register signatures) ranged from 60 per cent literate in Halifax (1754–62) to 77 per cent literate in Oxford (1799–1804). But improvement was not strictly linear. A period of large-scale immigration into a rapidly growing town could cause overall literacy rates to fall in the short term, as may have occurred in some of the booming industrial towns. In those cases, however, the scale of educational facilities, the utility of basic reading and writing skills, and the pressures of consumer demand, rapidly pushed literacy rates up again. Even the much-pilloried Sunday Schools were turned to account by working-class parents, who did not wish to deprive their offspring, who worked during the week, of a chance to acquire or improve basic educational skills (if not religious reformation).

In a more general sense, too, the towns were important centres for the dissemination of news, information, and discussion. Bookshops and circulating libraries were established in an increasing number of towns in the course of the century. Chapbooks, broadsheets, prints, songs, and ballads were widely available. The growth of the press in the eighteenth century saw many provincial towns follow London in acquiring their own local newspaper. The weekly *Norwich Post*, founded in 1701, was the first of these; and by 1760 as many as 130 papers had been inaugurated in

55 different urban centres, although turnover was rapid. Some towns had more than one paper, prompting some cut-throat journalistic competition; while other places, within the orbit of a larger town, often made do with their own local editions of the neighbouring press. With its rapid turnover of a large array of diverse information (often culled wholesale from the London press), the newspaper was the quintessential accompaniment to urban living. Copies were to be found not only in the coffee-houses and gentlemen's clubs, but in the very 'ale-house kitchens', where the illiterate could go to hear the papers being read aloud.

The social and cultural life of many eighteenth-century towns was vivid and variegated. Their clubs, societies, meetings, associations, were protean and innumerable. There were clubs for drinking and feasting. There were political associations, reform clubs, music societies, flower societies, and debating clubs. It was from this milieu that some of the formalized Institutes, Academies, and learned societies were established in the course of the century – not only in London but also in a number of major provincial towns. The best-known of these was the Birmingham Lunar Society, with its tradition of scientific and philosophical enquiry.

The towns increasingly diversified their formal venues for social gatherings and entertainments. Theatres, Concert Halls, Assembly Rooms, were built in many towns, in substitution for the private rooms in inns and grand houses that had been used before. And much popular entertainment also flourished in an impromptu fashion. Ballads were sung in the street, showmen travelled to markets and fairs, travelling players performed in inns and halls: 300 inhabitants of Bury (Lancs.) were injured in 1797 when a barn that was in use as a temporary theatre collapsed. Countless races, fights, and games were inaugurated, accompanied by bets and wagers, in the streets, market places, inns, and taverns.

It was not true that eighteenth-century towns – even those of latest growth – were without any popular entertainments. The notion that they constituted a cultural vacuum – between traditional rural sports and entertainments on the one hand, and the later national network of music halls and football clubs on the other – greatly underestimates the social vitality and diversity of these places. It is true that there was often opposition from local magistrates to violent pastimes, such as cock-fighting, and rumbustious games that appeared to challenge urban order; and eventually some traditional popular entertainments were indeed curbed. Bull-running in Stamford, for example, and the Shrovetide football game in Derby, which was held throughout the whole town and which often included satirical demonstrations against unpopular local figures, were two noted cases for hostility from the magistrates. The regulation (and suppression in the case of Stamford bull-running) of rowdy sports was, however, more of a mid-nineteenth-century phenomenon. By contrast the vitality of the eighteenth century's social life came from the conjunction of both rural and urban traditions – in towns that were full of recent migrants from the countryside.

The counterpart to opportunities, were, however, urban 'problems'. These were very widely defined – and, indeed, what were thought of as problems to some were opportunities to others. Yet, in a sense, the myths were as powerful as the actualities. One of the favoured targets of the critics of the urban environment was its alleged propensity to 'vice' and 'crime'. Those were very different things, but they made a dramatic combination. Fielding's *Enquiry into the Causes of the Late Increase of Robbers* (1751) was, for example, explicit on the progression from moral laxity to theft. Much attention was devoted to questions of moral and social reforms in the towns, although in practice reform campaigns came to focus less upon the vices themselves than upon their unacceptable public manifestations. The Societies for the Reformation of Manners, founded in London, Bristol, and some other provincial towns in 1699, for example, included among their aims a desire to give a 'Check to the *Open Lewdness* that was acted out in many of our Streets'. In the course of the century, public drunkenness in particular became increasingly frowned upon in the towns, rather more than the consumption of drink as such. The so-called 'gin mania' in the era of cheap grains in the 1730s and 1740s caused further worries, particularly in London; and gin-drinking was curtailed by an increased excise and the licensing of retailers in 1751, after heated polemical warfare between the distillers and the reformers, who therefore dramatically exaggerated the moral and physical damage caused by gin. 'We do not see the Hundredth part of poor Wretches drunk in the Streets, since the said Qualifications, as before,' it was noted duly in 1757. The licensing of alehouses and gin shops, therefore, remained a key, and contentious, issue in the intricacies of local politics – although in fact gin itself seems to have been most popular in London and among those working in indoor and sedentary trades. Elsewhere, in the west-coast ports, for example, rum or rum-and-water was the favoured drink.

In terms of their social order and general viability the towns were also much less violent, criminal, and anarchic than the critics feared. The very operability of town life depends upon a degree of trust, that numerous daily contacts with complete strangers can be conducted with reasonable safety. Marauding gangs who attacked people indiscriminately at night in the streets, such as the London Mohocks, who caused scares in 1709 and 1712, were unusual – and gained no popular support or cult status. Measures to reduce public violence were welcomed.

Crimes against property, by contrast, engendered a more complex attitude. Both rich and poor depended upon a degree of order and security – for example against arbitrary and malicious damage of goods; but in an acquisitive society, all could comprehend, if not approve of, theft and robbery. There was a certain promotion of popular cults, of particularly dashing or daring thieves or highwaymen; and a number of relatively minor crimes were condoned – especially in an era when official penalties for even minor offences were very severe. The 'problem' was not, however, one of an intrinsic urban criminality. In so far as detailed comparisons have been made by historians,[3] the per capita rates of indictments for crime seem to have been relatively low in the towns, as they were in the countryside in eighteenth-century England. The difficulties came in the sphere of legal and administrative changes: the creation of an effective police force; the establishment of an impartial magistracy rather than the 'trading' justices who made a living from fees and fines; the reform of the law.

Urban growth did not therefore herald a pathological breakdown of society; but it did pose new problems on an unprecedented scale, demanding reforms in the nature and administration of justice that were ultimately political in their implications. The insistent self-scrutiny of a mass urban society had arrived.

9 Urban politics

Political changes in eighteenth-century England in response to the emergence of the towns were subtle and indirect, under a superficial veneer of constitutional stasis and traditionalism. But, despite some appearances, it was an era of change, culminating in the political drama of organized urban lower-class radicalism in the 1790s. The view of eighteenth-century urban politics as a story of inertia, oligarchy, and corruption, punctuated occasionally by violent but ineffectual popular rioting, is greatly oversimplified. It underestimates both the degree of local adaptation and innovation taking place in the towns, as well as the extent and nature of their politicization. In fact, the accelerating process of urban growth posed new problems, on a greater scale, to local government authorities, calling for fresh administrative responses. It gave a new weight to urban pressure groups, in their national lobbying and general influence. It greatly extended the scope for popular participation and interest in politics. Not that corruption and oligarchy could not be found: on the contrary, there were plenty of examples of both. Yet that was not the whole story. The very structure of local politics itself became a political issue within many towns, heightened by the growing incongruity between traditional forms and new expectations.

In particular, it is important to distinguish between the experience of the towns (as defined by population and economic role) and that of the many smaller places of ancient title. The poor political reputation of the 'rotten' boroughs and of the 'decayed' corporations has tended to be taken as applying also to the towns. There was no direct correlation, however, by the eighteenth century between these three categories: the towns, the boroughs, and the corporations. Yet the overlap was sufficient to confuse the issue and, incidentally, to render the cause of reform highly complex. In terms of parliamentary representation the boroughs had not been enfranchised systematically, with reference to the merits of their own intrinsic claims, but haphazardly, over centuries, in response to a miscellany of factors, including, in the sixteenth and seventeenth centuries, gentry pressure for 'pocket' seats. Table XIII shows that in 1700, 17 of the 68 towns with populations of 2,500 or more had no direct representation in Parliament; with continuing urban growth the number of towns in that position had risen to 40 in 1750 and to 86 by 1801.

Furthermore, there was no uniformity in the composition of the electorate within those places that did return MPs. Some enfranchised boroughs were sizeable towns with large electorates – Norwich, Bristol, and the City of Westminster were often interpreted as the political touchstones for a wider public opinion – but others, although sizeable towns, had only small qualified electorates. Urban growth did increase the number of towns with at least some representation in Parliament (see again Table XIII) but without changing the size of their electorates. And yet other boroughs remained insignificant throughout. The borough of Old Sarum housed nothing but one farm, yet sent two MPs to Parliament. 'Who those members can justly say they represent would be hard for them to answer,' remarked Defoe in the 1720s. That was one of the most notorious cases, but it was not unique. Many parliamentary boroughs, especially a number in Cornwall and the south of England, were routinely described, even by their defenders, as 'rotten' or 'pocket' boroughs. They were tiny places, with only a handful of voters, while numerous large towns were completely without direct representation in Parliament. In the first cautious and unsystematic reforms of 1832, fully 56 boroughs were deprived of two seats and another 30 lost one, being replaced by two seats for 22 previously unrepresented major towns (or parts of conurbations) and one seat apiece for another 20.

Similarly, the acquisition of municipal status had evolved over the centuries, through custom, prescription, and chartered grant. It had not been undertaken upon any systematic basis (nor, indeed, had it been carried out in conjunction with the process of enfranchisement). There survived, therefore, by the eighteenth century, a great miscellany of places with corporate status. So various and venerable were their origins that their numbers (*c.* 200) were difficult to ascertain with precision. They included not only some very large towns but also many small and 'decayed' townships, whose major claim to fame was their proud retention of their ancient municipal title; while, again, some of the leading urban centres were without any formal incorporation. The 'decayed' corporations were not by any means the most corrupt or exclusive of eighteenth-century political authorities, but the contrast between their grand claims and their actual insignificance added a touch of near farce to the reputation of the municipalities. The radical *Political Dictionary* (1795) derided and denounced a corporation as 'an infamous relic of the ancient feudal system;... generally consisting of gluttons, idiots, and oppressors'. Therefore, as in the case of the boroughs, the notoriety of the corporations tended to obscure the actual political

Table XIII Towns (2,500+) and parliamentary representation in eighteenth-century England and Wales*

Towns	1700		1750		1801	
	Represented by at least one MP**	Not directly represented in Parl.	Represented by at least one MP**	Not directly represented in Parl.	Represented by at least one MP**	Not directly represented in Parl.
Over 100,000	1	–	1	–	1	–
20,000+	2	–	4	1	9	6
10,000+	4	–	10	4	18	15
5,000+	20	4	23	8	24	21
2,500+	24	13	26	27	50	44
All towns	51	17	64	40	102	86

* Based on comparison of towns in Table I with information in T. H. B. Oldfield, *An Entire and Complete History, Political and Personal, of the Boroughs of Great Britain* (1792), 3 vol.

** Elected under restricted franchise.

history of the towns. Indeed, the complexities of the old system created a web of powerful vested interests in opposition both to franchisal and to local government reform, although it also ensured that the eventual enfranchisement of the towns, in 1832, was closely followed by reform of the municipal corporations, in 1835.

In terms of their own local government, then, the eighteenth-century towns displayed great variety in their constitutional format. They included some boroughs and some corporations, but also some 'mere villages'. There was no attempt at a general overhaul or review of the system – not that the growing non-corporate towns displayed much sustained anxiety at their lack of formal municipal status. It was not true that the issue was unmentioned: a number of inhabitants in Birmingham in 1716, for instance, and in Manchester in 1763, had petitioned parliament for a local act of incorporation and, in the latter case, for parliamentary representation. But their lack of success in both cases was received very calmly; and the proposals were dropped without much local dissension or even debate.

Nonetheless, those well-established towns that were incorporated greatly valued their status. The dignity of their leading citizen – usually the Mayor, sometimes the Bailiff, the Alderman, the Warden, or the Portreeve – was jealously upheld and enshrined in local protocol. He wore rich robes and a chain of office. He was addressed officially as his 'Worship', a style that had evolved in the sixteenth century. Some cities – Newcastle (1691), York (1724–30), and the City of London (1738–52) – constructed a special Mansion House for the Mayor's residence, while Bristol (1781–6) purchased and refurbished a grand dwelling for that purpose. Everywhere the annual election or selection of the Mayor was the occasion for public processions, feasts, and festivities. Even the satirical election of Mock Mayors or Sham Corporations – which seems to have been as much a rural or small–town tradition as a metropolitan custom – paid an inverse tribute to the municipal dignity. Indeed, the position of Mayor, although costly, was often much sought after. 'He would go to Hell Gates to be Mayor of *Portsmouth*,' declared one candidate acrimoniously of another in 1711.

Furthermore, municipal incorporation also bestowed certain tangible legal and constitutional rights. In essence, it established the municipality as an independent legal entity, separate from the existence of the individuals who comprised its membership. That meant that a corporation could sue and be sued in the courts, could make and enforce its own by-laws (within the framework of statute and common law), and could ensure its own permanent succession. In practice, therefore, the municipal corporations constituted independent units of local government, with their own administration and jurisdiction, separate from that of the surrounding countryside. The formal power to revoke a municipal charter, while still technically a royal prerogative, fell into desuetude after 1689 and moved into constitutional limbo, in company with the royal veto over parliamentary legislation.

Corporative autonomy was therefore enhanced, in general constitutional terms, although that did not free corporations from political management and, in some cases, remodelling. A very few places themselves sought fresh charters in the course of the century. Meanwhile, the resolution of disputed actions – or lack of action – was left to the jurisdiction of the courts, where extensive litigation by numerous corporations built up a complex case-law on the scope and use of corporative powers. In a struggle at Cambridge no fewer than nine separate legal cases were initiated, by rival factions, in the years 1787–9. In Colchester a successful *quo warranto* challenge to the legality of local elections in 1742 actually caused the corporation to fall into complete abeyance until the granting of a new charter in 1764. For a while at Scarborough in the 1730s, by contrast, there were two rival sets of corporation officials and councillors, following a series of disputed elections and heated contests for local power.

The constitutions of these 'independent commonwealths', as they had been critically termed in 1682, were immensely diverse in detail; but in broad outline they shared some of the essential features of the national constitution in the eighteenth century. That is to say, they had a restricted rather than a universal franchise, from which was drawn a representative general assembly, to which in turn the executive branch was responsible. In practice, however, matters were much more complex. Not only did the composition of the municipal assemblies vary considerably – some were unitary authorities, others had two or even three tiers of membership, from the Common Councillor to the Alderman, all with a myriad of local variations in their titles – but so, most crucially, did their methods of recruitment, and the powers and size of the local electorate.

A major distinction was that between the 'open' and the 'close' corporations. In the former case, admission as a freeman was at least relatively open, being usually obtainable either by patrimony (descent from a freeman), apprenticeship to a freeman, purchase (as a 'foreigner' or an out-of-town candidate), by gift or co-option of the corporation, or by some combination of these qualifications. The freemen then chose annually some or all of the Councillors, and, sometimes, the Mayor; and in some places the Aldermen were also elected, though holding office for life. However, not all those who were technically qualified for the franchise actually sought the privilege, which was an essential prerequisite also for the honours (and costs) of municipal office. The number of freemen was liable to fluctuate considerably, languishing at times but at others rising in a flurry of politically inspired nominations before a disputed election. It was rare, however, in even the most 'open' of constituencies in the eighteenth century to find a local electorate that ran into many thousands, or that amounted to much more than one-third of the adult male inhabitants. (In some places the widows and daughters of freemen inherited some privileges, but not, in this period at least, their vote.) In addition, residence within the constituency, which did not constitute a franchisal qualification, was not required of the freemen voters, who could and did reside many miles from town, returning for the elections – especially when encouraged to do so by an affluent candidate.

On the other hand, the many 'close' corporations traditionally allowed no active role at all to even the residual popular elements in their constitutions. Recruitment to office for life was solely by co-option, those already in place nominating to fill vacancies as they occurred. Some of these corporations had no separate body of freemen at all; others had a restricted burgage franchise, where the vote was attached to certain property rights; in other cases, the freemen were admitted by purchase or service, but their numbers were kept low by the corporation. At Bath, for example, there were only about a hundred freemen at any one time in the eighteenth century, with no constitutional role to play, leaving the 'close' corporation of twenty Councillors and ten Aldermen to exercise unfettered powers of co-option to their own ranks. Such a system, which looked oligarchic even in 1700, when the city of Bath housed 3,000 inhabitants (perhaps 750 adult males), had by 1800, when its total population had risen to nearer 35,000, become a scandal – especially when it is recalled that the corporation of thirty individuals also constituted the entire ranks of Bath's parliamentary electorate before 1832. That was one of the most dramatic cases, which was, indeed, under respectful assault from Bath's own freemen at least by 1788, when they issued a 'Petition and Remonstrance' to the corporation over alleged maladministration of common lands. Yet there were many other anomalies, all starkly highlighted in towns where 'close' corporations were juxtaposed with rapidly growing urban populations. Leeds with a 'close' corporation of 36, Liverpool with 41, Coventry with a maximum of 31, and Leicester with 48 Common Councilmen and 24 Aldermen, provided other celebrated examples; while Bristol, which had a sizeable parliamentary freemen franchise, had alongside that a restricted 'close' corporation of 43 individuals, bitterly denounced in 1792 as 'a local tyranny . . . an immoveable, uncontrollable, unaccountable power'. At

Maidstone the Common Council themselves in 1764 curtailed the voting rights of the burgesses – a decision that was, however, set aside by the courts after litigation two years later.

At the same time, variety, idiosyncrasy, and oligarchy were equally the hallmarks of the local government of the non-corporate towns, and of those urban parishes within conurbations that were adjacent to, but outside, the physical boundaries of the ancient corporations. These places were administered by a plethora of different authorities. In one case, that of Sheffield, there were twin communal bodies, the Town Trust (established by charter from the lord of the manor to his freehold tenants or burgesses in 1297) and the Church Trust (a 'close' Council, established by royal charter in 1554), that virtually constituted between them an independent municipal administration, albeit without a royal charter of incorporation as such. Indeed, the Trustees were recognized at law; had a joint seal; their own Town Hall, constructed in 1700; and, in the eighteenth century, a 'Town Regent' or 'Town Collector' as a quasi-Mayor.

Elsewhere, in other non-corporate towns, administration was carried out by the surviving institutions of the manorial court. In some places they functioned without even the nominal suzerainty of a manorial lord, as in Birmingham. There, a Court Leet met annually to make appointments to a range of posts, while the selection of the Leet Jury was in the hands of the Low Bailiff, chosen by the previous court. But the Birmingham Leet itself was becoming increasingly moribund by the later eighteenth century, its position undermined by the activities of the new Lamp and Street Commission. Other places retained a degree of participation by the lord of the manor. In Manchester, for example, he continued to appoint a Steward and collect certain market and other tolls; while concurrently the Court Leet claimed the nominal attendance of an extensive franchise of local inhabitants. That annual meeting appointed numerous officials, headed by the Boroughreeve, whose status again approached that of a Mayor. Here, as in the case of Sheffield, a municipal structure of local government was emerging, despite the absence of the official title and sanction of incorporation.

Yet there were numerous urban parishes that fell completely outside the surviving manorial framework. They were administered solely by the very localized authority of the parish vestry; and here, too, there was great diversity in their composition and efficiency. Indeed, some of the greatest campaigns against oligarchic rule in the eighteenth century centred around the attacks on the 'close' vestries, in London and some of the other major conurbations. The 'petty tyrannies' of parish officials were most keenly resented. 'I shall not be unjust', wrote an onlooker in

1802, 'when I say they can pick the pockets of the rich and starve the poor with impunity.'

In fact, both corporate and non-corporate authorities in the local government of the towns were apt to be defended by the same appeal to tradition and the long acceptance of their powers. Eventually, both came under the same attack, as inefficient, corrupt, unaccountable, and oligarchic. The Birmingham Court Leet was attacked as a 'bastard power' and a select and unaccountable body, very much as were the 'close' corporations. Some contemporaries, it is true, did urge positive advantages in the condition of non-incorporation and non-representation in Parliament. 'A Town without a Charter, is a Town without a Shackle!' was the catch-phrase widely used in Birmingham. It was asserted to be a reason for their growth (but see argument above, pp. 90–3). In particular, their freedom from the costs and turmoil of extensive electioneering was claimed as a bonus to compensate for the absence of representative government, although it was also the case that the tiny franchise in many 'close' corporations spared them the business of electioneering. In the later eighteenth century, however, attention turned rather to the political, social, and moral aspects of the question. Eventually the 1835 municipal reforms, incomplete as they were, endorsed the legal and constitutional benefits of incorporation, while substituting a more systematic, if still selective, rate-payer franchise for the variegated and anomalous local electorates that had flourished earlier in both corporate and non-corporate towns alike.

Local governments in the eighteenth-century towns, then, had some common characteristics irrespective of their precise constitutional status. One of these was their undoubtedly oligarchic composition. None had democratic – or even full rate-payer – franchises; they based their authorities not upon popular mandate but upon tradition, custom, and the general acceptance of ancient rights. In some chartered towns it was not even always clear which of several charters was in operation, thus creating wide scope for litigation. The courts in the eighteenth century, however, generally accepted the appeal to established usage and custom. In a number of places the corporations themselves manoeuvred to reduce the independent powers of their freemen; and in the 1720s Sir Robert Walpole got away with some controversial internal remodelling of the constitutions of two major cities. In London the exclusive Aldermanic Court was given the power of veto over the Common Council in 1725 (though that right was greatly watered down in 1746); and in Norwich in 1730 the electoral system was revised, with the active concurrence of the local Whigs, to reduce (but not remove) the elective powers of the freemen.

Furthermore, some places were even more oligarchic in practice than they were in theory. The City of Bath in the mid-eighteenth century, for example, was so far under the political sway of Ralph Allen (himself Mayor in 1742) that it was known as the 'One-Headed Corporation'. There were many similar cases. A prominent merchant–manufacturer, Oliver Peard, dominated the political life of mid-eighteenth-century Tiverton, exploiting to the full his position as four-time Mayor of the 'close' corporation in 1721, 1733, 1744, and 1753, and as the local Receiver-General of the Land Tax (1744); at his death in 1765 his fellow members of the corporation celebrated the end of a monopoly. Less economically powerful, but nonetheless a controversial figure in Portsmouth, a local Alderman, Edward Linzee, established a record by becoming Mayor as often as eight times between 1745 and 1780. He was the Admiralty candidate, representing the naval interest in their attempt to 'garble' or pack the corporation, as a hostile witness reported. And some of the vestries in London, equally, fell under the sway of cliques and city 'boss' figures, such as Joseph Merceron in later eighteenth-century Bethnal Green. In general terms, the more restricted the local constitution, the greater the chances of a political monopoly; but it also occurred when an impoverished local electorate was vulnerable to the lure of bribery and political patronage.

Virtually everywhere the politically powerful were drawn from among the front ranks of the socially and economically influential citizens. Given the initial costs of office, that was hardly surprising. In London, for example, it took an Alderman some time to recoup his expenditure upon dinners and festivities, and a man with 'Insufficiency of Wealth' – set at £15,000 in 1737, £20,000 in 1799 – could decline to stand. Nor, indeed, given the well-entrenched nature of social and economic inequalities, was it a matter of much comment in the course of the eighteenth century. More controversial at the time was the denominational exclusiveness of local office-holders. Under the Corporation (1661) and Test (1673) Acts, which were not repealed until 1828, tenure of public office was confined to communicants of the Church of England. In some towns Protestant nonconformists took advantage of the special Indemnity Act, passed regularly after 1727, to assume municipal office; Nottingham, for example, had a large number of Dissenter mayors. But the formal legal barriers were considerably more than a mere irritant: much of the impetus for municipal reform in the later eighteenth century came therefore from middle-class Dissenters.

It would be misleading, however, to depict this as a period of uncontested and universal oligarchy in urban local government. Increasingly the composition and performance of the traditional institutions came under public scrutiny and debate – again in both corporate and non-corporate towns. Too ostentatious a monopoly of privilege or too flagrant an abuse of power attracted vocal criticisms and expressions of hostility. Particularly sensitive issues were maladministration of town funds or a town's common fields, or the corrupt licensing of alehouses, or nepotism in the use of corporation patronage. Movements for reform were strengthened in the course of the century – although, as will be seen, changes usually took the form of bypassing rather than recasting the traditional structures of municipal government. In a few rare instances, corporations began to reform themselves. At Plymouth in 1803 the 'close' corporation itself voted to revive the ancient freemen assembly, although that too was a relatively limited body.

The reputation of the eighteenth-century municipalities for 'corruption' thus stemmed, at least in part, from the increasing public attention paid to their performance and use of power. If not generally couched in terms of full democratic accountability, there was nevertheless a growing sense in the towns that public bodies were legitimate targets for public scrutiny and criticism. There was certainly no shortage of pamphlet and press comment. The term 'corruption' was used in many senses. For some radicals, by the later eighteenth century, it had become a shorthand term for the whole system of non-elective and unaccountable local government. But it was also used to refer to abuses and scandals within the system that troubled even those who were prepared, in general terms, to defend the traditional authorities. One target of criticism was a too blatant use of the power of patronage in the interests of one party or clique. In particular, the right to grant or withhold admission to the freedom of the city was often a source of controversy, particularly when there was an attempt to pack the electorate (in places with a freeman franchise) before local or parliamentary elections. For example, there was an outcry in Northampton following a surge of 396 admissions of non-resident freemen at three guineas apiece before the general election of 1733. In 1740 the corporation took the unusual step of disfranchising 49 freemen (44 were reinstated on petition). This reversal of policy was all the more striking in that one of the disbarred freemen was a powerful local magnate, Sir Edward Isham of Lamport. Indeed, one of the most touchy issues in eighteenth-century municipal politics, particularly early in the century, was the extent to which landed patrons managed to control or influence the municipalities. Conversely, by the later decades, there were reverse complaints from rural interests at the extent to which the towns were able to extend their political sway over the countryside.

But the most frequent source of complaint was fiscal corruption. Some of the 'close' corporations in control of extensive assets were notorious for allowing their members to line their pockets in office and for extravagant expenditure on feasting, festivities, and municipal embellishments. 'The sacred Office of a Common Councilman is prostituted to the lowest and basest Ends,' declared *City Corruption and Maladministration Displayed*, written by a citizen of London in 1738.

Nonetheless, the performance of the unreformed administrations in eighteenth-century towns in practice varied markedly from place to place. It is not really possible to establish a league table of relative fiscal and political corruption, since so much jobbery went on behind the scenes. Some corporations were bumbling rather than notorious – Leicester being a case in point. It is also clear from contemporary comment that a few municipal authorities had at least established good public reputations as reasonably impartial and effective bodies within the scope of their relatively modest functions. Their numbers even included two 'close' corporations, where the temptations were greatest. The municipal government of Leeds was sufficiently admired for a Reform Committee in Manchester in 1808 to propose the adoption of 'a local Government formed on the Model of that of Leeds', despite the fact that it was not a publicly elected body. Similarly, the 'close' corporation in Liverpool had established a reputation for energetic and innovative concern for local improvements. Its income, which included rents from property and port dues, was the greatest of any municipal authority in the country outside the City of London; but the Liverpool authorities were relatively free from accusations of fiscal corruption. The corporation was admired particularly for its investment in the dock-building that was essential to the growth of the port of Liverpool. No doubt part of the admiration, too, stemmed from the fact that its abundance of income from other sources helped it to keep the local rates very low. Liverpool Corporation remained, however, vulnerable to criticism for its social and denominational exclusiveness; and, later, its use of municipal influence and money against the opponents of the slave trade from 1787 onwards embroiled it in heated political controversy.

In general, it is notable that the budgets of most eighteenth-century municipal administrations were relatively small. Accounts were not usually published in the eighteenth century, as there was no legal requirement for authorities to do so; but even in 1840 evidence collected from 178 leading corporations showed an average annual municipal expenditure of only *c.*£5,400 apiece (though these figures excluded poor relief). Certainly, their functions were very constricted, by twentieth-century standards, and criticism of their performance and constitution was correspondingly mild.

But with the insistent pace of urban growth came new pressures for collective services, to provide at least the basic amenities for mass living. Important among these were the provision of fresh-water supplies, street-cleansing, -paving, and -lighting, refuse clearance, sewage disposal, and establishment of a watch or police force. The classic eighteenth-century response to such demands, often on petition from local inhabitants, was the creation of a new *ad hoc* local commission to carry out each special function. Flexibility was the keynote, even if sometimes at the cost of administrative confusion. For these special 'Improvement' commissions were widely established, in towns with their own corporations as in those without them; and the relationship between the multifarious overlapping jurisdictions was not always easy to define – even in cases where some or all of the members of the local corporation were given ex-officio membership of a commission. In rare cases, these special statutory powers were conferred solely upon the traditional institutions. The new bodies derived their authority not from tradition but each from its own local Act of Parliament. They had independent powers to levy local rates for the provision of special services or the hire of contractors. So although there was no general process of local government reform in eighteenth-century England, there certainly was a considerable amount of quiet innovation, in response to local demand. If the commissions were not institutionally the ancestors of the reformed municipalities of the nineteenth century, in many ways functionally they were exactly that.

In the detail of their format and composition Improvement Commissions shared the eighteenth century's constitutional eclecticism, although they tended to become more standardized over time. Some of the earliest ones were self-selected 'close' bodies. Later commissions were usually elective bodies, with a middle-class rate-payer franchise. They drew therefore from a wider and a socially somewhat more homogeneous stratum of the urban population than did the very disparate freemen franchises. They also had the advantage that they could be given authority over a number of traditionally separate administrative areas: that was often also the rationale behind urban Poor Law Commissions.

Reforms began, almost literally, in the street. Some of the earliest commissions were those established to cleanse and light public highways. After the mid-century there was a flood of local legislation, much of it imitative – one town's example inspiring the inhabitants of another. By the end of the century there were important Improvement Commissions in most of the large urban areas. At least a hundred commissions in towns, or parts of towns, had been established. By the 1830s only Leicester, Nottingham, Wenlock, and Wigan remained, among the municipal boroughs with populations of more than 11,000, without such a body. In places like Birmingham, the Lamp and Street Commission, established in 1769, played a more central role in local government than did the expiring powers of the antique Court Leet. Similarly, the Police Commissioners in Manchester, inaugurated in 1765, eventually became active in cleansing and improving the streets of both Manchester and Salford, as well as providing a local police force.

Nevertheless, the efficiency of the eighteenth-century Improvement Commissions should not be exaggerated. Some became as notoriously inactive as were the unreformed corporations, and in general it could not be said that eighteenth-century towns were very efficiently or effectively administered – or that they expected to be. But the promotion of these special bodies indicates in itself the force of pressure for change, even if it did not always achieve the desired result. Imperceptibly there developed an awareness of the need for communal responsibility for the provision of communal services, whether they were administered locally or farmed out to contractors. It was no longer practicable to leave to the individual householder the duty of, for example, cleansing and lighting the adjacent highway. The number of full-time officials paid by urban authorities began gradually to rise, and the debate over the proper extent and/or limits of government intervention had already begun, well before the end of the century. A number of voices were raised to suggest a more positively interventionist role, particularly in the case of doctors calling for medical or sanitary reforms. A few reformers in Liverpool in the 1790s, repelled by the city's dank cellar dwellings, urged that this was a social 'evil which has a strong claim upon the feelings of the magistracy for interference and redress'. And the optimistic Dr Lucas in Leeds had also proposed a revision of the anomalies and irregularities in the system of assessment and collection of local rates.

Nor was interest in municipal affairs confined to the towns themselves. The device of obtaining private legislation meant that an increasing amount of parliamentary time was being absorbed by urban issues. Alongside the numerous eighteenth-century private Bills for turnpike and enclosure commissions must be ranked a growing mosaic of special legislation directly affecting the towns.

In other words there was a concealed urban dimension to much of the eighteenth-century political world, at both national and local level. New social forces often come to the forefront of attention, sometimes disguised as 'problems' or 'questions', long before their importance has been enshrined in formal constitutional rights and before people from their own ranks have achieved highest office. The landed-gentry world of eighteenth-century England found itself insensibly becoming 'urbanized', in its politics as well as in its social life. The shift was often reluctant. 'What times do we not live in, when a parcel of low shopkeepers pretend to direct the whole Legislature,' was the shocked reaction of George III to a petition against the Cider Act, from the highly respectable Common Council of the City of London in 1763. Nonetheless, the King himself had assured the Council only a few months earlier, in 1762, that he too was very concerned about 'shopkeeping' issues of policy: 'the Prosperity of the City of *London*, and the extensive Trade and Navigation of my faithful Subjects, are, and ever will be, the constant Object of my unwearied Care and Attention.'

The growing political impact and centrality of urban issues came about for a variety of reasons and in a variety of ways. In part, of course, the sheer magnitude of commercial and industrial expansion directed governments' attention to its visible social manifestations. Yet much stemmed too from the active intervention of successive urban residents themselves, whether as behind-the-scene pressure groups and lobbyists for specific causes or as public critics and protagonists of reform. It is clearly not feasible here to investigate in detail all the intricacies of urban political life during a complex century. Nor, indeed, did every instance of local factional fighting and feuding – perhaps over the distribution of patronage – necessarily have any wider significance. In general, however, it can be observed that urban politics were not exclusively concerned with place and profit, and that the towns collectively acquired, in the course of the century, the sort of respect and admiration, closely mingled with fear and suspicion, that London had notably commanded in earlier centuries. And the City of London continued its tradition of independence and assertiveness. In fact, of course, many urban populations were themselves often uncertain and divided over political issues – between conservatism and reform parties in the 1790s, for example. Yet their dramatized and over-simplified reputation for assertiveness, independence, and occasional radicalism, did have a reality in its own right, alongside the simultaneous complexities of local politics.

The impact of the towns did not derive solely, or even chiefly, from an ability to oppose government. On the contrary, many civic élites were active and successful lobbyists for what they perceived to be the interests of their localities. They sent petitions, letters to ministers, deputations, and discreet behind-the-scenes canvassers. Such dealings, which often left only scanty traces in the records, were part of the manoeuvres needed to get government assistance, if only in terms of providing parliamentary time for the passage of private legislation. The quantity of special local Acts in the course of the eighteenth century, relating not only to special cases, such as the London and Norwich Anti-Calico Act (1722) or the Manchester Act (1736) but including many routine local improvements, attests to the responsiveness of Parliament on this sort of issue, in contrast to its slowness to endorse constitutional change. In the 1720s and 1730s, in particular, Sir Robert Walpole went to great lengths to buy off as many municipal interests as possible, to add urban props to his own patronage empire. He often worked in conjunction with local Whig politicians in the towns themselves to minimize the influence of popular critics of his government. One of the difficulties, of course, was that it was not always easy to satisfy all interests either simultaneously or permanently. A controversial issue, such as the conduct of a war, for example, could easily divide urban merchants into pro- and anti-war factions, and guarantee that, whatever policy was followed, some would find themselves in opposition. But it indicates one way in which urban interests received attention from aristocratic governments that were drawn from a narrow landed-gentry oligarchy. With time, too, growing numbers of non-enfranchised urban freeholders came to play a significant role in county elections; and rich town merchants and businessmen were able themselves to purchase 'rotten' boroughs.

To an extent, political expediency was supplemented by prevalent political theory. England's 'ancient constitution' enshrined a real, if circumscribed, degree of constitutionalism. Governments should not seem arbitrary or despotic, but should endeavour to rule in the interests of the 'people', who were all, by one means or another, 'virtually', if not directly, represented in Parliament. The theory, of course, allowed much latitude to governments in practice; but it did make them generally sensitive to public opinion, and it did demand a certain degree of outward respect for the electorate. Edmund Burke's celebrated speech to the electors of Bristol in 1774, explaining that, as their MP, he was a representative and not their delegate, did nonetheless explicitly acknowledge his obligations towards the 'people' in general and to his constituents in particular. As for that latter group, they in turn showed their own readiness to assess his unpopular performance as their representative by engineering his withdrawal from the Bristol seat at the election of 1780, to great local applause. In so far, therefore, as urban interests were recognized by the traditional constitution, they enjoyed a degree of leverage, if not predominance.

Yet their political influence was compounded and complicated by the strong element of fear and suspicion that underlay gentry attitudes to the independence and self-assertiveness of the urban populace. In a less genial mood in 1795 Edmund Burke explored those emotions, in a denunciation of the attention given to urban market riots in that year of dearth. 'The cry of the people in cities and towns, though unfortunately (from a fear of their multitude and combination) the most regarded,' he wrote, 'ought, in *Fact*, to be the *least* attended to on this subject.'

Agriculture, he explained, was a rural concern. Nonetheless, even Burke in his most conservative vein did acknowledge that the urban viewpoint had a magnetic 'pull', and that the towns' growing importance in terms of numbers had augmented their potentialities for concerted action. Furthermore, since the towns also constituted political pressure gauges for a wider public opinion, and were the nerve centres of the communication network, prudence as well as fear entailed that the threat of widespread urban disaffection was always taken seriously by successive central governments. In general terms, therefore, reactions in the towns helped to set the bounds of the politically possible, even though in many specific instances urban protest and radicalism was not successful in its wider aims.

Fears were sharpened by the many cases of lower-class or 'mob' disorder, disturbance, demonstration, tumults, and affrays, known generally, but loosely, as 'riots'. Mass assemblies were, indeed, a particularly characteristic way in which public opinion on matters of general concern was expressed in the eighteenth-century towns, where, of course, the bulk of the population were without the vote and not formally incorporated into the 'political nation'. Such demonstrations lacked continuous organization or a fully fledged political programme; but they had an immediacy and a mass force that often aroused disproportionate fears. On some issues, too, they might hope for some support and assistance from the magistrates. It is important to distinguish between minor affrays and mass demonstrations, as also between their aims, organization, and the extent of violence and anger involved. Some did develop into attacks on persons and property, although many crowds dispersed after a counter-display of official force, sometimes accompanied by promises of redress. Yet all gatherings placed pressures upon the local magistracy, whose handling of events could often exacerbate or calm passions, and whose enforcement powers were in practice very limited. The magistrates were therefore one of the prime filters whereby the force of public opinion and the extent of civil commotion was interpreted and transmitted to central government.

Indeed, the urban political leaders often acknowledged the force of crowd demonstrations as a show of strength; and sometimes used the tactic themselves in the context of a local power struggle. Defoe probably exaggerated his account of the literal faction-fighting in Coventry at the 1722 election: the Whigs and Tories lined up along the streets, facing each other across the central gutter or kennel, and then 'fell on with such Fury with Clubs and Staves, that in an instant the Kennel was cover'd with them'. But he was emphatic in reporting that their ranks included not merely 'the Scum and Rabble of the Town, but ... the Burgesses and chief Inhabitants, nay even Magistrates, Aldermen, and the Like'. Clearly, then, it cannot be assumed that all 'riots' were explicit challenges to authority, or that all assemblies were solely lower-class in their social composition. Quantification of disorder is therefore of little significance without consideration of the nature of the dispute. Yet any collapse of civic order, however brief-lived, did ultimately pose a threat to traditional authority and the fabric of the community. The civic élite were therefore generally cautious in their tactical deployment of crowd support.

By reputation, the urban inhabitants *en masse* were seen as a powerful but unpredictable force. Clearly, riots and disturbances did not involve all townsmen – nor all towns. Furthermore, many manifestations of public feeling were not overtly political in motivation and, when political, not always radical, as the celebrated Birmingham riots in support of 'Church and King' in 1791 revealed. A demonstration's latent threat could, however, be turned into an explicit challenge by a weak or clumsy response from local authorities. Much depended upon a subtle show of strength and counter-strength. 'But Troops alone, (If we had enough, wch. we have not) would not do the Business,' explained the Duke of Newcastle, commenting on the 1756–7 grain and militia riots in Sheffield, York, and the industrial West Riding, 'Except the Nobility and Gentry and principal Magistrates . . . will do their Part.'

Two of the most dramatic provincial confrontations between rioters and municipality began as demonstrations over economic grievances. In Newcastle upon Tyne in June 1740 the 'pitmen, keelmen, and poor of the town' combined to sack the Guildhall and destroy 'many of the publick writings and accounts', after their hopes had been raised and then dashed in the course of a market protest at the dearth of grain. In Liverpool in August 1775 a clumsily handled industrial dispute between merchants and seamen in the Africa trade led to the seizure of the Exchange (the heart of the city's commerce and also its Town Hall) by a crowd of sailors and townsmen, who fired cannon and small arms captured from shipping and gunsmiths' shops. Their recourse to fire-power caused an immense sensation; and, although the near-insurrection was eventually quelled by the army, the implications of the event were considered so serious that a virtual news embargo was imposed on reports in the local press. London also experienced a dramatic escalation from demonstration into challenge to established order in the case of the Gordon Riots, in the summer of 1780. Mass anti-Catholic rallies by the Protestant Association – not in itself a highly controversial cause in eighteenth-century England – were treated with too much complacency by the magistrates; and the disturbance to regular public order encouraged a progressive collapse of authority for several days, with rioting, arson, looting, an assault on the

Bank of England (defended by Alderman John Wilkes), and the highest loss of life incurred in the course of any civil disturbance in this period. That such a state of affairs could arise so rapidly and so unexpectedly throughout extensive areas of the capital city added to the shock.

There were also times when popular demonstrations were consciously used for political ends. The workforce in the manufacturing towns – particularly in the textile trades – had a tradition of organization and combination that was in some cases harnessed to political campaigns. In Tiverton, for example, the weavers had a long tradition of militancy. There were riots and public demonstrations, of greater or lesser significance, there in 1706, 1720, 1733, 1749, 1754, and 1765. The contraction of the staple industry sharpened criticisms of the policies of the 'close' corporations and their electoral monopoly. In 1754, for example, the weavers organized a powerful campaign to obtain the vote:

As soon therefore as they knew that the Parliament was dissolved [wrote a late eighteenth-century sympathizer], the principal Members of the ... Societies [of] Wool-combers, Weavers, Scribblers, etc. assembled daily at their Club-houses ... ; and at Night frequently beat brass Pans, as Signals for meeting together in larger Bodies, to strike Terror into the Minds of the Members of the Corporation, or any other Persons that might attempt to oppose their claim of electing the Members of Parliament.

They did not in fact succeed; but the account gives evidence of their organization and militancy. They continued to exert pressure on the Corporation, with further dramatic scenes in 1765, when the Mayor's house was invaded, his nose tweaked and his wig pulled off, by another angry crowd, which included, as in many demonstrations, large numbers of women.

The inhabitants of the towns, then, were more than just interested onlookers at eighteenth-century political life. Of course, not every individual townsman was keenly politicized, any more than was every country gentleman. Yet there were complex two-way linkages between national and municipal politics. Contests between Whigs and Tories in the early decades of the century, for example, were seen in refracted image in party contests in many towns, especially in those with large freemen electorates. Similarly, the mid-eighteenth-century equipoise under Walpole and the Pelhams, shot through as it was with protest and argument, also informed the municipal politics of that era with the same combination of oligarchy and challenge. On occasions, political demonstration by urban crowds – especially in London – had a specific impact on the course of national events. Among other examples, the Sacheverell riots in 1709–10 helped to oust the Whig government in 1710; the anti-excise riots in 1733 helped to force Walpole to withdraw the controversial Excise Bill; and popular anti-government feeling in the 1720s and 1730s was sufficient to keep the government worried with fears that opposition might turn into support for the exiled Jacobite cause (a conjunction that did not, in fact, materialize.) In the early eighteenth century none of these protests really developed into a permanent or nation-wide movement; but the nature and social composition of their support were both more broadly based and socially respectable than the notion of the ignorant rabble of legend, just as their political views were more articulated and complex than their opponents liked to pretend. There is no need, therefore, to insist on a continuity of organization or a linear progression of extra-parliamentary activism in order to identify its existence and its substance.

In the later eighteenth century the context of national and local politics was further transformed. The development of a nation-wide political consciousness, outside the ranks of the traditional gentry world, was fostered in the 1750s by Pitt and Beckford, City MP and Lord Mayor, who was prepared to stand up as spokesman for the 'middling sort' (despite the fact that he himself was a large landowner and an absentee sugar-plantation owner). It was powerfully stimulated, in the 1760s, by the inspirational politics of John Wilkes, who was able to broaden his stance on particular issues into a national rallying-cry of 'Wilkes and Liberty'. Much of the excitement and political activity was concentrated in London; but Wilkes's campaigns were a matter for interested discussion in many towns. In a relatively small place like Lincoln, for example, the Dean's wife thought initially that Wilkes's doctrines had made little impact. But, she recorded in April 1769, 'They say a few of the lower People begin to be a little infected with it here'; and her husband hastily preached a sermon on the duties of obedience.

Thereafter there were successive attempts at establishing organizations for parliamentary reforms, from the Wilkeite Society of Supporters of the Bill of Rights (1769) onwards. These were not campaigns that were sponsored solely, or even chiefly, from within the ranks of urban society. The politics of country and town were too closely enmeshed for simple dividing lines to be drawn. Yet clearly, urban populations were involved in the process. Not only did the towns contain many of the intellectual and middle-class protagonists of franchisal reform, but they were also social phenomena whose formal exclusion from national political life prompted much of the initial questioning of the traditional constitution. It was particularly the non-representation of urban wealth that worried many who were not democrats but supporters of the claims of property. The organization and articulation of reform movements helped therefore to keep urban issues continuously in play, bringing the debate repeatedly before Parliament. It also developed links between reformers in different parts of the country: London, the provincial towns, and industrial counties. Urban lobbyists had combined on specific issues before (for example, to make representations on industrial and commercial matters). And, indeed, it was a group of Birmingham manufacturers who attempted (in 1785-7) to organize a permanent industrialists' lobby, with a general Chamber of Manufacturers of Great Britain, in contact with local committees in Glasgow, Liverpool, Manchester, Norwich, Nottingham, Sheffield, and Stoke. But franchisal reform brought forward the common interests of towns as towns. Not surprisingly, therefore, the conscious promotion of reform also had an impact upon the complexities of local politics. Much of the pressure for change came from Whigs and Dissenters, especially in the large towns that were without parliamentary representation. They tended also to support proposals for local reform, while many of the traditional 'close' corporations, whose monopoly was under attack, became more defiantly conservative.

The emergence of organized lower-class radicalism in the towns in the 1790s was therefore in some respects a new departure. Yet it was an intelligible development – springing from existing traditions of independence, assertiveness, association, and protest among the urban populace. The artisan Corresponding Societies, Constitution Societies, Reformation Societies, and Revolution Societies that sprang up in London and many major provincial towns in 1792-6, were not born purely in response to events in France. Their political programme of far-reaching democratic reforms drew much from ideas already in circulation in the towns. Urban societies had been receptive to the impact of the American revolt and many middle-class reformers had propounded an optimistic belief in liberal progress in the 1770s and 1780s. To these ideas were added the semi-covert popular tradition of Levellerism (the name resurfaced in some radical posters in the 1790s) and the towns' tradition of a questioning dissent in religion. Middle-class criticisms of the established form of the constitution led therefore to consideration of more popularly based reforms. Similarly, the organizational base of the lower-class radical movement was that well-known urban phenomenon, the tavern and its social clubs: those 'infidel societies', as a critic termed them in 1800, where people met regularly to read the papers (or hear them read) and to discuss matters of common interest.

The new developments in the 1790s, however, lay in the articulation and the organization of a popular democratic movement in the towns, calling for a (male) universal franchise. The stimulus of the French Revolution and a widespread depression in the English economy proved the joint incubators. A richly textured radical literature of books, ballads, essays, journals, developed a national debate: the single most successful work was Tom Paine's combative *Rights of Man* (1791), which had an immensely wide circulation throughout the country. At the same time the radical clubs and societies, drawn from the ranks of small tradesmen, artisans, and 'Mechanicks', began to federate, not merely on a local basis but also into a nation-wide organization. There were at least a hundred such societies by 1795, many with their own local offshoots, in communication one with another. It was that, above all, that galvanized the government into an awareness of the potential power of the movement. Traditional gentry suspicion of the urban lower classes was immeasurably heightened by the threat of combination between, as well as within, the towns; even though, as the radicals found, it was very difficult to co-ordinate a mass movement when the pulse of discontent beat at a different pace in different parts of the country.

The early strength of urban radicalism was notably greatest in those manufacturing towns whose economies were most harshly hit by the economic depression and the effects of the wars against France. London, Manchester, Norwich, Nottingham, Derby, Coventry, Sheffield, and Stockport were among the major strongholds of the corresponding societies; even their 'Loyal Clubs' opposed the war. By contrast, the inhabitants of the dockyard towns, whose trade was war, were initially hostile to the radicals. Similarly, the popular response in Birmingham, with its variegated economy, including its reliance upon armaments, was distinctly divided. The 'Church and King' riots in the spring of 1791 profoundly shocked the reformist middle-class Dissenters, whose homes and property were attacked; and it put the early radical movement there very much on the defensive. But all mass political activity worried the authorities. It seemed more than a mere challenge to social discipline; it was regarded as a genuine threat of sustained and fundamental alteration to the established social and political order. 'Weep, ye who grind the Face of the Poor, oppress the People, and starve the industrious *Mechanic!*' commanded a Norwich wall-poster in 1793, attacking the wealth of the rich. 'Think of this, all ye who work hard and have hardly a *Crust* to put in your Mouths, think how many Wretches it would have made happy.' The impact of such arguments lay in the revelation of potentialities as well as of actualities. The prefiguration of nineteenth-century mass politics was clear.

The urban radicals were gradually making further efforts to co-ordinate movements within and between different towns; and by the mid-1790s popular support for the government had soured in many places. Particularly with the extensive dearth and economic problems of the mid- and later 1790s, considerable disaffection set in – even in previously 'loyalist' towns such as Birmingham and the dockyards. The London Societies sent a delegation specifically to these towns in 1796–7, canvassing fresh political ties. But by then William Pitt had dramatically curbed the radicals, with legislation against political associations and public meetings. The movement fell on to the defensive. Pitt had, furthermore, institutionalized political repression with a new programme of building permanent barracks for the army in a number of the leading provincial centres. Pointedly, army policy kept the units of men on the move between towns, so that they should not imbibe radical contagion from the local inhabitants.

That, indeed, pointed to the ultimate significance of the lower-class radicalism of the 1790s. It marked the emergence, at the forefront of the political calculus, of a powerful new force. Whether the urban working-class movement remained continuously organized or not, an impact had been made, a political reputation established, that long outlasted the specific and finite events of the 1790s themselves. Temporarily and publicly silenced by the end of the century, urban radicalism had acquired importance – both for its own supporters and for its political opponents. Significant events make their own history. London tailors, Norwich weavers, Manchester artisans, Sheffield cutlers, Birmingham nail-makers, Plymouth dockyard workers, had moved into the political arena in organized association. And, despite initial defeat, the urban working class was henceforth, in presence or in absence, a factor in political equations.

Reactions to that, both within the towns and in the political world of the gentry, became the new stuff of politics. 'Hearken! O ye Poor of the Land!' urged the Stockport Friends of Universal Peace and the Rights of Man, in January 1794, '. . . Claim as your inalienable *Right* universal Suffrage and annual Parliaments . . . and whenever you have the Gratification to chose a Representative, let him be from among the *Lower Order* of Mankind.' A few long-sighted radicals in the English Revolution of the 1640s had called, in their defeat, for the growth of towns and trade to create a new political constituency as the only basis for success. In the course of the eighteenth-century that political force emerged; and by the 1790s that challenge had become explicit.

10 The urban environment

The emergence in this period of a distinctive nation-wide urban identity, transcending many perceptible local variations, consolidated the influence and centripetal force of the towns. Their growth in size and number, up and down the country, accentuated their physical, as well as social, cultural, political, and economic impact. London, although unique, no longer seemed quite so exceptional or aberrant. While the refracting images of specialist towns became more sharply differentiated into 'Coketown', 'Bath', or 'Barchester', the towns also developed a strongly marked collective identity as towns.

Their physical form was studied as visible proxy for other changes. This period saw the acceleration of the modern torrent of writing, discussion, and analysis, as well as prints, drawings, and designs, relating to the understanding and improvement of the urban environment. (The building, planning, design, and architectural development of eighteenth-century towns remain by far the most intensively studied aspects of their history.) Money was invested, as well as time and attention. The relative abundance of capital in eighteenth-century England, and the prevalence of low rates of interest, meant that investment in the urban fabric was not only feasible but also comparatively attractive. The building and, equally important, the rebuilding of eighteenth-century towns absorbed considerable investment capital. There was a multitude of undertakings, both large and small. Funds were also channelled on a considerable and increasing scale into the refurbishing, or new foundation, of those public buildings that have come to be so characteristic of the towns. In their varying permutations, the town centres housed a guild-hall, market hall, and Exchange, as well as purpose-built theatres, assembly rooms, concert halls, literary institutions, not to mention, in the wider urban context, workhouses, hospitals, prisons, and court-houses. The scale of institutional building also accelerated, particularly from the 1750s onwards: by 1801, for example, every large centre, the manufacturing town as well as resort, had its own purpose-built theatre – as did some small regional centres, such as Stamford (population 4,000). The urban 'improvements' to basic amenities, such as lighting, paving, cleansing, and water-supply, additionally generated a growing financial commitment, particularly as the rising scale of urbanization dramatically multiplied the problems.

One of the most striking aspects of that urban 'identity' was its association with crowds, noise, bustle, and, literally, with light. In the period before the invention and diffusion of gas- and later of electric-lighting, the entire countryside was dark by night. The illuminated towns, by contrast, stood out like beacons – and, indeed, their modern counterparts still cast a glow into the night sky that is observable even from a less-than-completely dark countryside. The provision of street lighting prolonged the hours of accepted public activity, especially in the winter months. Without it, communities lived by the rising and setting of the sun, and phased their evening activities by the light of the moon. The name of Birmingham's Lunar Society bespeaks its origin. In the emergent industrial town of St. Helens in the later eighteenth century, too, the Book Club meetings were held on the night nearest to the full moon. Some of the members of that Club – who included many prominent local industrialists – were themselves later active in the promotion of the town's first Gas Light Company (1832) and the St. Helens Lighting and Watching Act (1836).

Artificial lighting therefore represented power for the citizens in more way than one: little wonder that the provision and improvement of street lighting were matters of much public concern in the eighteenth-century towns. Improved street lamps, burning rape-seed oil and incorporating reflective glass, were patented for outdoor use in the later seventeenth century. As already noted, in the course of the eighteenth century numerous towns acquired local Street Lighting Acts, whereby private contractors and/or local commissions were authorized to provide for oil-burning street lights in the main thoroughfares and public places – usually between October and March (but in some places all year round). Other sources of illumination were also relied upon: shopkeepers put lamps in their windows; some individual householders hung out lanterns; and, in the larger towns, link-boys, carrying torches, could be hired to accompany the traveller. But the principle of public lighting was increasingly widely accepted in the eighteenth-century towns.

Attempts at imposing an evening curfew were everywhere abandoned. Urban 'night life' began to acquire its own reputation, and specialist descriptive literature. Country visitors often eulogized the brilliance of the towns' nocturnal illuminations, even while the blasé city residents complained (accurately enough) that the lighting did not extend into every dark corner and alleyway. If, by the standard of later technologies, the light cast by the oil-burning street lamps was feeble, to contemporaries their massed effect was striking. 'Nothing, indeed, can be more superb,' enthused Von Archenholz, of the lighting of London's West End in the 1780s. A 'Very Young Lady' was inspired to verse, in her manuscript journal (1805), by the bright lights of the very much smaller city of Colchester (pop. 11,500):

> As our Stay was but short, I shall only remark,
> That the Shops blazed with Light, though the evening was dark.
> The Lamps were so splendid, the Street was so wide,
> It resembled taking a peep at Cheapside.

Identity was confirmed by the mass and density of urban settlement. The larger cities, with their multiplicity of resources clustered into one huge area, constituted a world of their own. Contemporaries joked more than half-seriously about the chronic self-absorption of London society in particular. And, although the towns varied in density of settlement – there were also marked variations between different areas within the towns – they shared the impact of crowds and bustle. A few of the long-established cities were very literally separated from the countryside. They still retained their encircling walls and gates, although many urban fortifications had been destroyed in or after the seventeenth-century civil wars. Some walled cities in the early eighteenth century (Norwich, Exeter, York) persevered in the old tradition of closing the gates on Sundays and at night. But that policy, however easily circumvented in practice, eventually conflicted with the need for ready access to town, and was discontinued. Mediaeval city walls had not yet acquired tourist glamour. Nor did the selective glance of the controversial 'Gothic Revival' in the later eighteenth century fall with favour on their cause. In many places, therefore, large sections of crumbling fortifications were pulled down piecemeal in the course of urban expansion (Bath, Hull, Leicester, Newcastle upon Tyne, Nottingham, Worcester, among others); while the Corporation of Norwich, in a miscalculated attempt at 'modernity', decided in the early 1790s to demolish its complete set of city gates, and to allow the collapse of most sections of its encircling flintstone walls.

Other towns were less manifestly separated from the countryside; but they also displayed a relatively compacted and nucleated form. Even those that were growing most rapidly did so by means of considerable infilling as well as by geographical extension of the built-up area. There were, needless to say, many local variations in topography, and imponderables in the release of land for construction purposes, so that the towns did not simply expand in a neat pattern of widening concentric circles. But even those whose growth was the most asymmetrical retained a certain mass and density in that new development, although the centre of gravity shifted. Urban boundaries, if mobile, were therefore readily identifiable. A town, whether walled or not, was visible from afar as a town. The many eighteenth-century prints of urban 'prospects' and 'panoramas' often depicted a densely clustered settlement, viewed across green fields. By contrast, the lack of a single focus to the Potteries conurbation was always a matter of comment, and to this day its component towns retain their separate identity.

In general, the essential pressure towards nucleation was that of the prevailing transport technology. Most people walked around the town on foot. Sedan-chairs and hackney cabs were certainly owned and available for hire in the bigger places; and, with growing area specialization in the larger conurbations, it is probable that there was an increase in mean distances daily travelled. There were several signs of intensified demand for internal transport services within the towns. Many *Directories* listed numbers of cab-owners, while London had its own *Hackney-Coach Directory* (1770). Indeed, municipal authorities in London and Bath found themselves faced with the need to license carriages and chairs, and to regulate the scale of fees, in order to avert consumer discontent, such as that evinced by the angry general at Bath who was 'kept Prisoner in a Chair, with the Top lifted up, in a hard, rainy Night' for refusing to pay the bearers what he regarded as extortionate fees. However, it was convenience rather than distance of travel that was offered by the sedan-chairs. The horse-drawn cabs and carriages similarly did not cater for mass transit; and they later ran into considerable logistical problems in the supply of hay and horses when they began to do so in Victorian towns.

Eighteenth-century towns therefore saw only a limited expansion of suburban development at any distance from the city centre. The poorest industrial suburbs were usually adjacent to the towns, and were often swallowed up in the course of subsequent urban growth. Some of the largest towns did, however, generate an affluent upper- and middle-class residential suburbia, situated a long carriage-drive away from the city centre. Consumer demand for lower residential densities, views of green fields, and cleaner air, proved a pointer to future urban aspirations, when transport mobility improved. It was certainly a distinctive change from earlier times. But the growth of suburbia did not constitute a real flight from the town – whether the move be viewed in geographical or in social and cultural terms. It denoted, on the contrary, a further example of the emergence of specialized residential areas within a greater conurbation. As Defoe, among others, pointed out, the affluent citizens retired, not to the wilds, but to join select groups of other wealthy citizens. Their way of life remained highly urbanized; and residences were often situated on or close to the main roads into town. The poet Cowper waxed sarcastic at their fond delusion that they had found the real countryside:

> Suburban Villas, highway-side Retreats,
> That dread th' Encroachment of our growing Streets,
> Tight Boxes, neatly sash'd, and in a blaze
> With all the July Sun's collected Rays,
> Delight the Citizen, who, gasping there,
> Breathes Clouds of Dust, and calls it Country Air.

The scale of the urban population growth in densely settled town centres during the century suggested that problems of mass living could not solve themselves by spontaneous adjournment to the suburbs. As the quantity of smart town housing constructed in the eighteenth century indicates, the upper and middle classes had by no means abandoned the towns. Fashion reinforced necessity. Increasingly, therefore, attention began to be directed towards the conscious ordering and improvement of the urban environment.

Of course, neither the theory nor the practice of town planning, in any of its guises, was a pure product of the eighteenth century. Nor was the general growth of English towns in that period in any way the result of any conscious policy objective. England's eighteenth-century 'Renaissance' in planning, design, and improvement was not exclusively applied to or derived from the towns: numerous landscaped parks and redesigned country estates testify to that. But the town became a legitimate and increasingly challenging preoccupation within that developing tradition. Most of the inspiration came, it should be noted, from private citizens and local authorities rather than from central government or the crown. National political and military requirements did not call for a wholesale remodelling of English towns; wholly new 'plantations' were essentially colonial, both in concept and actuality. Eighteenth-century London, for example, an imperial capital and seat of royalty, was never planned as a whole; and John Gwynn's appeal for comprehensive renewal, in *London and Westminster Improved* (1766), did not strike a response from central or local government or, indeed, from the crown. The last remaining private royal 'King's Road', which ran through south-west London, was increasingly encroached upon by an impatient public (there was a thriving trade in counterfeit travel passes) before it was officially thrown open. Furthermore, the Prince Regent's own lavish patronage of urban development in early nineteenth-century London and Brighton marked the crown estate's late adhesion to the ranks of improving aristocratic landowners rather than a new affirmation of royalty. It was much more a monarchical celebration of the town than the reverse.

Some of the most magnificent 'grand designs' in eighteenth-century English towns were privately built and sponsored estates of town housing. These were to be found in the fashionable residential areas of prosperous cities and in the newly-expanding resort centres. The fine crescents, circuses, parades, and squares of Bath were the most celebrated exemplars. It was not so much their novelty – for there were earlier examples – but their style and scale that impressed. Yet even here, it should be noted, they were by no means co-extensive with the entire urban area. These grand developments were cases of estate- rather than of full town-planning. John Wood's dreams of refashioning the whole city of Bath were never realized. The old centre or 'lower town', with its narrow streets and alleyways and its crowded housing, was rebuilt only gradually and in piecemeal fashion; while there were also small single-site developments in the 'upper town', attracted there by the glamour of Wood's initiatives.

Nonetheless, the eighteenth-century redevelopment of Bath in particular had an immense impact. Its reputation, indeed, was much greater than the physical extent of the new building would suggest. The modelling of the townscape by the Woods and other speculative developers indicated a conscious process in which individual requirements were blended with collective social goals. Stylistically, the Woods in particular, with their fluent use of contour and variety of forms (squares, crescents, circles), were highly influential. In practical terms, their use of the restrictive covenant in the building lease also indicated one key device whereby, in the absence of standard planning regulations, general supervision could be retained over diverse sectional interests. In even more prosaic detail, they showed how local capital could be attracted to invest in imaginative developments. Above all, their invocation of the classical tradition, in style and planning, appropriated for the eighteenth-century towns the antiquity and majesty of a legitimating civic vision. The senior John Wood's *Essay towards a Description of the City of Bath* (1749) laid particular stress upon the inspiration of Roman town-planning, but in the context of native urban growth. He endorsed with enthusiasm Bath's claims to a legendary foundation by the ancient British King Bladud. New styles were to be blended with long-standing British traditions. For Wood, the whole process reflected a divine harmony, that was in turn displayed in the building process. He sought an equipoise of form and style, use and beauty. As he explained in his remarkable testament, *The Origin of Building* (Bath, 1741): 'In the Works of the DIVINE ARCHITECT of all Things, we find nothing but perfect Figures, consisting of the utmost *Regularity*, the sweetest *Harmony*, and the most delightful *Proportion*.'

Eighteenth-century attitudes to town design, therefore, increasingly assimilated European classicism into an English tradition – of expectations, if not achievements. Towns were thought of as environments that were consciously man-made, to be viewed, celebrated, and adapted. Not only was the most common civic emblem of cultural activity the theatre, but the town itself was to be a social theatre. Perceptions of the favoured scale and layout of the townscape were considerably changed. Streets were to be broad, accessible, panoramic, rather than small, winding, and crowded. Building façades were to be regular, uncluttered, cohesive if not symmetrical, and visually impressive. Open prospects were to lead to public open spaces, or to some central point of reference. Churches now, for example, also doubled as visual props in the urban street scene. The particularly English contribution to this style was the harmonious deployment of the town square, with a central paved area, or, increasingly, a leafy garden. If its most classical exposition in England was found in the development of the 'upper town' in Bath, its most complete application came in neighbouring Scotland, in the later eighteenth century, with the building of Edinburgh's New Town.

The style has been described, following the perceptive insights of Lewis Mumford, as a civic 'architecture of the carriageway'.[1] It not only facilitated the movement of wheeled traffic through the towns, but was also best viewed from a fast-moving, smooth-rolling coach or chariot. Yet it was simultaneously an architecture of the stoutly built brick or stone town house, that did not depend substantially for shelter and insulation upon close massing and grouping with other properties. The town house was itself an object of social display. The concomitant of the broad and open, but often windy and wet, public carriageway was the warm and well-insulated private house (and, out of doors, the umbrella, whose use was less-and-less thought of as an eccentricity).

Closely associated with the new design, therefore, was the creation of the classical image of the Georgian town house. In fact, of course, very far from all eighteenth-century urban town housing was constructed or rebuilt to the highest standards of fashionable design. Nor were the new styles themselves as uniform as the later standardized image of 'mock Georgian' might suggest. In particular, there were still many key variations in local traditions and especially their building materials: from the red brick of the west Midlands to the mellow stone of Bath and the high-quality limestones of Stamford. Yet the eighteenth century saw the emergence of a conscious and nation-wide idiom in town housing, replacing earlier traditions of regional vernacular. That substitution was sometimes very literal. Much old timberwork housing was refronted or partially rebuilt, in imitation of the new style. In Nottingham it was observed in 1751 that 'many of the Inhabitants have taken to new Fronting their Houses after the newest Fashion, some with Parapet Walls.' In the much smaller Chichester it was noted that by the 1780s the whole place had been 'new built or new faced'. The emphasis was upon an overall regularity and symmetry, into which individual diversities could be set. It conveyed dignity, permanence, solidity.

In terms of building materials, the new styles encouraged the abandonment of timber, plasterwork, and thatch, in favour of brick or stone, and tiles. The switch was strongly endorsed by local by-laws, intended to curb the risks of fire; and it was made possible by an increasing provision and abundance of coal for urban brick-kilns. Little wonder that Newcastle upon Tyne was one of the earliest towns to effect an extensive change to brick buildings. Nuances of fashion in town housing themselves changed with time. The more ornate 'Queen Anne' houses made fashionable by Wren in the early eighteenth century gave way to the simple classicism of the Palladian school in later decades. By that time, pattern books were available for even the humblest jobbing builder. It was, above all, the adaptability of the style into terrace form that demonstrated that desirable residences could be created even at high urban densities. In particular, the brick-built London terrace house, with its narrow street frontage, porticoed doorway, carefully proportioned sash-windows, and high parapet wall concealing the roof line, came to stand as prototype. Such developments helped to strengthen traditional English preferences for the house, rather than the flat or apartment, as the staple unit of accommodation, even in the high densities and crowded environments of the city centre.

Many towns were transfigured in the course of the eighteenth century. Bath, although unique in its social configuration, was by no means a solitary case. Indeed, rather the contrary: the extent of fashionable townscaping, smart housing, and dextrous refronting of older buildings was apparent in many towns. In the very early eighteenth century, for example, Bristol Corporation itself had laid out the huge Queen Square (1700–27), leasing the surrounding building plots for fashionable residences; and they were rapidly emulated by private developers, with St. James's Square (1707–16) and Orchard Street, quickly and fashionably renamed Orchard Square. In the same decades the rebuilding of parts of central Warwick, after a major fire in 1694, made it for a while the cynosure for new standards in town building, under the supervision of a specially instituted local Rebuilding Commission. Its elegant surroundings confirmed its role as a social centre of the minor gentry; and Warwick fostered a number of locally distinguished architects, one of whom, Francis Hiorn, became thrice mayor in the later eighteenth century. Another unusually extensive rebuilding also followed a major conflagration at Blandford Forum in 1731: the Bastard brothers remodelled the small but growing township on spacious lines, incorporating a new church and civic buildings. It showed how widely diffused were the new styles and aspirations.

Some places achieved an elegance of ambiance without much conscious direction or new road building. Eighteenth-century Stamford reconstructed and embellished its dignified stone housing in the new styles as adapted by local craftsmen. It consolidated its role as a social centre for the gentry and a 'thoroughfare town' astride the busy Great North Road. But in many places the special Improvement Commissions began to turn their attention specifically to widening streets and regulating house frontages, especially in the city centres. Some of the London commissioners were among the most active here; but provincial commissions also responded with zest. In later eighteenth-century Oxford the local commission in 1771 instituted a wholesale street clearance programme, supported with approval by the Revd Edward Tatham, later Rector of Lincoln College, who sniffed that: 'Our forefathers seem to have consulted petty Convenience and monastic Reclusiveness, while they neglected that Uniformity of Design, which is indispensable to Magnificence, and that Elegance of Approach, which adds half the Delight.'

Even in less glamorous towns, many expanding sites were developed with at least a modicum of regulation and estate-planning, notably in the case of aristocratic estate-development. There were very few real shanty towns, of impermanent structures built by squatters. The scale of urban growth in eighteenth-century England was not sufficient to overwhelm the building industry, while the pressures of demand tempted many estates into the development market. Elements of planning often included the layout of main streets, the promotion of some focal points, the regulation of building frontages, and, sometimes, the provision of sewers. The London Building Acts (1774) were important milestones in that process. A detailed study of the building of England's provincial towns[2] has shown that these procedures were widely followed there – whether tenure of land was predominantly freehold or leasehold, and whether the initiative came from the local corporation or from private landowners. The uniformity of plan was much influenced by the size of the estate. Places with many small plots (such as Leeds, Nottingham, Hull) tended to grow in a more intricate jigsaw than did those with a few larger ones. In Birmingham and parts of Manchester, for example, large private estates were attracted into the market: they were surveyed and laid out by the owners, and then conveyed on building leases to builders and developers, many of whom sub-let part of the property in turn. While in Liverpool one of the most sizeable promotions in any eighteenth-century English town was instigated by the Corporation, on large parts of the huge 1,000-acre Corporation Estate (on long lease from the Earls of Sefton and purchased outright in 1776). Much of the detailed development was left to the subsidiary building lessees, but the Corporation's Committee of View retained some general supervision and began to take a keener interest in the quality of housing and amenities provided from the 1780s onwards: a General Surveyor was appointed in 1786, with his own salaried staff. In Newcastle the Corporation had made a similar appointment as early as 1746.

Planning was, however, partial and incomplete. Very few urban communities in eighteenth-century England were completely planned from the start; and they certainly were not devised for formal reasons of planning policy (in the manner of later garden cities, or 'overspill' new towns). Here there was a striking contrast with continental Europe, which saw some noted examples of formal town planning (often for military or political reasons). The motives for town foundation in eighteenth-century England tended to be prosaic; and their groundplan was devised accordingly, often in a version of the simple gridiron street pattern. Undoubtedly the most successful example of these was the novel promotion of Whitehaven by the Lowthers, on one large estate. Their original plans incorporated a network of houses with backyards and gardens, on a gridiron of narrow streets, with the establishment of some communal institutions (an Anglican church, a chapel, a school). In the long term, however, population growth blurred the merits of the scheme, particularly as densities rose; but it showed that the promotion of a new town could work when it discovered an adequate economic base. It was not surprising that a neighbouring landowner attempted to emulate the Lowthers by building a grid of houses and a dock on his estate at Maryport (1749); nor that he found it very difficult in fact to replicate Whitehaven's unusual commercial role. In many ways, however, although workaday Whitehaven never achieved anything like the great fame of Bath in the conscious history of English town-planning, it was a forerunner of many later plans for new commercial and industrial estates.

Most widespread of all conscious adaptations to the immediacies of town life was the growing formalization of provision for staple amenities: lighting, paving, cleansing, water supply. By 1715 legislation (confirmed in 1736) had empowered Justices of the Peace to appoint scavengers to clean the streets, in cities and market towns where that was not being done. And Samuel Roberts has left an amusing account of the entertainment to be derived from communal efforts at cleansing in later eighteenth-century Sheffield. Every quarter, the water from Barker's

Pool was sent flooding through the streets, at a designated time, and people came out to wash their houses, streets, and animals, in a 'constant Babel-like uproar'. The array of formal institutions and authorities commissioned in the eighteenth-century towns for 'improvements' has already been noted. It indicated that these services were thought of increasingly as essentials to be collectively organized for the community rather than as amenities to be provided by the private citizens. Here concern for health, environment, safety, utility, and economic efficiency all overlapped and coincided. 'A general spirit prevails', asserted an onlooker in London in 1771, 'for correcting ancient errors and establishing new improvements' – the very concept was redolent of innovation and confidence.

Intention, needless to say, should not be confused with efficiency of implementation. The application of these 'improvements' was often patchy and partial. As noted elsewhere, the supply of water, for example, could be a highly contentious issue between neighbouring urban communities. Some towns continued to experience difficulties in supply. It took much time and travail to devise fully efficient systems. This was particularly a problem in the case of street cleansing and refuse clearance. In some places the scavengers amassed the muck into huge and unfenced heaps by the roadside, which then waited days for collection. In many towns there were frequent complaints that the night-carts slopped their contents as they made their rounds to clear the privies. Everywhere there was great uncertainty as to legal responsibility for the yards, courts, and backland premises, that were off the public highway. In other words, then as now, expectations of 'improvement' were often raised more rapidly than they could be fulfilled.

Townscape design, urban 'improvement', provision of basic utilities: the sum of these activities did not amount to a full planning tradition in the broadest sense. Even in terms of the minimum regulation of individual building standards, controls were only very patchily applied; few improvements were systematically available; and administrative structures were not geared to giving attention to an urban area as a whole. Nevertheless, these plans, both the prestigious and the prosaic, indicated the diffusion of a conscious response to the development of an urbanizing environment – and a growing preoccupation with its 'problems'.

For, at the same time, the accelerating pace of urban growth was creating an urban reality that was very complex, very disorderly, and very crowded – and that on an unprecedented scale. The fastest-expanding industrial centres and great sea ports, in particular, were dramatic exemplars of the problems inherent in mass living on a large scale –

becoming, with some notorious parts of London, the 'shock cities' of their generation. They were cramped, crowded, polluted, unhealthy, and often ugly. Their inhabitants lived in dwellings later defined emphatically as defective – cellars, back-to-back houses – and next to polluting factories. Yet this urban growth also sprang from the same processes as did the more elegant growth of the resorts, and reflected some of the crucial weaknesses, as well as the strengths, in eighteenth-century attitudes to town building. In particular, the absence of general planning provisions, for example relating to density of habitation, land-use zoning, and control of pollution, meant that while some areas flourished, others did the reverse – although formal planning cannot be said to have solved all these problems subsequently. Some of the poorest of the working-class districts accumulated a variety of environmental problems – thereby accentuating the pressures for greater residential segregation.

The crowded and noxious industrial 'Coketowns' of the early Industrial Revolution did not, therefore, represent a sudden forgetfulness of earlier good planning practice, as reproachful town-planning historians sometimes appear to imply. Patterns of urban growth did not even demonstrate a straightforward contrast between 'aristocratic' estate-planning on the one hand, and 'commercial' or 'industrial' *laissez-faire* on the other. Many peers, merchants, industrialists, and, indeed, municipal corporations, had a hand in estate promotion in many towns, while almost everywhere much of the actual development was carried out by local lessees – small builders, craftsmen, tradesmen. But the scale of urban growth placed immense strains upon these *ad hoc* procedures; just as some towns and areas within the towns showed the process at its best, others were less than ideal.

Some of the difficulties were practical ones. Schemes did not always work out as planned. Developers sometimes failed to gauge correctly the state of demand or the value of their location. The market for high-class residential property was necessarily limited, but as that was often thought to be the most lucrative form of development, it attracted most attention and thought. The interests of the main developer and his tenants might also differ. For example, in Liverpool a local surveyor and entrepreneur, Cuthbert Bisbrown, failed in 1773–4 to promote a stylish residential 'new town' on land leased from the Earl of Sefton at Toxteth Park. His problems stemmed to a large extent from weak drafting of the sub-leases, which enabled his tenants to cram high-density cheap housing on backland sites; as well as from the fact that he had been too optimistic about the state of middle-class demand in a not-so-fashionable area of town. Instead of the 'lofty Turrets' and 'spacious Fabric' that were promised in the poem that launched the scheme in the *Advertiser*, there sprang up a maze of 'close, gloomy courts' with cramped housing, off mean, narrow streets. Bisbrown himself went bankrupt in 1776.

Bisbrown's experience pointed to another key feature of the eighteenth-century *ad hoc* tradition of town building. While the economics of speculative development made spacious upper-class residential accommodation an attractive option in some towns, by the nature of things not all land could be developed successfully in that manner. An alternative option was to build cheap housing at high densities, to cater for mass demand from the growing working-class population. Small-scale developers, like Bisbrown's lessees, tended to adopt this course. There was no national framework of statutory requirements to stipulate minimum standards for such developments: no zoned densities, building regulations, drainage and road layout conventions, lighting and ventilation standards. Local by-laws intended to prevent 'nuisances' were imperfectly framed and enforced – and certainly not intended as a framework for urban growth. Hence eighteenth-century towns also saw the piecemeal promotion of areas of highly intensive settlement, in a maze of densely packed dwellings, around courts and off narrow streets and alleys, without systematic provision of public amenities and open spaces.

It was a mode of development that followed from, and reinforced, existing patterns of high-density living in the nucleated town centres. Indeed, the first impact of rapid population expansion was often to promote infilling of the backland of properties fronting on the established street pattern, long before the built-up area began to expand outwards into new areas. As has been pointed out in the case of Leeds,[3] a considerable expansion of population (to over 16,000) was initially accommodated by infilling within the existing confines of the old centre, which had housed less than half that number a century earlier. No entirely new street of houses was built in Leeds between 1634 and 1767; and the subsequent development of high-density plots of back-to-back housing was a continuation of existing patterns of high-density, tightly packed housing. The same experience was found in the very much smaller centre of Kendal. A century's population growth intensified settlement on existing street patterns, long before there was a physical expansion of the urban terrain. Even the notorious case of Nottingham, one of the most densely crowded of all town centres by the end of the eighteenth century, sprang from the same tradition of intensification rather than extension of the urban fabric. Its problems were certainly accentuated by the fact that it was confined by a ring of unenclosed common fields; but growth outside the town centre was not completely impossible, and had in fact begun to some extent before the common fields were eventually enclosed. Only gradually did the multiplication of such densely packed developments reveal the full dimensions of the health and environmental problems thus created, and thereby promote the case for planning to avert the worst, as well as to produce the best.

In particular, there was in the eighteenth century only a relatively muffled debate over the quality of working-class housing. John Wood the Younger was being consciously innovatory when he produced *A Series of Plans for Habitations of the Labourer... adapted as well to Towns as to the Country* (1781, and many later editions). His designs were for one- to four-roomed housing; his most radical suggestion that each dwelling should have its own privy. But the major changes in urban working-class housing in the eighteenth century were not so much in design as in the use of new building materials. Lath and timberwork housing began to be replaced by brick dwellings, even if often 'jerry-built' with inferior materials (as in the 1790s). There was, however, criticism of some forms of housing. For example, the damp and unhealthy cellar-dwellings found in Liverpool and Manchester had already achieved notoriety. The early back-to-back houses, on the other hand, which were constructed on some scale in the northern and Midland industrial towns from the 1780s onwards, did not attract much initial controversy. Often solidly built, they extended the tradition of 'blind-back' and infill courtyard dwellings. These occurred on a large scale in Nottingham, for example, with its highly fragmented pattern of small units of property. In Leeds some of the earliest new plots of back-to-backs were constructed for their own artisan occupants, via the agency of their building societies. As housing, in other words, the back-to-backs were not thought of, in the first instance, as a degenerated form of development. Some observers were prepared to praise the style of housing for its warmth; and again, it permitted, even at high density, each family to have its own front door at ground-floor level – in very faint echo of the grand style.

In general, it seems that new units of housing in the expanding towns were supplied at a rate broadly equivalent to the overall growth of the urban population: Table XIV, showing the mean number of inhabitants per occupied house, as recorded in eighteenth-century enumerations, demonstrates that in many cases the figure remained relatively stable before 1801. The number of people per house actually fell in some towns in the later eighteenth century; although it did rise more noticeably in crowded cities like Liverpool, where land values were high, or in places of sudden growth. The much smaller Carlisle in the later eighteenth century saw very rapid Irish and Scottish immigration, in response to the expansion of cotton-spinning there. That placed exceptional pressure upon housing supply, which contributed to cultural tensions. Too much significance cannot, however, be accorded to the figures in Table XIV, as definitions of what constituted a 'house' were often imprecise and, of course, information about their mean number of habitable rooms is lacking. But it seems that the expanding urban populations were being accommodated in a multiplication of small dwellings rather than by a subdivision of larger properties into multi-occupied housing. It was, however, the crowding and under-servicing of whole areas of the towns, as much as their individual housing, that came to constitute the 'problem'. The existence of the 'slums' certainly predated their name, which was given to them in the 1820s and referred, of course, to the whole environment of inadequate housing and poor services.

With time, attention began to be turned increasingly to the nature of the urban environment as a whole. An additional hazard was posed by the unprecedented expansion of industrial works and domestic heating that depended on the burning of coal. That was especially a problem in some of the major manufacturing towns and in the ports with substantial refineries. Already, by the 1720s, the glassworks of Newcastle upon Tyne and the salt-pans at Shields had made the area 'not the pleasantest place in the world to live in'. These problems were augmented by expansion and the effects of other industrial waste and pollution. There were no clearly developed land-use conventions or effective zoning to move noxious industry away from residential accommodation. Traditional regulations to control the location of urban tanneries and slaughter-houses were quite inadequate to deal with the new scale of problems. Some landowners of fashionable estates did, it is true, attempt to impose covenants to exclude all industrial and commercial users from a few privileged areas. But these were the clauses that proved most difficult to enforce on a large scale. Indeed, it was a difficult distinction to make throughout the town, when much production was carried out in the home or in a backyard workshop. Some work processes had always necessitated a specialized venue (shipbuilding being one obvious example), but many other manufacturing jobs were still domestic in their location. The concept of the specialized work environment emerged only very gradually.

It therefore seemed natural when factories were developed, as well as advantageous for transport, to site them cheek-by-jowl with housing. The strength of that attitude was demonstrated when some master manufacturers initially built grand residences close to their industrial plants. The eventual departure of their descendants, however, indicated that it was easier for one affluent family to escape the consequences than it was for an entire industrial workforce. There was little initial understanding of either the medical or the environmental implications of pollution on a large scale. Indeed, it took some time for the cumulative effect of blight

Table XIV Mean number of inhabitants per house, from eighteenth-century urban enumerations and 1801 census*

Towns** ranked by 1801 population size	Date	Enumerated population	Mean inhab. per occupied house (empty houses excluded)	Population	Mean inhab. per occupied house (empty houses excluded)
		Enumeration		*1801 Census*	
Manchester	1773	27,246	6.4	84,020	6.7
„ (excl. Salford)	1788	42,821	7.2		
Liverpool	1773	34,407	5.8		
	1790	55,732	6.8	77,653	6.8
Birmingham (town)†	1750	23,688	5.7		
	1770	30,804	5.1	73,670	5.1
Norwich	1752	36,169	5.1	36,832	4.6
Sheffield (town)†	1788	26,538	4.5	31,314	4.8
Nottingham	1739	9,890	5.5		
	1779	17,584	5.5	28,861	5.8
Coventry	1748	12,117	5.9	16,034	5.5
Chester	1774	14,713	5.1	15,052	4.8
Shrewsbury	1750	8,141	4.3	14,739	5.3
Wolverhampton	1751	7,434	5.2	12,565	5.4
Bolton (town)†	1773	4,568	4.8	12,549	5.1
Worcester	1779	13,104	5.4	11,352	5.1
Derby	1791	8,563	5.2	10,832	5.1
Warrington	1781	8,791	4.5	10,567	4.7
Carlisle	1780	6,299	7.1		
	1796	8,716	6.7	10,221	7.8
Maidstone	1781	5,650	5.1	8,027	6.0
Northampton	1746	5,136	4.7	7,020	5.3
Taunton	1790	5,472	4.9	5,794	5.1
Chesterfield	1783	3,335	4.3		
	1788	3,626	4.4		
	1791	3,987	4.6	4,267	4.8

* As shown in 1801 Census and those enumerations that also recorded housing.
** Partial listings, of single parishes only, have been excluded.
† Old town only, i.e. not including whole conurbation.

to become apparent, as it did to document the links between health and environment. Much early industrial pollution was therefore considered to be an unpleasant 'nuisance' but not actually harmful. For example, Dr Moss's *Familiar Medical Survey of Liverpool* (1784) displayed a determined optimism about the city's noxious refineries. The effluvium from the salt-works covered its neighbourhood in 'Soot and Obscurity' but was harmful only if inhaled in excess, he reported; the smell of the oilhouse was 'in the highest Degree nauseous' but not inimical to health; nor did the fumes from the tan-yards or soap manufactory constitute a hazard; while the sulphur from the copper refinery was not dangerous, although he agreed it did produce 'a disagreeable and unpleasing Effect of an incessant Stream of Smoke'. These were, he concluded, but *'occasional Circumstances'*, and not *'immediately, generally,* and in a *material Manner* injurious to the health'. Liverpool's high incidence of chest infections (asthma, coughs, consumption) he attributed to other factors – including, rather conventionally, the city's variable climate and its breezy environment.

Such complacency and ignorance were widely shared, as was the evident reluctance to press criticisms on environmental grounds alone. By-laws against creating nuisances were weak weapons in the face of the might of industrial development, especially when local authorities themselves were often composed of industrialists. A number of industrial and refinery towns were therefore gradually blighted by acrid smoke, stunted vegetation, blackened buildings, polluted rivers, industrial waste. The forges of the metal-manufacturing towns and kilns of the Potteries were among the worst offenders; but glass-, copper- and chemical-works, with their poisonous wastes, also had devastating effects, especially when one successful factory was followed by imitators. The process was, however, slow and difficult to detect in advance. St. Helens in Lancashire, later celebrated for its blighted landscape, was still in 1797 described, without irony, as 'a very neat, pretty country Town': and that was some twenty-five years after the foundation of the first huge Ravenhead plate-glass works (1773) and the first large copper refinery (1780). The impact of industrial blight was therefore accepted almost as a force of nature: insidious, ubiquitous. Indeed, in the history of town planning a marked time-lag can be seen in the eventual adoption of formal intervention to improve the urban environment as a whole: legislation on sanitation and housing standards, in the nineteenth century, considerably preceded legislation on land-use zoning and environmental improvements, in the twentieth century.

In the eighteenth century, then, the powerful and protean identity of the town was declaring itself ever more insistently: the bright lights, the crowds, the bustle, the pickpockets at the market, the sense of many things going on. In London, a visitor 'at first imagined that some great Assembly was just dismissed, and wanted to stand aside till the Multitude had passed; but this human Tide continues to flow, without Interruption or Abatement, from morn, till Night.' In lesser Lincoln, too, the Dean's wife found life was busier than she had at first supposed. She recorded in 1771 that 'in the Course of this Week, we have been asked to four

Dinners, two Assemblys, a Play, and a Concert, not to mention Company we have had at our own House.'

.The towns were noisy: the sounds of people, horses, traffic, the tapping of wooden pattens on cobbles, street cries, ballads and 'town music', clocks striking, church bells. In the greatest towns the practice of tolling a passing bell for every death had eventually to be stopped: its too frequent occurrence caused 'a *real* Disturbance to the Sick, Nervous, and Hypochondriack'. There were also the sounds of work: the construction and demolition of housing, the click-clack of the loom, the resonance of the forge, the clamour of the docks and shipyards, the intent hum of the market place.

The towns were noxious and smelly: from rubbish and dung in the streets, plus slops from scavengers' carts and midden heaps; from privies and ash-pits in backyards, and closets at the foot of indoor stairwells; from industrial and human effluents in rivers, and in drainage ditches and streams; from the smoke of coal-fires, kilns, and forges; and from the dank odours from overcrowded urban graveyards. Even in an elegant town house in St. James's, London, Jonathan Swift (who was hypersensitive on a subject that was rarely referred to) detected 'a thousand stinks in it'.

The towns even felt distinctive under foot: their street surfaces were paved, cobbled, or hard packed by countless passers-by. As walking was a favoured entertainment as well as the staple means of transport, complaints at sore feet were common. The cobbles of Kendal were 'so slippery that the inhabitants acquired a catch in their walk as if on ice'; while *A Walk through Leicester* (1804) apologized to its readers for taking them over the 'rough forest stones of our streets'. Sight, sound, smell, touch; even the after-taste of smog in the lungs: the towns' impact was all-pervasive.

Conclusion

The dynamism of expansion brought an increasing confidence and self-consciousness to urban society in the course of the eighteenth century. It is true that there was no distinctive appellation for English townsmen or their middle class that could compare with the flavour of the French 'bourgeois'. The term 'cit' (pronounced as in the first syllable of 'citizen') had some continued currency, usually with contemptuous overtones. But the urban experience in England proved too pervasive in a mobile society to gain an exclusive nomenclature.

The towns had become pace-setters for rural England. 'Is there a Creature in the whole Country but Ourselves that does not take a Trip to Town now and then to rub the Rust off a little?' enquired a plaintive Goldsmithian heroine in 1773. The very words 'civility' and 'urbanity', which originally referred to the characteristics of life in towns, also acquired, in the course of the seventeenth and eighteenth centuries, specific connotations of politeness, suavity, and social polish. The editor of the *Gentleman's Magazine,* founded in London in 1731, adroitly awarded himself the dual pseudonym of 'Sylvanus Urban', to suggest a metropolitan as well as pastoral sensibility. And that epistolary advocate of polished manners, the Earl of Chesterfield, urged his son in 1739 to cultivate the social graces in order to avoid the fate of being mistaken for 'a mean Fellow, or a country Bumpkin, [who] is ashamed when he comes into good Company'.

The inhabitants of the towns showed much interest in their own evolving traditions. The local town history and guide developed in this period into a successful and distinctive literary genre. Few large towns lacked such a compilation by the end of the eighteenth century – the relatively enclosed societies of the dockyard towns and the diffused Pottery towns were the least well served in this respect. Some of these local histories contained little more than pious listings of antiquities, notable buildings, town worthies, and local 'great events'; yet many conveyed fresh and vivid impressions of the physical and social ambiance of the developing towns. The guides to the resorts in particular were explicitly propagandist for the urban way of life. Chroniclers of the non-incorporated towns were as eager as those of the ancient corporations to insist on their traditions. 'Though the town has a modern appearance,' wrote Hutton of Birmingham in 1781, 'there is reason to believe it of great antiquity,' tracing its history to the 'remote ages of the ancient Britons'. Whitaker in Manchester in 1771 had also traced the origins of Manchester back to pre-Roman times, when it was 'the British town of Mancunium . . . distinguished by the general appellation of *Mancenion* or the Place of Tents'. John Wood adopted the legend of Bath's foundation by King Bladud. So marked was the fashion for urban claims to antiquity that Deering found himself positively defiant, when he published in 1751 his careful researches into the history of *Nottinghamia Vetus et Nova*, which led him to strip it of 'a considerable number of chimerical Ages, during which the Town is supposed to have had its pretended Being'.

A number of these publications also doubled as handbooks and guides to the contemporary towns, detailing postal and transport services, the dates of markets and fairs, the names of banks, the nature of the local government, and a miscellany of topical data. As the towns grew in size and complexity, the need to formalize and standardize useful information in accessible works of reference increased. The histories and guides were supplemented by the new specialist town directories, which often contained detailed descriptions of the town as well as listings of names, addresses, and occupations of leading tradesmen and citizens. The first of these publications was a list of London merchants, in 1677. It was not emulated until 1732, when *The Directory; or List of Principal Trades in London* was published by Henry Kent; but by 1800 there had ensued at least thirty such works for metropolitan London alone, many of them in numerous editions. The leading provincial towns followed suit, with local directories for Birmingham (1763), Liverpool (1766), Manchester (1772), Sheffield (1774), and Bristol (1775). In 1784 Thomas Minshull declared that he 'almost blushed' that Shrewsbury lacked such a useful compilation, before proceeding to supply one himself in 1786. By 1800 most of the largest towns had their own directories, and much of this local data was aggregated into the first national collections, with Bailey's *British Directory* in 1781 and Barfoot and Wilkes's *Universal British Directory of Trade and Commerce* in 1790. Many trades and services also acquired their own specialist directories and handbooks, as the growing range of information to be absorbed and assimilated suggested the need for categorization and classification.

Such publications helped to service the workings of complex urban societies. The information network could no longer rely upon word-of-mouth alone. Strangers and all those journeying across towns needed systematic guidance. For the same reasons, most eighteenth-century towns began the practice of standardizing and signposting street names, and numbering the houses. By the 1760s London directories were listing house numbers as well as streets, to aid identification; and the practice spread, though it was some time before enumeration was carried out fully and systematically. A degree of self-conscious ordering of the environment accompanied the growth of large-scale urbanism. The rhythm of life in towns implied an awareness of man-made timekeeping. Clocks and timetables were its hallmark. Conscious effort was needed to co-ordinate and synchronize the diverse patterns of work, leisure, travel. 'God made the Country, and Man made the Town', ran Cowper's celebrated dictum. The proposition was philosophically dubious but it expressed a profoundly felt belief about the nature of towns.

As they were thought of as man-made, so the towns were open to change and adaptation. The proliferation of debate about their merits and problems sprang from and expressed the fusion of opportunity with anxiety. Their variety of relationships and roles at once attracted attention, and defied easy generalization. Many observations could be made about the towns, and be as promptly disagreed with. Debate and contradiction were part of an urban experience. Local songs of praise for the town, such as 'Shrewsbury for Me', or 'Sheffield's a Wonderful Town, O', could easily be inverted into songs of satire and criticism with a change of inflection and tone. Such ballads were very popular in the eighteenth-century towns – and were used both affectionately and sardonically. Indeed, humour, wit, satire, paradox were very characteristic modes of expression in urban societies. They assumed the existence of a knowing audience, while simultaneously they were not averse to laughing at the confusion of the country cousin who failed to get the joke.

Even the poets' idealization of the physical countryside – often carried out from the safety of the towns, as satirists enjoyed pointing out – did not generally extend to much urban enthusiam for the inhabitants of rural England. Although there were many criticisms of the towns, there was nothing like the virulence of the anti-urbanism found in some intellectual traditions (as in nineteenth-century America, for example). English towns were accepted – and also seen as open to change. Their achievement was a positive one. With all their perplexities and potentialities, they increasingly became pace-setters for the wider society. Their influence was oblique in some respects, direct and unmistakable in others; but their collective impact exercised a profound gravitational force. The towns of modern Babylon had arrived.

Notes

Chapter 1

1. See, for example, a summary of the debate in E. Jones, *Towns and Cities* (Oxford, 1966), pp. 1–12.
2. Other estimates differ in detail but strongly confirm the general trend of these figures. Compare C. W. Chalklin, *The Provincial Towns of Georgian England: A Study of the Building Process, 1740–1820* (London, 1974), pp. 3–54, and C. M. Law, 'Some Notes on the Urban Population of England and Wales in the Eighteenth Century', *Local Historian*, x (1972), 13–26.
3. Estimates of the total size of the country's population also differ. Some adopt higher overall totals of 6 million inhabitants in 1700 and 6.5 million in 1750. In that case the pace of urban growth in the first half of the century is rendered more impressive: from 16 per cent in 1700 to 21.5 per cent in 1750. But there are grounds for thinking that those estimates (particularly of the total population in 1700) are too high. See the calculations in E. A. Wrigley and R. S. Schofield, *The Population History of England, 1541–1871: A Reconstruction* (London, 1981), esp. pp. 207–10, 577, 587, showing a population (for England only) of a little over 5 million in 1700, and close to 6 million in 1750.
4. P. Clark and P. Slack, *English Towns in Transition, 1500–1700* (Oxford, 1976), esp. pp. 33–45.

Chapter 2

1. D. Davis, *A History of Shopping* (London, 1966); and S. I. Mitchell, 'Urban Markets and Retail Distribution, 1730–1815, with particular reference to Macclesfield, Stockport, and Chester' (unpublished D. Phil. thesis, University of Oxford, 1974).
2. See A. Everitt, 'The Marketing of Agricultural Produce' in J. Thirsk (ed.), *The Agrarian History of England and Wales. Vol. IV: 1500–1640* (Cambridge, 1967), pp. 480–6; and idem, 'The Food Market of the English Town, 1660–1760', *Third International Economic History Conference: Munich, 1965* (Paris, 1968).

3. A. J. Reiss, 'Functional Specialization of Cities' in P. K. Hatt and A. J. Reiss (eds.), *Cities and Society* (New York and London, 1951), pp. 555–75.

Chapter 3

1. The figures are imperfect, but internally consistent enough to furnish a general guide: see R. Davis, *The Rise of the English Shipping Industry in the Seventeenth and Eighteenth Centuries* (London, 1962), esp. pp. 403–6.
2. Local customs were collected in twenty-one regional centres or 'headports', while national accounts were compiled in the ledgers of the Inspectors-General of Imports and Exports. Trade with Scotland (after the Union in 1707) was not considered as foreign trade, while that with Ireland was. See G. N. Clark, *Guide to English Commercial Statistics, 1696–1782* (London, 1938), esp. pp. 6–11, 40–1, 52–6.
3. Eighteenth-century trade statistics in general provide a better guide to the volume of trade than to its value, as customs valuations were calculated at fixed official rates that did not reflect variations in actual marketability: see Clark, op. cit., pp. 33–42; and E. B. Schumpeter, *English Overseas Trade Statistics, 1696–1808* (Oxford, 1960), pp. 2–5.

Chapter 4

1. J. H. Plumb, *The Commercialization of Leisure in Eighteenth-Century England* (Reading, 1973).

Chapter 5

1. By 1801 the 'greater' conurbation of London included not only the Cities of London and Westminster, but also a number of Middlesex parishes whose population returns were collected in the London 'Bills of Mortality', plus the Borough of Southwark, and adjacent suburbs in Lambeth, Camberwell, Bermondsey, and Rotherhithe. See S. J. Neele, *A New Plan of London, Twenty-Nine Miles in Circumference* (1797), and M. D. George, *London Life in the Eighteenth Century* (1925; paperback reprint 1966), pp. 1, 73–8, 397.
2. See figures in Tables I and II. There are margins for disagreement over the precise size of London, in population terms, but all estimates agree that, in proportionate terms, its share of the total population was not substantially increasing in the course of the eighteenth century. George, op.cit., pp. 37–8, 319, gives a higher estimate for the London population in 1700, so that London's proportionate share of the country's population would have fallen between 1700 and 1750. Most authorities, however, accept a lower figure for 1700: see E. A. Wrigley,

'London's Importance in Changing England's Society and Economy', *Past and Present*, no. 37 (1967), 44.

For 1801, most historians compute figures of between 900,000 and 1,000,000 inhabitants for the London conurbation: the lowest calculation is 864,845 (or 9.73 per cent of the total), the highest is 1,117,000 for 'greater London' including all Middlesex (or 12.6 per cent of the total population of England and Wales). See A. F. Weber, *The Growth of Cities in the Nineteenth Century* (New York, 1899), pp. 46–7, and B. R. Mitchell and P. Deane, *Abstract of British Historical Statistics* (Cambridge, 1971), pp. 19–20.

Chapter 6

1. E. P. Thompson, 'Time, Work-Discipline, and Industrial Capitalism', *Past and Present*, no. 38 (1967), 56–97; and also urban data in J. Rule, *The Experience of Labour in Eighteenth-Century Industry* (London, 1981).

2. Contrast with the typology of the 'new towns' of the sixteenth and seventeenth centuries, as suggested by P. Clark and P. Slack, *English Towns in Transition, 1500–1700* (Oxford, 1976).

3. M. J. Daunton, 'Towns and Economic Growth in Eighteenth-Century England' in P. Abrams and E. A. Wrigley (eds.), *Towns in Societies: Essays in Economic History and Historical Sociology* (Cambridge, 1978), pp. 245–77.

Chapter 7

1. E. J. Buckatzsch, 'The Places of Origin of a Group of Immigrants into Sheffield, 1624–1799', *Economic History Review*, 2nd series, II (1950), 303–6. Buckatzsch's proportionate calculations of distance travelled are often quoted; but it should be noted that they do *not* refer to all cutlers apprenticed in Sheffied but only to the non-Sheffield immigrant apprentices, who were a small minority of the total numbers joining the industry.

2. At the time of the first census in 1801 parish totals of baptisms and burials were collected for selected years during the eighteenth century, but these so-called 'Parish Register Abstracts' were not a very reliable compilation – and by chance happened also to cover years when mortality was unusually high. For problems in this source material generally, see M. W. Flinn, *British Population Growth, 1700–1850* (London, 1970).

3. See, for example, calculations of Nottingham's birth and death rates by comparison with population totals, in J. D. Chambers, 'Popula-

tion Change in a Provincial Town: Nottingham, 1700–1800' in L. S. Pressnell (ed.), *Studies in the Industrial Revolution* (London, 1960). Since urban birth rates themselves fluctuated considerably, there are major difficulties in reversing the exercise and attempting to calculate urban populations from their baptismal rates, applying a standard multiplier to very 'non-standard' figures.

4. There has been considerable discussion about the extent of burial under-registration. But, if even the most generous adjustment rates that have been proposed are applied to these urban estimates for 1801, the corrected death rates in Leeds, Nottingham, and Exeter still do not catch up with the corrected birth rates. (Only in Norwich did the picture differ and its population experience in the 1790s was anyway unusual – with people then moving from the city.) See generally J. T. Krause, 'The Changing Adequacy of English Registration, 1690–1837' in D. Glass and D. E. C. Eversley (eds.), *Population in History* (London, 1965); and comments in Flinn, op. cit., pp. 27–8.

5. The *Lancet's* calculations constitute much of the basis for the very optimistic picture of improvements to London's health drawn by M. D. George, *London Life in the Eighteenth Century* (London, 1925; paperback ed. 1966).

Chapter 8

1. Cited in H. Perkin, *The Origins of Modern English Society, 1780–1880* (London, 1969), pp. 20–1.

2. R. G. Wilson, *Gentlemen Merchants: The Merchant Community in Leeds, 1700–1830* (Manchester, 1971), p. 20.

3. See, for example, J. M. Beattie, 'Crime and the Courts in Surrey, 1736–53' in J. S. Cockburn (ed.), *Crime in England, 1550–1800* (London, 1977), pp. 155–86, with breakdown of indictments for 'urban' and 'rural' Surrey parishes.

Chapter 10

1. L. Mumford, *The City in History: Its Origins, its Transformation, and its Prospects* (London, 1961; paerback edn. 1966), pp. 421–4.

2. C. W. Chalklin. *The Provincial Towns of Georgian England: A Study of the Building Process, 1740–1820* (London, 1974).

3. M. Beresford, 'The Making of a Townscape: Richard Paley in the East End of Leeds, 1771–1803' in C. W. Chalklin and M. A. Havinden (eds.), *Rural Change and Urban Growth, 1500–1800* (London, 1974), p. 282.

Select bibliography

General

P. Abrams and E. A. Wrigley (eds.), *Towns in Societies: Essays in Economic History and Historical Sociology* (Cambridge, 1978), esp. essays by Daunton and Wrigley.

P. Borsay, 'The English Urban Renaissance: The Development of Provincial Urban Culture, *c.* 1680–*c.* 1760', *Social History*, v (1977), 581–603.

C. W. Chalklin, *The Provincial Towns of Georgian England: A Study of the Building Process, 1740–1820* (London, 1974).

C. W. Chalklin and M. A. Havinden (eds.), *Rural Change and Urban Growth, 1500–1800: Essays in English Regional History* (London, 1974), esp. essays by Millward, Chalklin, Neale, Beresford.

P. Clark (ed.), *The Early Modern Town: A Reader* (London, 1976), esp. essays 8–14.

A. Everitt (ed.), *Perspectives in English Urban History* (London, 1973), esp. essays by Everitt and Whyman.

G. H. Martin and S. McIntyre (eds.), *A Bibliography of British and Irish Municipal History* (Leicester, 1972).

L. Mumford, *The City in History: Its Origins, its Transformation, and its Prospects* (London, 1961; paperback 1966).

M. Weber, *The City* (Glencoe, Ill., 1958; paperback 1966).

R. Williams, *The Country and the City* (London, 1973; paperback 1975).

Victoria County Histories:

Oxfordshire, IV: *City of Oxford* (1979).

Warwickshire, VII: *City of Birmingham* (1964); and VIII: *City of Coventry and Borough of Warwick* (1969).

Yorkshire: East Riding, I: *City of Kingston-upon-Hull* (1969); and *The City of York* (1961).

Chapter 1

P. Clark and P. Slack, *English Towns in Transition, 1500–1700* (Oxford, 1976).

D. V. Glass, *The Town and a Changing Civilisation* (London, 1935).

E. Jones, *Towns and Cities* (Oxford, 1966).

C. M. Law, 'Some Notes on the Urban Population of England and Wales in the Eighteenth Century', *Local Historian,* x (1972), 13–26.

R. L. Meier, *A Communications Theory of Urban Growth* (Boston, Mass., 1962).

C. A. Moser and W. Scott, *British Towns: A Statistical Study of their Social and Economic Differences* (London, 1961).

D. Read, *The English Provinces, c. 1760–1960: A Study in Influence* (London, 1964).

Chapter 2

W. Addison, *English Fairs and Markets* (London, 1953).

D. Davis, *A History of Shopping* (London, 1966).

A. Everitt, 'The Food Market of the English Town, 1660–1760', *Third International Economic History Conference: Munich, 1965* (Paris, 1968).

C. Gill, *History of Birmingham, Vol. I: Manor and Borough to 1865* (Oxford, 1952).

D. Hey, *The Rural Metal Workers of the Sheffield Region* (Leicester Occasional Papers, series II, v, 1972).

W. G. Hoskins, *Industry, Trade, and People in Exeter, 1688–1800* (Manchester, 1935).

W. G. Rimmer, 'The Industrial Profile of Leeds, 1740–1840', *Thoresby Society Miscellany, 14,* 1 (Leeds, 1968), 130–57.

M. B. Rowlands, *Masters and Men in the West Midland Metalware Trades before the Industrial Revolution* (Manchester, 1975).

R. B. Westerfield, *Middlemen in English Business, particularly between 1660 and 1760* (New Haven, 1915).

R. G. Wilson, *Gentlemen Merchants: The Merchant Community in Leeds, 1700–1830* (Manchester, 1971).

Chapter 3

D. C. Coleman, 'Naval Dockyards under the Later Stuarts', *Economic History Review,* 2nd series, vi (1953/4), 134–55.

R. Davis, *The Rise of the English Shipping Industry in the Seventeenth and Eighteenth Centuries* (London, 1962).

R. Davis, 'English Foreign Trade, 1770–74', *Economic History Review,* 2nd series, xv (1962), 285–303.

F. E. Hyde (ed.), *Liverpool and the Mersey: An Economic History of a Port, 1700–1970* (Newton Abbot, 1971).

G. Jackson, *Hull in the Eighteenth Century: A Study in Economic and Social History* (Oxford, 1972).

W. E. Minchinton (ed.), *The Trade of Bristol in the Eighteenth Century* (Bristol Record Society, xx, 1957).

J. Presnail, *Chatham: The Story of a Dockyard Town* (Chatham, 1952).

T. S. Willan, *The English Coasting Trade, 1600–1750* (Manchester, 1938).

J. E. Williams, 'Whitehaven in the Eighteenth Century', *Economic History Review*, 2nd series, viii (1955/6), 393–404.

Chapter 4

A. Barbeau, *Life and Letters at Bath in the Eighteenth Century* (London, 1904).

D. Gadd, *Georgian Summer: Bath in the Eighteenth Century* (Bath, 1971).

E. W. Gilbert, *Brighton: Old Ocean's Bauble* (London, 1954).

L. Melville, *Society at Royal Tunbridge Wells in the Eighteenth Century and After* (London, 1912).

R. S. Neale, *Bath: A Social History, 1680–1850* (London, 1981).

J. A. R. Pimlott, *The Englishman's Holiday: A Social History* (London, 1947; reprinted 1976).

J. H. Plumb, *The Commercialisation of Leisure in Eighteenth-Century England* (Reading, 1973).

T. B. Veblen, *The Theory of the Leisure Class* (New York, 1899; many reprints).

Chapter 5

J. G. Broodbank, *History of the Port of London* (London, 1921).

M. Byrd, *London Transformed: Images of the City in the Eighteenth Century* (New Haven, 1978).

E. Beresford Chancellor, *The Eighteenth Century in London: An Account of its Social Life and Arts* (London, 1920).

M. D. George, *London Life in the Eighteenth Century* (London, 1925; paperback ed. 1966).

D. J. Olsen, *Town Planning in London: The Eighteenth and Nineteenth Centuries* (New Haven, 1964).

S. E. Rasmussen, *London, the Unique City* (Copenhagen, 1934; Eng. trans. 1937).

G. Rudé, *Hanoverian London, 1714–1808* (London, 1971).

J. Summerson, *Georgian London* (London, 1945; paperback 1962).

Chapter 6

M. A. Bienefeld, *Working Hours in British Industry: An Economic History* (London, 1972).

M. E. Falkus and E. L. Jones, 'Urban Improvement and the English

Economy in the Seventeenth and Eighteenth Centuries', *Research in Economic History*, iv (1979), 193–233.

J. D. Gould, *Economic Growth in History: Survey and Analysis* (London, 1972).

J. R. Kellett, 'The Breakdown of Gild and Corporation Control over the Handicraft and Retail Trade in London', *Economic History Review*, 2nd series, x (1958), 381–94.

T. G. McGee, *The Urbanisation Process in the Third World: Explorations in Search of a Theory* (London, 1971).

P. Mathias, *The First Industrial Nation: An Economic History of Britain, 1700–1914* (London, 1969).

E. P. Thompson, 'Time, Work-Discipline, and Industrial Capitalism', *Past and Present*, no. 38 (1967), 56–97.

Chapter 7

F. Beckwith, 'The Population of Leeds during the Industrial Revolution', *Thoresby Society Miscellany*, *12*, xli (Leeds, 1954), 118–96.

E. J. Buckatzsch, 'The Places of Origin of a Group of Immigrants into Sheffield, 1624–1799', *Economic History Review*, 2nd series, ii (1950), 303–6.

J. D. Chambers, 'Population Change in a Provincial Town: Nottingham, 1700–1800' in L. S. Pressnell (ed.), *Studies in the Industrial Revolution* (London, 1960).

C. Creighton, *A History of Epidemics in Britain* (Cambridge, 1891–4; revised edn Cambridge, 1965).

M. W. Flinn, *British Population Growth, 1700–1850* (London, 1970).

R. Mols, *Introduction à la Démographie Historique des Villes d'Europe du XIVe au XVIIIe Siècle* (Louvain, 1954–6).

R. A. Pelham, 'The Immigrant Population of Birmingham, 1686–1726', *Trans. Birmingham Archaeological Soc. for 1937*, lxi (1940), 45–80.

R. Pickard, *The Population and Epidemics of Exeter in Pre-Census Times* (Exeter, 1947).

E. A. Wrigley and R. S. Schofield, *The Population History of England, 1541–1871: A Reconstruction* (Cambridge, 1981).

Chapter 8

C. R. Dobson, *Masters and Journeymen: A Prehistory of Industrial Relations, 1717–1800* (London, 1980).

A. D. Gilbert, *Religion and Society in Industrial England: Church, Chapel and Social Change, 1740–1914* (London, 1976).

J. L. and B. Hammond, *The Skilled Labourer* (London, 1919; reissued 1979).

J. J. Hecht, *The Domestic Servant Class in Eighteenth-Century England* (London, 1956; reprinted 1979).

J. W. F. Hill, *Georgian Lincoln* (Cambridge, 1966).

J. Money, *Experience and Identity: Birmingham and the West Midlands, 1760–1800* (Manchester, 1977).

N. Rogers, 'Money, Land, and Lineage: The Big Bourgeoisie of Hanoverian London', *Social History*, iv (1979), 437–54.

J. Rule, *The Experience of Labour in Eighteenth-Century Industry* (London, 1981).

G. Simmel, 'Metropolis and Mental Life' in K. H. Wolff (ed.), *The Sociology of Georg Simmel* (Glencoe, Ill., 1964).

L. Stone, *The Family, Sex, and Marriage in England, 1500–1800* (London, 1977; abridged edn 1979).

A. J. Taylor (ed.), *The Standard of Living in Britain in the Industrial Revolution* (London, 1975).

R. F. Wearmouth, *Methodism and the Common People of the Eighteenth Century* (London, 1945).

Chapter 9

J. Cannon, *Parliamentary Reform, 1640–1832* (Cambridge, 1973).

A. Goodwin, *The Friends of Liberty: The English Democratic Movement in the Age of the French Revolution* (London, 1979).

R. W. Greaves, *The Corporation of Leicester, 1689–1836* (Oxford, 1939).

A. Redford, *The History of Local Government in Manchester. Vol. I: Manor and Township* (London, 1939).

N. Rogers, 'Popular Protest in Early Hanoverian London', *Past and Present*, no. 79 (1978), 70–100.

W. J. Shelton, *English Hunger and Industrial Disorders: A Study of Social Conflict during the First Decade of George III's Reign* (London, 1973).

F. H. Spencer, *Municipal Origins: An Account of English Private Bill Legislation relating to Local Government, 1740–1835* (London, 1911).

J. Stevenson (ed.), *London in the Age of Reform* (Oxford, 1977).

J. Stevenson, *Popular Disturbances in England, 1700–1870* (London, 1979).

L. S. Sutherland, 'The City of London in Eighteenth-Century Politics' in R. Pares and A. J. P. Taylor (eds.), *Essays presented to Sir Lewis Namier* (London, 1956).

E. P. Thompson, *The Making of the English Working Class* (London, 1963; paperback 1968).

S. and B. Webb, *English Local Government: The Manor and the Borough, Vols. I–II* (London, 1908; reprinted 1963) and *Statutory Authorities for Special Purposes* (London, 1922).

Chapter 10

W. Ashworth, *The Genesis of Modern British Town Planning: A Study in the. Economic and Social History of the Nineteenth and Twentieth Centuries* (London, 1954).

M. Aston and J. Bond, *The Landscape of Towns* (London, 1976).

T. C. Barker and J. R. Harris, *A Merseyside Town in the Industrial Revolution: St. Helens, 1750–1900* (Liverpool, 1954).

A. F. J. Brown, 'Colchester in the Eighteenth Century' in L. M. Munby (ed.), *East Anglian Studies* (Cambridge, 1968), pp. 146–73.

C. W. Chalklin, 'Capital Expenditure on Building for Cultural Purposes in Provincial England, 1730–1830', *Business History*, xxii (1980), 51–70.

S. D. Chapman (ed.), *The History of Working-Class Housing: A Symposium* (Newton Abbot, 1971), esp. essays by Beresford and Chapman.

M. E. Falkus, 'Lighting in the Dark Ages of English Economic History' in D. C. Coleman and A. H. John (eds.), *Trade, Government, and Economy in Pre-Industrial England* (London, 1976), pp. 248–73.

J. D. Marshall, 'Kendal in the Late Seventeenth and Eighteenth Centuries', *Trans. Cumberland and Westmorland Antiquarian and Archaeological Society*, new series, lxxv (1975), 188–257.

I. C. Taylor, 'The Court and Cellar Dwelling: The Eighteenth-Century Origin of the Liverpool Slum', *Trans. Historic Soc. Lancashire and Cheshire*, cxxii (1970), 67–90.

F. Vigier, *Change and Apathy: Liverpool and Manchester during the Industrial Revolution* (Cambridge, Mass., 1970).

Index

More OPUS books

What is Theology?

Maurice Wiles

'Professor Wiles's book makes a first-rate introduction to the subject. It has the honesty, the quiet persuasiveness and the penetration which we have come to associate with his work. Let those who undervalue theology read it and then ask themselves if theology is either a soft option or an irrelevant pastime.'
Times Literary Supplement

'It is a lively, stimulating, and surprisingly thorough treatment, and one which certainly conveyed to me 'the worthwhileness and the excitement of the subject', which is indeed one of the author's aims.' *Theology*

The Voice of the Past
Oral History

Paul Thompson

'Oral history gives history back to the people in their own words.
And in giving a past, it also helps them towards a future of their own
making . . . It thrusts life into history itself and it widens its scope.
It allows heroes not just from the leaders, but from the unknown
majority of the people.'

Paul Thompson argues that oral history can help to create a truer
picture of the past, documenting the lives and feelings of all kinds of
people, and that its value has been badly neglected by conventional
historians. It can juxtapose professional opinion with
interpretations of events drawn from all classes of society. In
addition, the effect of collecting oral evidence can be to bind
together communities, promote contact between generations, and
give people a sense of roots in their own historical past.

'a pioneering and valuable book' *New Society*

Ethics since 1900

Mary Warnock

'In this lively and fascinating book Mrs Warnock tells with admirable clarity the story of the development of English moral philosophy in the twentieth century . . . most attractively written, spontaneous, forthright and unfuzzy.'
Times Literary Supplement

'The book is a classic among handbooks: unpretentious, but very individual, with a vigour and clarity which make it as attractive to read as it is instructive.' *Christian World*

Moral Philosophy

D. D. Raphael

Do moral philosophers have anything to say that is useful, let alone comprehensible, to the majority of us who have more down-to-earth concerns? An emphatic 'yes' is the reply given by Professor Raphael in this new book, whose purpose is to introduce moral philosophy to those with little or no acquaintance with the subject. In it he explains and discusses various doctrines such as utilitarianism, naturalism, and rationalism, stressing that far from being a purely esoteric subject, moral philosophy can and does have a bearing on practical problems experienced by those concerned with government, law, and social service. No one who reads this book is likely to make the mistake of thinking moral philosophy irrelevant.

Modern Spain

Raymond Carr

Taking as its starting-point the 'September Revolution' of 1868, *Modern Spain* looks at that country's troubled history over the last century. Professor Carr argues that much of modern Spanish history is explained by the tensions caused by imposing advanced liberal ideas and institutions on a conservative society. The various political regimes failed to win the allegiance of the masses, and the sudden political mobilization of the Second Republic of 1931 brought to the surface conflicts which previous regimes had buried and which the Republic itself could not master.

This important book synthesizes twenty years' work, incorporating much new research, and includes an examination of the present democratic regime and the problems it faces.

'This volume will be widely welcomed. He compresses with great skill and judgement in less than two hundred pages a comprehensive survey of the last hundred years giving particular attention to the period 1875–1930.' *Contemporary Review*

Change in British Society

A. H. Halsey

Most of us claim that we believe in liberty, equality, and fraternity –
but is it possible to achieve them without creating anarchy? Can
democracy survive increasing bureaucratic control over our lives? Is
Britain doomed to progressive economic and political decline?
Distinguished sociologist A. H. Halsey attempted to answer these
vital questions in a series of six Reith Lectures given in 1978. The
subject of much discussion and debate, they explored the ways in
which British society has changed since the beginning of the
century, and proposed solutions to major problems that are at once
sane and radical. The revised edition of this important book
includes a postscript by the author on developments during the last
two years.

This book is an Open University set text.